SynchroFile

Other Books by Raymond E. Fowler

UFOs: Interplanetary Visitors

The Andreasson Affair

Casebook of a UFO Investigator

The Melchizedek Connection [A Novel]

The Andreasson Affair—Phase Two

The Allagash Abductions

The Watchers

The Watchers II

The Andreasson Legacy

UFO Testament—Anatomy of an Abductee

SynchroFile

◆

Amazing Personal Encounters With Synchronicity And Other Strange Phenomena

Raymond E. Fowler

iUniverse, Inc.
New York Lincoln Shanghai

SynchroFile
Amazing Personal Encounters With Synchronicity And Other Strange Phenomena

All Rights Reserved © 2004 by Raymond E. Fowler

No part of this book may be reproduced or transmitted in any form or by any means, graphic, electronic, or mechanical, including photocopying, recording, taping, or by any information storage retrieval system, without the written permission of the publisher.

iUniverse, Inc.

For information address:
iUniverse, Inc.
2021 Pine Lake Road, Suite 100
Lincoln, NE 68512
www.iuniverse.com

ISBN: 0-595-31589-5

Printed in the United States of America

Dedicated to David R. Harris, my dear friend and *adopted* brother, who is responsible for so many good things that have happened to me and to my family.

Contents

Preface xi
Introduction xv
CHAPTER 1 SynchroFile's Mother of Synchronisms 1
CHAPTER 2 Coincidence Categories 5
CHAPTER 3 Concurrent Coincidences 10
CHAPTER 4 Corresponding Coincidences 27
CHAPTER 5 Converging Coincidences 72
CHAPTER 6 Clock Coincidences 96
CHAPTER 7 Family Coincidences 115
CHAPTER 8 Supernatural Synchronisms? 123
CHAPTER 9 Flying Saucers 145
CHAPTER 10 Stigmatic Synchronicity 163
CHAPTER 11 UFO Abduction Dreams and Synchronicity 173
CHAPTER 12 Metaphysical Musings 209
CHAPTER 13 Conclusions 231
APPENDIX A Book Review: Quantum Leaps in the Wrong
             Direction 237
APPENDIX B The Other Faces of Synchronicity 239
APPENDIX C A Recommended Reading List 247

Notes 251
List of Photographs 257
About the Author 259

Acknowledgments

I am indebted to family members who allowed their synchronistic experiences to be recorded in this book. I am especially grateful to my niece, Deborah Wheaton, who spent many hours editing the manuscript for publication.

Preface

> *People commonly equate the word "coincidence" with the word "chance"; they often make statements to the effect that they "don't believe in coincidence". From that statement alone, however, it is impossible to tell whether such a person is a skeptic or a mystic! Their confusion arises out of their ignorance of the distinction between the terms "coincidence" and "synchronicity."*
>
> —Stephen J. Davis
> *Synchronicity: Trick or Treat?*

On Wednesday, September 11, 2002 (9-11-02), the New York State Lottery winning number was 911. Is this a highly improbable coincidence or is it debatable? Statisticians would quickly remind us that the probability that 911 would be the winning number upon that date is 1 in a 1,000. Thus, the probability is not that high.

However, some would argue the lottery number is just one half of the equation. This coincidence did not happen on just any date. It coincided with a highly known and emotional event. It was the date of the greatest attack ever made upon the United States of America. In addition, it would be pointed out that there were other coincidences regarding the number of 11 in this now portentous date.

1. September 11 is written 9–11, the telephone number for emergencies.

2. The sum of the digits in 9–11 (9 + 1 + 1) equals 11.

3. September 11 is the 254th day of the year, the sum of (2 + 5 + 4) equals 11.

4. After September 11, there are 111 days left in the year.

5. The Twin Towers of the World Trade Center looked like the number 11.

6. New York was the 11th State added to the Union.

7. New York City has 11 letters.

8. The flight number of the first plane to hit the towers was (you guessed it) Flight 11.

9. Flight 11 had 92 people aboard—(9 + 2) equals 11.

If the above coincidences are not enough to make one ponder—here is another of similar ilk. The winning New York Lottery number was 587 on November 12, 2001. This was the very day that Flight 587 crashed into the Queens section of New York. The real question generated by these coincidences is whether they are mystical, paranormal, or merely a by-product of statistical possibilities. Proposed answers for this question revolve around the word *perceived*.

On one end of the spectrum, some perceive such coincidental happenings as supernatural guidance to decision-making by some outside force that interfaces with our reality. Others perceive them as overt mystical hints of an *interconnectedness* of reality. Still others would believe that such events occur all the time but our busy lives usually fail to recognize them.

On the other end of the spectrum, statisticians perceive such events as being merely the product of chance. They would state that when dealing with large numbers of people and experiences, the likelihood of something unusual happening to someone, somewhere, some day, is actually very high. Statisticians would also point out that people who believe such coincidences are something mystical never take note that non-coincidences are occurring in our midst most of the time. They would state that such a neglect of non-coincidental happenings would make those who experience coincidences think that they are something special. In short, statisticians would conclude that such coincidences only seem improbable or mystical to those who experience them.

Such reasoning seems to make sense if statistical analysis is applied to explain one or two remarkable coincidences in one's life. However, what if a person's life is full of synchronistic happenings? What if the improbability of their happening is so great that ascertaining a cause for them seems to be beyond human understanding? *I am such a person.*

It is my opinion that statisticians would be hard-pressed to account for the abundance of strange coincidences that I encounter in my life and in members of my family. Such experiences are what this book is all about. It is written mainly to entertain and to stretch the mind of its readers. It is the type of book that one would bring on vacation and perhaps read while on a plane or train. The coincidences contained within will also make good tidbits for conversation and discussion. Aficionados of the subject may be tempted to read it through in one or two sittings! Lastly, its contents provide a gold mine of first-hand accounts of synchronicity, for use as source material for professional analysts.

It is not the purpose of this book to go into much detail regarding the theories about what the catalyst and purpose might be for such amazing coincidences. As mentioned, experts in this field of inquiry have already written much on these aspects. I found that the range of subjects used to explain the phenomenon stretch between the paranormal and quantum physics. However, I would be remiss if I ignored the theoretical aspects all together. So, such theories will be summarized and discussed in layman's language in the introduction. Later in this book, I will also provide a sufficient recommended reading list for those who wish to probe further into this fascinating phenomenon. [Refer to Appendix C.] The name of the book itself, *SynchroFile*, is derived from the term *Synchronicity*. What is meant by synchronicity? Who coined this descriptive term and why? The answers to these questions are found in the introduction to the book that follows.

Introduction

Synchronicity

So Man, who here seems principal alone, perhaps acts second to some sphere unknown. Tis but a part we see, and not a whole.

—Alexander Pope
Essay on Man

The question—*What is Synchronicity?*—This is easy to answer in a descriptive sense. The *Journal of Religious Thought* defines it in modern terms as "a meaningful coincidence of two or more events, where something other than the probability of chance is involved."

It is the latter part of the above definition that posed a problem to early researchers of the phenomenon. The problem, of course, was the "something other" that produced synchronicity; that is, a highly improbable coincidence called a synchronism.

Causation, or the law of cause and effect, ruled on the throne in early studies of this phenomenon. Mainstream science then and now has no place for any explanatory theory of a phenomenon that is not causal in nature. It insists that all forms of synchronistic events, no matter how improbable the circumstances surrounding them, have to be a product of chance.

How did causation become so embedded in modern science? Why were primitive ideas about synchronicity rejected for centuries by rationalism? Why are primitive beliefs about reality suddenly appearing in the forefront of a variety of advanced scientific studies? How has a deceased psychologist named Carl Gustav Jung influenced them? The answers to such questions will give the reader a basic understanding of the development of Jung's theories and how they apply to the synchronistic experiences recorded in *SynchroFile*.

The cultural belief systems of primitive societies in the past, and even to this very day, are wed to the synchronistic practices of casting spells and the interplay of placating or controlling nature and spirits by sacrifices and ritual magic. The synchronistic practice of Voodoo on the island of Haiti is but one example. Real or imagined results from such practices were attributed to supernatural causes and the interconnectedness of reality. These were also believed to be the cause of the appearance of eclipses, comets and other misunderstood natural phenomena.

Before the Age of Enlightenment, European society still echoed the above primitive belief systems that found meaningful connections between historic and natural events. The cause for such connections continued to be believed as supernatural in nature. Facts were less important than apparent patterns and synchronistic interconnections of individual events.

The location of the starry constellations of the Zodiac coinciding with human birth gave meaning to human personalities and direction for living. Eclipses and comets that occurred at or during coronations, births, plagues and important historic events were interpreted as meaningful coincidences. The Norman invasion of England, for example, coincided with what we know as Halley's Comet today. A star that shined with extraordinary brilliance coincided with King Charles of England's coronation on May 29, 1610. It was interpreted as an omen and it was named *Cor Coroli* [Heart of Charles] after him.

Such beliefs began to erode when the Age of Enlightenment ushered in a remarkable change in thinking about the mind. The philosophical thoughts of men such as Rene Descartes (1596–1650) declared that the capacity to think should be the primary mover behind human endeavor and the ultimate expression of individuality. Philosophers Baruch Spinoza (1632–1677), Thomas Locke (1632–1704) and Rene Descartes substituted a system of mechanical interpretations of physical phenomena for the vague spiritual concepts of the past.

Their thoughts and writings taught that natural phenomena are not regulated by divine or supernatural intelligence. They taught that such phenomena are adequately explained by the mechanical cause and effect laws of chemistry and physics. There were, of course, marked differences among these and other thinkers of that period, but the one thing all had in common was complete faith in the power of human reason and causation.

Such a way of thinking was practically demonstrated in the discoveries of scientists such as Nicolaus Copernicus 1473–1543), Galileo Galilei (1564–1642), Johannes Kepler (1571–1630), Tycho Brahe (1571–1630) and Isaac Newton (1642–1727). Building upon each of their predecessor's discoveries, man, through the power of human reason, was able to overthrow mystical and theological beliefs about the solar system and man's place in it.

Such knowledge did not come easy because competing philosophies made them difficult to hold by society as a whole. Some were imprisoned for their views and others were hampered by government censorship and attacks by the church. The church, holding to a rigid literal interpretation of Genesis and a theology wed to the ancient philosopher Aristotle, forbade such teachings and forced Galileo to recant upon the threat of excommunication.

On the other end of the spectrum, a movement called Romanticism rebelled against the cold, unfeeling mechanistic worldview of rationalism. Romanticists held that that the human passions are placed at the heart of our existence rather then reason. The Romantic poems of Samuel Coleridge (1772–1834) and William Wordsworth (1770–1850) and the musical compositions of Ludwig Van Beethoven (1770–1850) and Franz Peter Schubert (1797–1828) reflected the ideals of romanticism. They resurrected the subjective feelings of primitive cultures that all of life was interconnected in some unknown way.

However, by the 19th century, the tension that existed between Romanticism and Reason eased due to the influential works of Jean Jacques Rousseau (1712–1778). He brilliantly defended his view that the kind of civilization built upon reason alone had corrupted humankind. He boldly declared that the natural or primitive state was morally superior to the civilized state that had evolved out of the *Age of Enlightenment.*

Rousseau's philosophy appealed to the deepest emotions of man and thus appealed to the masses that were not scientifically oriented. It became a bridge between the 18th century Enlightenment's emphasis upon reason and individual rights, and early 19th century Romanticism, which espoused subjective experience against rational thought.

By the end of the 19th century, both Romanticism and Rationalism enjoyed a relative peaceful co-existence. Scientific experiments and philosophical writing became fashionable among wide groups in society, including members of the nobility and the clergy. However, within the domain of mainstream scientific enquiry, the power of reason and the law of cause effect reigned supreme. Woe to any scientist stepping outside of these boundaries who would dare to suggest that anything other than chance could be responsible for synchronistic events. At this juncture, enter Carl Gustav Jung! Jung was a man who was willing to stake his career and reputation on the belief that synchronistic events were *acausal* in nature. The term acausal simply meant without a natural cause. His coming to this conclusion, however, evolved over many decades of time. In brief, who was Jung and why did he come to this conclusion?

Carl Jung was born July 26, 1875, in the small Swiss village of Kessewil. When a boy he attended boarding school in Basel, Switzerland. Later, he went on to study medicine at the University of Basel and settled on psychiatry as his career.

After graduating, he took a position at the Burghoeltzli Mental Hospital in Zurich under Eugene Bleuler, an expert on (and the one who named) schizophrenia. In 1903, he married Emma Rauschenbach. He also taught classes at the University of Zurich, had a private practice, and invented word association at this time!

Jung was a long-time admirer of the famous psychoanalyst, Sigmund Freud. He met Freud in 1907 and an instant friendship developed between them. Freud became a father-like mentor to Jung and soon concluded that Jung was his choice to carry on his theory and method of psychoanalysis. However, Jung, although much impressed by Freud, was not convinced of Freud's theory. When Jung became involved in parapsychological phenomena, his relationship with Freud began to wane.

When Jung told Freud about this involvement, Freud rejected such reported phenomena as nonsense. He feared such interests would cause him to reject Jung as heir apparent to his theory. He told Jung that his theory was an unshakable bulwark against the occult. During what became an angry encounter, a loud bang erupted from Freud's bookcase. Jung told Freud that it was an example of psychic phenomena caused by his stress. To prove that this was the case, Jung predicted that another loud noise would again come from the bookcase. It did, and although Freud would not accept it as being paranormal at the time, he later became privately involved in researching such phenomena himself. Jung's hesitancy to accept Freud's theory and his ongoing interest in the occult finally led to the end of their close relationship. He went on to develop his own theory of psychoanalysis.

I am not a psychologist or psychiatrist. My only claims to fame in this area are psychology courses on an undergraduate level and self-study. Jung's theories are complex and hard to understand even by those who are educated in these areas. This is especially so as his views changed over the years and often seemed to contradict each other. This being the case, for the reader's sake and mine, I will only briefly summarize the psychology of Carl Jung. I will mention only the primary terms used by Jung in his work. This is chiefly a book about personal experiences. Jungian psychology is secondary. It will be used sparingly to acquaint the reader with its basics and to categorize and typify my encounters with synchronicity.

Freud had discovered what is called the individual or *personal unconscious*. This is that part of our mind that functions as the center of thought, emotion and behavior. It contains repressed thoughts and forgotten experiences. It is formed from impulses and wishes below the threshold of consciousness.

Jung found that the deeper he probed an individual's unconscious, the more it began to look as if some universal collective phenomenon existed. Déjà vu, the immediate recognition of certain symbols and meanings of certain myths, could all be understood as the simultaneous conjunction of our outer reality and the inner reality of a universally shared collective domain. He believed that such a realm would explain the spiritual experiences of mystics and the universal parallels found in dreams, fantasies, mythologies, fairy tales and literature.

Jung named this theorized domain the *collective unconscious* from which the *personal unconscious* emerges.

The boundaries of this mysterious realm remain unknown. They are collective because its mental contents are shared by all human beings. Whereas the *individual unconscious* contains personal life-experiences, the *collective unconscious* embodies all of the common *objects* and *experiences* from the distant past that the evolving human mind share. Jung called these primordial images or *Archetypes*. They formed during the development of human consciousness and the physical evolution of humankind from lower forms of life. Thus, according to Jung, every person inherits the same Archetypes. These manifest themselves in personal cultural experiences and in the forms of myths, dreams, tribal lore, fairy tales, visions, scientific discoveries, numbers, religions, philosophies, historical developments, etc.

Jung inferred the existence of Archetypes from studying the dreams of his patients. During therapy sessions, he found that the contents of dreams expressed themselves as symbols from the unconscious that were manifestations of the unconscious Archetype. Such manifestations of the Archetype were not limited to the symbols extracted from dream analysis. They come in many forms from all the cultural activities by which man has expressed himself.

> Jung writes that: "Meaningful coincidences...seem to rest on an archetypal foundation. At least all the cases in my experience—and there is a large number of them—show this characteristic." [1]

Jung believed that known forms of causality were incapable of explaining some of the more improbable forms of such coincidences. When no causal connection could be demonstrated between two events and a meaningful relationship existed between them, Jung believed that a unique type of principle was operating. He called this principle *Synchronicity*.

During his research into the phenomenon of the collective unconscious, Jung came across many coincidences that appeared to defy the calculations of probability. One of many demonstrative examples from Jung's case studies concerned a woman he was finding psychologically impossible to help because of her extreme rational know-it-all personality. He finally was able to break through her defense system when something very irrational occurred. It had a transforming effect upon both the patient and Jung himself. Describing the improbable meaningful coincidence responsible for this, Jung writes about the following incident. It occurred during a psychoanalytical session with this woman:

> I was sitting opposite her one day, with my back to the window…She had had an impressive dream the night before, in which someone had given her a golden scarab—a costly piece of jewelry. While she was still telling me this dream, I heard something behind me gently tapping on the window. I turned around and saw that it was a fairly large flying insect that was knocking against the windowpane from outside in the obvious effort to get into the dark room…I opened the window immediately and caught the insect in the air as it flew in. It was a scarabaeid beetle whose gold-green color most nearly resembles a golden scarab. I handed the beetle to my patient with the words, "Here is your scarab." This experience punctured the desired hole in her rationalism and broke the ice of her intellectual resistance. The treatment could now be continued with satisfactory results. [2]

Who or what was responsible for this synchronism—Jung, the patient or chance? Such a question presupposes a chain of causal events. However, Jung concluded that all known forms of causality were absent from this experience. The coinciding arrival of the scarab with the patient's dream had no determinable cause. It instead complemented the "impossibility" of the analysis that Jung was attempting with his patient. Jung believed that his experience with the scarab and similar experiences were truly acausal meaningful experiences. He writes that:

> Meaningful coincidences are *thinkable* [italics mine] as pure chance. But the more they multiply and the greater and more exact the correspondence is, the more their probability sinks and their unthinkability increases, until they can no longer be regarded as pure chance but, for lack of a causal explanation, have to be thought of as meaningful arrangements…However, their "inexplicability" is not due to the fact that the cause is unknown, but to the fact that cause is not even thinkable in intellectual terms.[3]

Such is the case regarding an example culled from my personal diary, *SynchroFile*. The person Margaret in the diary entries, unless specified otherwise, is my wife.

May 13, 2000: I got up around 5:30 a.m. and went for a two-mile jog around the golf course that borders our dead end street. Margaret got up later and soon after began suffering unusual chest pains, a feeling of weight on her chest and difficulty in breathing. She felt alone and helpless and wondered what was wrong with her. Margaret flicked on the TV to take her mind from the pain.

Shocked, there before her very eyes was a man describing the typical symptoms of a heart attack, which matched exactly what, was happening to her at that very time. He urged those who suffered such symptoms to get to a doctor immediately! At that very point, I arrived back from jogging. I raced her to the hospital emergency room where she was hospitalized for several days and treated for a mild heart attack!

Jung insisted that such improbable synchronisms are often the catalyst for profound changes in the lives of those who experience them. This was certainly so for Margaret and me who felt that the *concurrent coincidence* between the TV commentary and her heart attack was a Godsend.

This was also true in the life of Jung's patient whose extreme rationality had made her psychologically inaccessible to Jung's efforts to help her. The irrational magic-like appearance of the scarab-like beetle transformed her attitude toward the paranormal. Jung was able to break through the block of rationality that prevented him for helping her psychologically. It also greatly influenced Jung to begin intense research into this and other paranormal phenomena.

Jung of course wondered about the *why* behind synchronistic experiences and over time evolved a theory to explain the stimulus for them. According to Jung, when an Archetype is activated by an emotionally charged event, other related events tend to draw near and coincide with it. In this way the Archetypes become a doorway that provide us access to the experience of meaningful and often transforming coincidences

Concurrent with Jung's concept of synchronicity was his belief [like the Romanticists of old], in the ultimate "oneness" of the universe. He believed that synchronistic phenomenon revealed a "peculiar interdependence of objective elements among themselves as well as with the subjective (psychic) states of the observer or observers." Jung found additional evidence for this interdependence in his research into parapsychological phenomena. These included precognitive dreams, thoughts and visions, telepathy and near death experiences. All seemed to indicate a kind of absolute knowledge contained within the collective unconscious. Jung believed that such phenomena, along with other forms of synchronicity, were indications of how nature and we are interconnected through the collective unconscious.

As I end the Introduction, I must mention that Margaret's synchronistic warning about her heart attack is only one of hundreds of amazing coincidences that make up the warp and weft of my life. They are indeed meaningful to me and continue to transform my views of reality. There are times when these repetitious coincidental circumstances make me feel like a pawn in some complex predetermined chess game. Sometimes, even after applying cold logic to such a thought, it is not at all easy to dismiss it. In the past, my objective, logical mind rebelled against the practical significance of subjective experiences such as hunches and synchronisms. However, the frequency of such incidents gradually changed me from a skeptic to an agnostic to a believer. I concluded that something very strange was really happening in my life.

I wish that I had recorded all of these amazing synchronisms just as they occurred. I finally felt constrained to begin to do so in 1995. Some that you read in this book were gleaned from memory, but the bulk are recorded examples from *SynchroFile*. It is my hope that they will provoke the same enchanting feeling of awe and oneness with reality that I experience when I encounter the inexplicable. We will start with *SynchroFile*'s "Mother of Synchronisms."

1

SynchroFile's Mother of Synchronisms

Mysterious coincidences cause the reconsideration of the inherent mystery that surrounds our individual lives on this planet...forcing us to transcend our rational, scientific, materialistic attitudes.

—James Redfield
The Celestine Prophecy

Synchronistically enough, this incredible coincidence involves a real mother—my wife's mother. However, I am getting ahead of the story. In a sense, it started in England back on June 1, 1953, the day before the coronation of Queen Elizabeth II. I was in the United States Air force, stationed on a top-secret base electronically spying on Russia under the auspices of the National Security Agency. On that day, I was sitting on the barrack steps when several of my friends asked me to go to London to view the coronation. We had been warned that there were no accommodations in London because of the massive crowds. I protested but finally was persuaded to go.

When we arrived, I could hardly believe what I saw. The streets that usually seethed with commerce were filled with throngs of people, all anxious to find their observing sites along the path of the coronation parade. The route was cordoned off so that one could walk along it freely, but the crowds behind the fence filled the street completely. There was no room for the likes of a group of American servicemen.

My formerly exuberant companions soon lost their enthusiasm as they realized our folly. There was no place to spend the night. Hotels had been booked for weeks ahead. We had no food, umbrellas or rain gear. Several of my companions left our motley group for parts unknown. This left me and my buddy Gene to fend for ourselves.

It was then, and only in sheer desperation, that I conceived of a possible but improbable way out of our predicament. I suggested that we look for young women who had a good location from which to watch and who had food. We were hungry! I would add that such a suggestion was completely out of character for both of us. All of us were churchgoers and sought to live by high moral standards. We wondered what kind of girls would invite American servicemen to spend the night on the pavement with them!

In any event, as we trod along the coronation route, we actually came across the very scenario that I had envisioned. There, immediately to our right, were several English ladies with blankets, umbrellas, and hopefully food. We stopped and introduced ourselves as Americans who were intensely interested in seeing the Queen and her Prime Minister, Winston Churchill. We conversed further and soon found they appeared to be well groomed, articulate young women. Surprisingly, and to our great relief, they welcomed us to join them.

Gene and I seemed to click with two of the girls. He took up sidewalk residence with Joy and I with Margaret Pike. The others left us alone to talk and get to know one another. We found this was difficult because of differences with our accents.

The night was noisy with rowdy people. English Bobbies were continually pressing people closer together to make room for arriving latecomers. We got little sleep. At dawn, everyone was told to stand until the coronation parade started at 2:00 p.m. We had waited for about twenty-hours for the event. It was spectacular. We saw the Queen and Winston Churchill pass by at close hand. Winston Churchill waved his famous "V for Victory" sign as the horse-drawn carriage passed by.

However, the coronation was memorable for more than one reason. Margaret and I exchanged addresses and telephone numbers. Later, we had our first date canoeing on the Thames River, and the rest is history. Our marriage took place on June 25, 1955. Upon returning to the U.S., I was discharged and entered civilian life. We finally settled at 13 Friend Court in Wenham, Massachusetts. Then there was College, 25 years with GTE, four children, ten grandchildren and trips to visit Margaret's parents in between in Cottingham, East Yorkshire, England.

In 1996, Margaret's mother, now a widow and age 96, entered a nursing home. Her house was put up for sale. Howard Peach and Margery James purchased it shortly after. Margaret visited her mother at the nursing home in February 1997. On February 24, Margaret dropped by for a sentimental visit to her mother's former home, located three miles from the nursing home. She hoped that the new owners would be cordial. Howard and Marjorie gave her a hearty welcome and invited her in for tea. During the conversation, Margery asked Margaret where she lived in the United States. Margaret told them that she lived in a small town that they would never have heard about called Wenham, Massachusetts. [Current population: 4212]

Marjorie's jaw dropped and her face showed total amazement. Marjorie told Margaret that she had visited Wenham more than once! She explained that her cousin's husband's sister Evelyn [now deceased] had lived in Wenham, Massachusetts. Dumbfounded, Margaret asked Marjorie where Evelyn had lived. Her answer would strain anyone's credulity. Marjorie told Margaret that Evelyn lived on a street called Friend Court! Friend Court is the very street that we had lived on in Wenham since 1961! Margaret then asked her what the number of Evelyn's house was on Friend Court. Then the improbability of this amazing coincidence escalated further. Marjorie said that Evelyn had lived on 16 Friend Court. We live on 13 Friend Court. Number 16 is the house directly across the street within a stone's throw of our house!

It was then that Margaret realized that Marjorie was referring to our former neighbor and friend [now deceased] Evelyn Yeaton! I checked later with Marjorie and found out that she had visited Evelyn in 1971 and 1973. We may have even seen Marjorie from our house just a bare thirty feet across the street from Evelyn's house. However, her personage would not have given us the slightest idea what her portentous visit held for Margaret's mother's future. But, the amazing synchronistic revelations did not end there. Margaret had scarcely recovered from that shock when Marjorie told her that Evelyn's brother-in-law [now deceased] had also lived in Wenham. His name was Raymond Fowle! A name that was just one letter different from my own!

The grand finale came when Marjorie told Margaret that her cousin Irene lived in the next town of Essex, Massachusetts, just several miles from Wenham. Our son, David, lived in Essex, so naturally Margaret asked where Irene lived. Again, her answer was hard to believe. Marjorie told Margaret that Irene lived on the corner of Lakeside Drive and Western Avenue. This was just four houses from where my son lived at that time!

What are the odds for such thought-provoking synchronisms to happen? Marjorie's visits took place in the late 50s and early 60s. The population of the United States was 178,554,916 according to the 1960 census. Also, Howard and Marjorie were the first and only people to respond to the advertisement for the sale of Margaret's mother's house. They did this on the very day that it was posted. Prior to purchasing the house, they had lived in Hull, which borders Cottingham. Using a formula employing latitude and longitude, the distance between Cottingham/Hull and Wenham is approximately 3,215 miles. At that time, Howard and Marjorie were complete strangers to both sides of our family.

Happily, this is no longer the case. We both visited them on the occasion of Margaret's mother's 100th birthday. We often correspond with one another by email. This wonderful synchronism caused Howard and Marjorie to begin regular visits to Margaret's mother. They brought her fruit, snacks and flowers. In short, they did everything distance prevented Margaret from doing. Margaret's mother died on March 15, 2002 at the marvelous age of 103.

One senses the enactment of a mysterious guiding personal force behind this interconnected event, but what [or who] is it? There is no natural cause for such a coinciding event. One thing only is certain: If ever there were an *improbable acausal meaningful coincidence*, this particular one fills the bill. Now you see why I have called it SynchroFile's *Mother of Synchronisms*.

2
Coincidence Categories

If your belief system is such that intuition and synchronicity are real and significant, you will notice them. If your belief system is that they're hogwash, you won't.

—Carolyn North
Synchronicity: The Anatomy of Coincidence

Carl Jung initially defined synchronicity as simultaneous *acausal meaningful coincidences*. [What he meant by their being *meaningful*, as we have seen in the Introduction, was how they affected one's personality and worldview]. Jung was criticized for initially limiting synchronicity to just simultaneous events. This was especially true when Jung began to label non-simultaneous happenings as synchronistic in nature. Physicist Wolfgang Paul and others criticized Jung for this inconsistency. In a letter to Jung, Pauli wrote the following concerning Jung's initial definition of synchronicity:

> Initially it refers expressly to phenomena that are supposed to be *simultaneous* in definitions in the usual physical sense. Later, however, you try to include phenomena such as predicting the future, which do not occur at the same time. The word "synchron" thus seems to me somewhat illogical, unless you wish to relate it to a chronos that is essentially different from normal time. This seems to me to be a difficulty that is not just one of formal logic but also a factual one. For it is by no means easy to see why events that "express the presence of one and the same image or meaning" have to be *simultaneous*. [1]

In response to his critics, Jung expanded his definition to cover non-simultaneous types of meaningful acausal coincidences. These included precognition, telepathy, near death experiences and [as we shall see later] even the UFO phenomenon. *SynchroFile* will address all of these types of coincidences.

Jung concluded that all synchronistic phenomena could be grouped under three categories. I will classify the entries from my diary under these same categories, although in some instances, circumstances may cause some overlapping. Jung's three categories are as follows:

> 1. The coincidence of a psychic state in the observer with a *simultaneous* [italics mine] objective, external event that corresponds to the psychic state of content, where there is no evidence of a causal connection between the psychic state and the external event, and where, considering the psychic relativity of space and time, such a connection is not even conceivable. [2]

I will simply refer to this type of synchronism as a *concurrent coincidence* that has no apparent cause. The following coincidence is an example extracted from my diary involving my best friend:

> **September 29, 2002:** My friend, Dave Harris, called to tell me about an unnerving synchronism. Yesterday, he telephoned his son, Phil Harris, to check on his health. Dave told me that Phil had cancer. During the telephone conversation, he mentioned my name to Phil. **At that very moment, Phil was watching me on** TV! It was a rerun of a program on UFOs. [Note: Another synchronism occurred just after I typed this in my diary. I signed on to *Outlook Express* to go on the Internet. The first thing that appeared on my screen was an email. My server's processing information blocked the top part of the email message out. The first line under the square read: **"Does anyone know whether this is just a coincidence?"**

Jung's second category of synchronistic phenomena is:

> 2. "The coincidence of a psychic state with a corresponding (more or less simultaneous) external event taking place outside the observer's field of perception, i.e. at a distance, only verifiable afterward." [3]

I will simply refer to this type of synchronism as a non-simultaneous *corresponding coincidence* that has no apparent cause. An example of this type from my diary is noted below. It is one of three synchronisms that occurred on that date. It involved a Renaissance painter.

> **April 10, 1996:** I phoned...Betty Luca to tell her about a painting that I had seen in a magazine that depicted angels holding hands and dancing in a circle. The artist of the painting was the famed Renaissance painter, **Fra Angelica**. In

the meantime, my wife was downstairs picking through a pile of old books that we were going to sell to a dealer. She knew nothing of my conversation to Betty.

When I came downstairs, I found her looking through one of the old books that was entitled: *Roses in Bloom* published in 1876 by Louisa M. Alcott. I mentioned to her that I had just got off the phone with Betty about a painting by **Fra Angelica**. She looked up in disbelief and told me that she had just read a sentence in the book that mentioned **Fra Angelica**! This would have been about the same time that I had mentioned his name to Betty while on the phone. I asked her to find the passage in the book for me. She did and I read these words—"Have you given up your painting, she asked rather abruptly, turning to a gilded **Fra Angelica** *Angels,* which leaned on the sofa cover?"

[Note: For the readers' interest, today is October 12, 2002. Just after I typed the above entry from my diary into the manuscript for this book, my wife called out and asked if I wanted to watch ***Touched by an Angel*** with her! She had no idea that I was typing up the above entry about **Angels**.]

Lastly, Jung's third category of synchronistic phenomena is:

> 3) "The coincidence of a psychic state with a corresponding, not yet existent future event that is distant in time and can likewise only be verified afterward." [4]

I will simply refer to this type of synchronism as a future *converging coincidence* that has no apparent *physical* cause. They often appear precognitive or telepathic in nature.

The following excerpt from a 1954 diary that I kept while stationed on an USAF base in England is a good example of a *converging coincidence*. At the time I wrote this entry, Margaret and I were preparing to leave for the United States where I was scheduled for discharge from the Air Force prior to Christmas 1955. I had been in England for two years and eight months and had not been home during that time:

> **December 2, 1955 [Friday]:** The Orderly room says I may leave before or after the 21st. We packed lots of things and still got to bed early. **I dreamed that I returned home without Margy.** Mom asked me where she was and I said she was coming later

December 3, 1955 [Saturday]: I had a most vivid dream of my returning home and having a happy reunion. When everybody asked where Margy was, I told them that the government was sending her later. This is the second dream about this!

December 5 [Monday: Had an inspection today. I went to the Orderly Room to see when we were going home and I was directed to Sgt. Hunt. On my way to see him, the Lord spoke to me [a voice in my mind] and told me to prepare myself for a shock as I was just about to be told that **Margy could not go with me**. This seemed impossible, yet when I entered the building, I was told that very thing!

I still remember exactly where I was when that telepathic-like message entered my mind. I was passing the large bulletin board of the Orderly Room. I can remember Sergeant Hunt looking up from his desk and saying something like, "I'm sorry to inform you that your wife cannot travel with you, as there will not be enough room on the aircraft. She will have to join you later." So, I returned to the States alone. It gave Margaret another Christmas to spend with her family.

As it turned out, there was plenty of room on the plane as there were a number of empty reserved seats for officers. As it was, Margaret would have been terrified had she flown with me. We flew across the Atlantic from Scotland into a terrific storm. The aircraft experienced terrible turbulence and frightening air pockets. These sent the plane careening downward like an out-of-control elevator. The pilot had to make an emergency landing at Goose Bay, Labrador because of lack of fuel. We then proceeded to Brooklyn Air Force Base, New York where I was discharged. Margaret joined me a few months later.

I would call these three categories of coincidences *mainstream* categories. They are universally recognized by researchers of synchronicity. In addition to these, I am adding [independently] a fourth category, which I call *counter coincidences*.

These categories of synchronicity involve circumstances where an experience is opposite or counter to natural law. They occur in instances where two events that should naturally coincide do not. These experiences may appear supernatural to the percipient even though there may be a yet-to-be recognized rational explanation for them. Whichever may be the case, at that point in time, events that normally should coincide do not!

I have invented this descriptive term in order to categorize events of this nature recorded in *SynchroFile*. Such coincidences are rare in my own experiences. My studies indicate that they are also rare in the lives of others. The following is an example from my diary. It happened on the same day as a *corresponding synchronism* mentioned later under that category:

April 23, 1997: In the afternoon, something extraordinary occurred that involved Margaret. She went into the shed to get a rake. The rake handle was tangled with a large wooden stepladder that hung directly above her. When she pulled on the rake, the ladder became dislodged. It should have come down on top of her. She instinctively ducked. When she looked up unscathed, the ladder was standing in the middle of the shed with its legs apart and set up. This ladder is not easy to set up. It easily jams when one pulls the legs apart. How it got in the middle of the shed all set up is beyond us!

There is no [at least recognized] reason why the falling ladder should not have coincided with the location of my wife. She was directly under it. There is no explanation for it opening by itself in another location. These events were counter to what should have naturally occurred. Additional *counter coincidences* will be highlighted later.

3

Concurrent Coincidences

[There are] two Fundamental Types of Synchronicity. 1. One in which the compensatory activity of the archetype is experienced both inwardly and outwardly. **[The event seems to emerge from the subconscious with access to absolute knowledge, which cannot be consciously known]**. *2. One in which the compensatory activity of the archetype is experienced outwardly only.* **[These convey to the ego a much-needed wholeness of the self's perspective, they show one a new perspective]**.

—Robert Aziz
C. G. Jung's Psychology of Religion and Synchronicity

Concurrent coincidences take place [for all intents and purposes] simultaneously. They are mirror images of one another. In fact, Craig S. Bell dubs them "Mirror Coincidences" in his book that explores synchronicity. [1]

Such coincidences involve mirror-like reflections of proper names, other words, numbers and circumstances. However, many coincidences like these are not synchronisms. The stimuli for such coincidences are easily ascertained. Two people may think of the same person, place or thing at the same time because of a word association, a smell or other circumstance that connects them. For example: Margaret and I may both bring my father up simultaneously in conversation. Initially we might remark in amazement that we must have been thinking on the same wavelength! However, after a little reflection we would realize the catalyst for the coincidence. It could be attributed to a brand of tobacco that Dad smoked. Conversely, it might be the mention of a person, place or thing closely associated with him.

Such coincidences have a recognized cause. They are not true synchronisms that are acausal in nature. I have excluded coincidences of this kind from *Synchro-File*. Those recorded have no apparent mental or physical connection between the source and receiver of concurrent information. In some cases, radio, television and telephones may be the link between the two.

Radio and television sets obviously differ from people. They are not organic in nature. They obviously do not think! These boxes of interconnected electronic components merely provide a mode of communication between persons at a distance. Communication from persons appearing on radio and TV is one-way to us. Thus, there is no possibility of a coincidence involving radio and TV transmissions being caused by word association or circumstance. The following *concurrent coincidences* are selected examples from my *SynchroFile*:

OF THE RADIO KIND

Sometimes a coincidence involves the simultaneous connection between exact *words*.

> **March 18, 1996:** I was listening to the radio and picked up a note to read from one of my students. As I did so, a medical doctor mentioned a person whose last name was **Kezar** just as I glanced at the note, which was from a Janet **Kezar**.
>
> **March 23, 1998:** I was typing on the computer while listening to the news [on the radio]. Just as I was typing the word **Mexico**, the narrator said the word **Mexico**. Later he said the word **computer** just as I was looking at the word, **computer**. This has happened on a number of occasions.
>
> **December 7, 1999:** I was listening to the radio and typing on my word processor. Just as I clicked the cursor on "Style **Gallery**" in Microsoft Word, the host on the radio said the word **Gallery**. Sometimes I forget to record these kinds of synchronisms, but they occur often.
>
> **December 14, 1999:** While listening to my headset radio and working on my income tax, I turned to an item that I had purchased from a company named **Learning** Express at the same time that the radio announcer mentioned the word **Learning** twice. Seconds later, the same announcer said the word **just** at the exact moment I typed the word **just**.

At other times, there is a connection between what is being *said* by a radio host and what a person happens to be *doing* at the exact time.

> **September 5, 1997:** While vacationing in Kennebunkport, Maine, my wife and I turned on Boston radio station WBZ to hear the news. Just as we were

passing the driveway of former President **George Bush**, the newscaster announced that **George Bush** had accepted an invitation to write an article for a fishing magazine.

January 13, 1998: [At that time] I rarely ever eat an **apple**—maybe once a year—but I was hungry before going to bed...[I] brought one up to eat while listening to the news in bed. Just as I took the last bite of the apple, an ad on the radio said, **"How good it was to eat apples!"**

Three synchronisms were recorded on the following date. One involved what was being broadcast on the radio dovetailing with what I was doing at the exact same time. The other two involved TV and are recorded elsewhere.

September 20, 1999: 1. While brushing and bagging potatoes that I had harvested, I had put on my headphone radio to break up the boredom. I also was in the habit of putting dog food pellets out for several **crows** that I have befriended. They were up on the roof cawing for food. At the time, I had inadvertently turned on the Howie Carr Talk Show. He was complaining about being given a wrong kind of donut—a kind that he did not like—from a takeout place. At the exact moment I placed the dog food **for the crows** on the picnic table, Howie said that he "put the donut out in his backyard **for the crows**"!

September 21, 1999: While **jogging** at Bradley Palmer State **Park**, I was changing stations on my headset radio to find something interesting as I jogged along. I turned to a station to hear the host saying that he would like to go **"jogging in the park"!**

December 10, 1999: I was listening to my headphone radio and went outside for a moment. While outside, I noticed that the **birdfeeder** needed to be tipped to release more seed to its shelf. Just as I tipped it, the announcer said the words—**"You like birds"**—during something that he was talking about!

Another type of *concurrent coincidence* involves the concurrence of *thought* about a person, place or thing at the exact time something is said about the same person, place or thing by a person broadcasting on a radio.

February 7, 2000: Often I will be doing something or looking at something while listening to the radio and will experience synchronisms. Today I was at the computer looking at an article entitled **wealth and poverty** just as the radio mentioned the **rich and poor**. Later, I was looking at a clip art selection on a computer program named Print Shop. The clip art piece was called **din-**

ing out. Just as I glanced at it, the radio commentator said, "**dining out** at the Hearthside Restaurant." This happens when I am not at the computer. I forget to record it unless I made a note of it to record later.

April 13, 2000: While jogging and listening to my headphone radio, I was mulling over how the placement of a comma in the original Greek text of a certain Bible verse has caused two conflicting **theological** positions in the church. Just as I was thinking this thought, the hostess on the secular radio station that I was listening to used the word **theology**.

A simultaneous connection between what is *said* by a radio announcer and what a person is *seeing* is another type of *concurrent coincidence*.

June 10, 1999: I was in the car waiting for Margaret to do some shopping. I was parked in front of **a video rental store** listening to music on WBUR. A large sign on the video store was advertising a movie entitled **Gods and Monsters**. It was near 5:00 p.m., so I switched to WBZ to wait for the news to come on. Just as I did, a commentator was urging people **to rent God and Monsters** from a **video rental store** at the very same time I was staring at the video store at what was written on the sign in front of me!

October 29, 2002: I was jogging along Maguire road listening to my headphone radio. As I jogged, I was looking down at the pavement. I had just passed through a section where the rising sun was blinding my eyes. I quickly glanced up as I noticed something in my path. It was a large yellow sign, which read, among other things, *Children at Play* in big black letters. Just as I looked at the word **children**, the radio program host said the word, **children!**

November 26, 2001: [Two synchronisms occurred on this date. One was a *concurrent coincidence*.] I was jogging on the golf course listening to the news on my headset radio. At the exact time that the newscaster made the statement that "thousands are traveling by trains," a passenger train roared past me on tracks that border the golf course.

November 5, 2003: I was driving along a highway, which had speed signs posted at 45 mph. The radio was on. I happened to look up at a new sign increasing the speed limit up to **50** mph. Just as I was reading the sign, the announcer on the radio said **50** three times in a few seconds.

Obviously, TV, like radio, can also be the medium that transmits the stuff that makes up *concurrent coincidences*. However, it may sometimes add startling *visual* impact to the already amazing audio synchronicities via radio transmission.

OF THE TV KIND

As in *concurrent coincidences of the radio kind*, television at times provides the link between one's *thoughts* about a person, place or thing at the exact time something is *said* about them on TV. Some examples follow:

> **December 10, 1995:** I was typing a sentence today and listening to the TV at the same time. Amazingly, the news commentator said the **same five to six words** that I was typing at that very moment. This happens often. [By the time I finished what I was typing, I had forgotten what the exact words were.]
>
> **December 16, 1997:** I typed the word **China** just as someone on the TV said **China.** This happens often.
>
> **September 20, 1999:** [Two of three synchronisms recorded on this date]. While watching television, I was wondering where I had misplaced some **fishing lures** that I had bought for my son. At that very moment a TV ad flicked on for Dodge automobiles showing **fishing lures**! [There was no prior hint that this type of ad was coming on.]
>
> Later, while watching Tom Brokaw on the TV news, I was mulling over finances in my mind. Just as I thought of **ten** dollars, Tom Brokaw said the number **ten** at the exact same moment. These types of things happen often, but I do not always record them in the diary.

Some *concurrent coincidences of the TV kind* involve the observer and the TV performer doing exactly the same thing simultaneously.

How would you feel if you walked into a room and glanced at the TV screen to see a mirror image of exactly what you were doing? This can be spooky to the observer and I, of course, was the observer! The following incident took place in England while visiting Margaret's mother:

> **September 10, 1995:** I entered the living room where Margaret and her mother were sitting watching TV. I sat down with a copy of *The Holographic Universe* **book in one hand and a large yellow marker in the other.** I then glanced up at the TV and saw a man holding a **book in one hand and a yellow marker in the other**! If this were not enough, I had just been reading on page 78 about the synchronism experienced by Carl Jung that was the catalyst for his investigation into the phenomenon of synchronicity!

Another similar synchronism took place at home while watching *X-Files on TV*.

February 1, 1998: This morning I woke up to find a fresh **scab on the back of my neck**, which sometimes itched. This evening I was watching a movie entitled *The Love Letter*. During a commercial, I decided to flick to another channel to see what I was missing on the *X-Files* program. I flicked to the channel and **began scratching the scab at the back of my neck**. When I glanced up at the screen, *X-Files* TV character Scully suddenly touched a **scab at the back of her neck**. She was being told that it was the location of an implant inserted during her abduction by aliens!

Another synchronism took place at the exact moment that I opened some mail. I pulled the same item out of an envelope that suddenly appeared on the TV screen at that very moment!

April 3, 1999: Two synchronisms. [One I recorded in another chapter.] I was watching TV. During commercials, I finally got around to glancing through my mail. One of the envelopes contained a **Maine Vacation Information Packet.** Just as I opened it up, I glanced up to see the same **Maine Vacation Information Packet** advertised on the TV screen!

At other times, I have experienced a pertinent connection between what is said [or seen as words] on TV and pertinent information about myself. The following incident occurred when I happened to walk into the living room and glance at the TV screen. I was shocked to see something that was very pertinent to me:

June 16, 1998: When I joined my wife to watch the evening news, I saw a man being interviewed. His name appeared on the lower section of the screen in big letters—**RAMOND FOWLER!**

April 14, 2000: I went into the living room to listen to the news. I had brought a copy of the April 5, 1966 House Armed Services Committee **Congressional Hearings** on UFOs to look up something in it for someone during commercials. Just as I sat down with the document, the TV announcer said the word **"Congressional Hearings."** Then, as I continued browse through the document, I read the word **Martians** just as the TV announcer began to talk about the failure of the **Mars** Lander.

January 26, 2001: This morning, I turned on the Today Show on the TV and went back into the kitchen to get some cereal. As I did, I for some reason started singing a few old gospel songs that I had sung in a quartet at churches while stationed in England. I wondered why these songs from over 50 years ago suddenly popped into my mind. Both songs were about life after death in a heavenly place. This subject immediately turned my mind to the phenomenon of the Near Death Experience [NDE]. I had been reading about the oft-reported **light at the end of a tunnel**, which people report during an NDE. At the exact same time that I was thinking of this proverbial light, I heard Matt Lauer on the *Today* TV show say the words **light at the end of the tunnel**. He was referring to California finally getting some relief from an electric power shortage.

March 22, 2001: I was listening to TV and typing on my computer's word processor at the same time. Just as I placed the mouse's cursor on the word **SAVE**, the TV host, Kelly O' Donnell said, **Save, Save, Save!**

March 21, 2002: [Two synchronisms occurred on this day. One was a *concurrent coincidence*.] Margaret and I were watching TV. Just as she said my son's name, "**Raymond**", the name **Raymond** appeared on the TV screen!

January 3, 2004: I was upstairs in my study addressing an envelope. The TV was playing loud enough for me to hear an announcer speaking. Just as I was writing **Arizona** on the envelope, the announcer said the word **Arizona**.

January 6, 2004: Synchronism. This evening Margaret was crocheting a large scarf for a granddaughter. She had just finished one like it for another granddaughter. I was watching TV and turned and asked her if her fingers ever hurt from crocheting so much. She answered that once in a while her thumb got sore. Just as she said **thumb**, the TV newscaster began talking about **thumb** prints.

Telephones, like radio and TV sets, are inanimate non-thinking inorganic devices. However, unlike radio and TV, they provide two-way communication between persons. They also provide the means for *concurrent coincidences* to occur.

OF THE TELEPHONE KIND

Have you ever thought about a person moments before they telephoned you? For some reason, this type of coincidence is better known than others. This type usually falls under the category of a *corresponding coincidence,* as the synchronicity is not instantaneous. However, I do have several *concurrent coincidences* that I remembered to record in *SynchroFile*. The first one provided currently needed information to both parties involved in the coincidence.

March 2, 1995: In the midst of writing a letter of enquiry to obtain **John Carpenter's** address, the telephone rang. It was **John Carpenter's** associate calling to obtain information from me. She gave me John's address. She then asked if I had Jacques Vallee's telephone number, which had been changed. I had just received the new number two days ago and gave it to her!

March 6, 1995: I was sorting through letters from [a certain **person**]. The telephone rang. It was [the **person**].

Other than chance being the cause for such coinciding events, we are left with the possibility of the telepathic transformation of thought. If so, what is the cause behind telepathy? Jung is right in stating that:

> People…talk of…clairvoyance, telepathy, etc, without, however, being able to explain what these faculties consist of or what means of transmission they use in order to render events distant in space and time accessible to our perception. All these ideas are mere names; they are not scientific concepts that could be taken as statements of principle, for no one has yet succeeded in constructing a causal bridge between the elements making up a meaningful coincidence. [2]

April 24, 2002: A few weeks ago, I received only half of the seed potatoes that I had ordered but was charged for the whole order. I telephoned the responsible company and complained. They apologized and said that they would send the rest of my order. However, over a week passed and the potatoes had not arrived. Today I telephoned to complain to the company. At the **very moment** that I reached the company representative on the telephone and began to complain, my wife shouted that UPS had just come to the door with the potatoes.

The above *coincidence of a telephone kind* and the ones to follow may be related to chance. However, the possibility of chance decreases with the sheer number of times such coincidences happen to me. Some, like the one that follows, [to use a colloquial expression] *blow my mind* for their sheer incredulity!

May 27, 2002: [Two synchronisms occurred on this date. Of the two, the one that follows is a *concurrent coincidence*.] This morning I was on the deck reading a book entitled *The Holographic Universe* for the second time. Such a universe, according to the originator of the theory, could explain a number of inexplicable phenomena such as *synchronicities*.

At the time, I was reading about an experiment by a Russian scientist, Nikolai Bernstein when Margaret handed me the telephone. The call was from one of my granddaughters who wanted help in identifying an unfamiliar bird that had appeared on a bird feeder. She told me that it looked "like a sparrow with *a* **black head** and a **white dot** painted on top of it". I was shocked! At that exact moment, I was reading the following sentence describing a Bernstein experiment: "people in **black leotards** upon which Bernstein had painted **white dots."**

What can be behind these other-worldly-like connections? Is there an intelligence working behind the scenes and if so, for what reason? Can it be that similar thoughts are attracted together by unknown means when circumstances are right for a telepathic path to be opened between them? If so, what would be the circumstances that would open this pathway?

Pondering such questions evokes similar feelings to those caused by experiencing the synchronisms themselves—a feeling that all of reality is interconnected. Sometimes, for some unknown reason, we suddenly find ourselves being part of a *psychic* connection between like thoughts, acts or circumstances. The telephone, as in the continuing examples, provides the *physical* connection:

August 11, 2000: I received a telephone call from a friend today who called to tell me about some strange **synchronisms occurring in his life**. He had no idea that at that time I had just written about an abundance of **synchronisms occurring in my life**.

June 23, 2002: Ed. S. was supposed to phone us sometime during the week, but we had not heard from him. I asked Margaret to call him. As she was looking up his telephone number, **Ed. S** phoned us.

September 7, 2002: Margaret received a phone call on our answering machine **from Del** in the morning. He needed some information about Sunday school materials. Since we were busy with company, Margaret decided not to call him back until the evening. This evening, just as she looked up Del's phone number, the phone rang. **It was Del**. This was a repeat of the September 4th entry.

December 21, 2003: I was on the computer working on this book when the telephone rang. I heard Margaret answer it upstairs. Her voice became excited as she talked to the person on the other end of the line. The thought that it was an old girlfriend from England named **June** came to my mind. However, I quickly dismissed this as she had only called a few times since Margaret left home to live in the United States in 1956. Later, I went upstairs to eat supper and asked who had been on the phone. She told me that it was a transatlantic call from **June**!

Other *concurrent coincidences* concern various kinds of simultaneous *circumstances*. Some examples are as follows:

OF THE CIRCUMSTANTIAL KIND

These kinds of *concurrent circumstances* involve the names of persons, places or things that are being seen, thought or talked about. They, unlike radio, TV and telephone, take place *directly* between two persons or parties. I had recorded an example of this type in a diary that I kept while stationed at a USAF base in England. The rest are recorded from *SynchroFile*.

> **October 15, 1954:** One day, a while back, while waiting for a bus to go from Bedford to London to see Margaret, a man stopped in his car and picked me up. Amazingly, his route took him within just three minutes of Margaret's apartment! Today I again was waiting for a bus with a friend. I told him about the man that had picked me up and how his business route brought me almost to the door of Margaret's apartment. **At the very moment that I was telling him this**, the same man stopped and gave us both a ride to London!

It may have come as a surprise to some readers that I have been investigating the phenomenon of unidentified flying objects for over forty years. I have authored ten books on the subject. More will be said about this in a later chapter. I mention this now because during investigations and writing about UFOs, I have experienced some fascinating synchronisms. The following is an example of a *concurrent coincidence* that I experienced on the way home from an investigation:

This enigmatic experience took place on May 22, 1980. I was driving home from Cheshire, Connecticut, where I had attended a hypnosis session with UFO witness Betty [Andreasson] Luca. It was late at night and there were no other cars on the road. I was finding it hard to believe the bizarre experiences that Betty had relived under hypnosis. So, in fun, I shouted—"If these experiences are real, show me a sign!" *Instantly*, the whole sky lit up from horizon to horizon sending rippling chills through my body!

A number of synchronisms have taken place when I am teaching. The following is an example:

> **January 12, 1995:** I am currently teaching one of three courses on UFOs for North Shore Community College at Danvers, Massachusetts. This evening I started the first lesson by taking attendance. I found to my astonishment that two women, sitting one in front of the other, **both raised their hands** when I asked if Elizabeth Riley were present. They too were surprised and even more so when they asked each other for their middle name. Both had **Ann** for a middle name.

November 17, 1996: We were out on a walk and decided to take a path that intersected a main road. As we walked onto the road, we merged with a couple of old friends [whom we had not seen for years] who were taking a walk on the road.

June 15, 1997: I was sitting at the dining room table talking to Margaret and my daughter and son-in-law. We were talking about a **mattress** that was given to my son Ray that reeked of the smell of cigarettes. We were discussing how to advise him of getting rid of the smell. At that moment, a noise outside caused me to glance out the window behind me. Amazed, I saw large letters spelling ***MATTRESS***. A truck belonging to a mattress company had just parked on the street in front of the window! [A mattress was being delivered to the house across the street.]

February 12, 1998: Margaret and I were preparing to leave for the airport and an interesting synchronism took place. I was in the kitchen putting on my coat and she was in the hall. I noticed an old cleaning **tag** on my jacket. Just as I **ripped it off**, Margaret who was in another room, simultaneously said—"I'm **ripping off** this old **tag** from my suitcase."

February 24, 1998: I went out to check the mail. I was expecting a CD-ROM, but it had not come. I thought to myself that it would probably be sent by **UPS**. At the very moment I thought the acronym **UPS**, a **UPS truck** drove by the window that I was facing.

March 12, 1998: While translating from my Greek New Testament, I had to use a lexicon to find the meaning of a word. When I picked up and opened the lexicon at random, I inexplicably turned to the correct page and found myself **looking at the very word.** This was incredible. The lexicon is 449 pages in length and contains over 24,000 words!

May 21, 1998: I was thumbing down a list in a telephone book. Margaret yelled to tell me that she was **giving our dog a bone** at exactly the same time that my eye fell on a service called: **A dog's best friend.** I was looking up the number of a hardware store with no connection to a dog.

July 1, 1998: A repeat synchronism from the past. [See March 12, 1998.] When translating from Colossians in Greek, I had to look up a word in my Greek lexicon, which is 449 pages long. I picked it up and randomly somehow opened it to the **exact word** that I was looking for!

July 29, 1998: Around 9:40 p.m., I went into the bedroom to put washed clothes lying on my bed into drawers. The window was open. Someone with a loud voice was talking on a portable phone across the street. I turned the lights on, put the shade down, and began placing the clothes into drawers. Just as I was placing **T-shirts** in a drawer, the person began talking about **T-shirts** in a loud voice.

I recorded two synchronisms on October 17, 1998. One was *a concurrent coincidence of the circumstantial kind*, which is as follows. The other was a *corresponding coincidence* and is recorded in the next chapter.

October 17, 1998: In the evening, during my Astronomy for Beginners course, an interesting synchronism occurred. I had announced on the blackboard that there would be no class on 11/11. This was an official holiday for North Shore Community College, which sponsored the course. I also told the class that 11/11 was my birthday. Immediately the student closest to me announced that 11/11 was his birthday and that he was born on 11/11/65. I laughed and said that I was going to be 65. He laughed and said that he was going to be 33. I retorted that I was born in 33. When we were finished with our bantering, another student chirped that her birthday also was on 11/11!

January 12, 2000: I was thinking about making an appointment with the dentist for my six-month teeth-cleaning appointment. As I looked at my records, I found that my last visit was *on* **June 28,** 1999. At the same time I happened to be looking directly at the clock, which read **6:28.**

March 13, 2000: Yet another synchronism. This type happens often but I usually forget to record them. I was working in a computer program called Textbridge. Just as I put the mouse cursor on an icon named **GO**, I heard my wife [who was downstairs] scream "**Go**" at the exact same time. Curious, I yelled and asked her why she had yelled this word. She said that she had shouted at a cat near our bird feeder.

May 18, 2000: I had a long dream, which kept involving the time **5:36 a.m**. I cannot remember what else was involved in the dream except that it was repetitious. Then, I dreamt that I woke up inside of my dream and told Margaret about a clock chasing me in the dream that read **5:36 a.m**. At that very moment, I really woke up with a start and glanced at the clock. It read **5:36 a.m.!**

September 7, 2000: Margaret and I are staying at a bed and breakfast establishment in England near the nursing home where her mother resides. When we told the proprietor of the establishment that we have daughters named **Sharon** and **Beth**, she told us that her daughter is named **Sharon** and her granddaughter is named **Beth**.

October 27, 2000: This evening I presented a planetarium show to an adult group. Although it was a star show, the subject of UFOs came up during the question and answer period. During a discussion, I mentioned that I had gotten in trouble with the USAF when I released data about UFOs disrupting the Minuteman missile. [I worked at GTE and was on the Minuteman Production Board.] I told the group that I had given this information to a staff reporter for the *Christian Science Monitor* named **Stephen Webbe**.

I was taken aback when a distinguished gentleman in the audience spoke right up and said that he was the editor-in-chief for the *Christian Science Monitor* and a friend of **Stephen Webbe**!

January 7, 2001: In the evening we were watching the movie *The Sound of Music* in which there was a **thunderstorm** scene at the same time a thunderstorm was in progress. **Thunderstorms** are exceedingly rare in the month of January.

January 10, 2001: I was using a hammer and pounding nails in a room that I was re-modeling. The mother of one of my wife's piano students passed nearby chatting with my wife. She was describing her child's piano playing. Just as she said the words **one finger**, I hit **one finger** with the hammer!

February 24, 2001: This morning I decided to download some topographical **maps** from the computer but first clicked on the local weather station. When it came on, the first word I noticed was **maps.**

April 9, 2001: Margaret and I save last year's Christmas cards. She randomly selects one each day from a pile in a bag. We say a prayer for their sender at dinnertime. Today, I came for dinner and sat down. Before praying, I told Margaret that a friend had just called to tell me that **Barry Greenwood** was dating Sue, a former secretary for MASS MUFON. Margy looked shocked. She said that the card in her hand was from **Barry Greenwood**! This was amazing especially. since almost exactly a year ago the same thing happened involving another name. [That April 25, 2000 entry is in *SynchroFile* and is in the *converging coincidence* category.]

December 22, 2001: I emailed a business associate to ask some questions. I left the computer for awhile. When I came back to it, I found an email from this associate. However, the person did not mention the email that I had sent, which I thought very strange. I checked my Internet server records to see what time I had sent my email and what time she had sent hers. **Amazingly both were sent at 4:06 p.m.!** No wonder she did not answer my first email. We were both emailing each other at the same time.

February 18, 2002: This morning, Margaret was swimming at the YMCA in Sanford alongside a woman in the next lane. The woman glanced over at her and called out her name. It was **an old friend** that she knew decades ago who had moved to Sanford.

April 23, 2002:.I took a break from gardening and was sitting on our front porch having a snack. I unwrapped and started eating **ice cream** [a fudgicle], at the exact time an **ice cream** truck passed right by in front of me.

May 2, 2002: This morning I had an appointment with my dentist at 8:00 a.m. and my doctor, Dr. **Shill,** at 10:00 a.m. Just as I arrived at the receptionist area at the dentists, the receptionist called out for someone else to call Mrs. **Fowler** and that Dr. **Shill** had cancelled his [dental] appointment. She was referring to another Fowler but the same Dr. Shill.

October 2, 2002: While hiking up a rugged trail to a waterfall, Margaret remarked that she could really use a **walking stick.** At that moment, I had stepped up and over a boulder to see a **walking stick** at my very feet that someone had left behind!

October 29, 2002: A month or so ago I emailed members of the local astronomy club that I had just installed an astronomical observatory on my property. I invited members to come and see it. This afternoon, I decided to take a break from writing a book. I decided to **go to the observatory** to see if some shelves would fit inside it. As I approached our front door, I saw a man through the window. He was starting to walk away from the door. [He had been ringing a doorbell that does not work and thought we were not at home.] I quickly opened the door and asked him what he wanted. He said that he was a club member and would like to see my observatory just as I was about to leave the house **to go to the observatory.**

It would appear that just as the man started knocking on the door [which I did not hear] I got the sudden impulse to leave my writing to go to the observatory! Was this impulse telepathic in nature? A number of similar coincidences in SynchroFile could be explainable by telepathy.

Two synchronisms took place on the date recorded below. One was a *converging coincidence.* It is recorded under that category. One was a *concurrent coincidence* and is as follows:

November 12, 2002: When I typed the word **book**, one of the women meeting in the living room with Margaret said the word **book,** which startled me.

December 30, 2002: This morning I was typing and pasting information onto a page of my new book manuscript when I experienced a synchronism.

Just as I pasted the word **love** onto a page of the manuscript, I heard my visiting daughter who was upstairs say the word **love.**

January 10, 2003: A telepathic synchronism? Margaret and I were playing cards. I was munching on some peanuts. I was just about to say, "**I wonder if the birds would like peanuts**" when she said, "**perhaps the birds would like peanuts**"! Neither of us had been talking or thinking about feeding birds up to that point in time.

January 19, 2003: I was listening to the news on channel 6 but flicked to channel 13 to see what it was covering. As channel 13 flicked on, the host said the words, "Mary Jane **Fowler**"!

February 2, 2003: I was watching Channel 6 and flicked to Channel 8 to see what was on. As I did, I saw the name Travis **Fowler** displayed.

February 7, 2003: I was listening to the news on TV and went to the window to see how hard it was **snowing** out. At the same time, I flicked the TV to another station. Just as I glanced out at the falling snow, the TV newscaster said the words, John **Snow!**

February 17, 2003: Today I brought in some photographs to be developed at Ocean Exposures in Kennebunkport. The clerk filling out the order form asked me my name. When I replied **Ray Fowler**, she looked shocked. She said her friend was named **Ray Fowler.**

March 24, 2003: I was reading the word **friendly** in a letter when the TV host said the word **friendly** at the exact time I read this word.

March 25, 2003: I was listening to radio station WBZ this morning while addressing an envelope. Just as I typed the word **south**, the news commentator said **south**.

April 25, 2003: Margaret and I vacationed in Rockport, MA and traveled to Beverly to do some shopping at CVS. Beverly is only several miles from our former home in Wenham. As we exited CVS, I thought to myself that perhaps we will see some **friends** that we know. Simultaneously, we heard people shouting at us from two different directions. We looked and *saw* **old friends** approaching in the CVS parking lot who had recognized us.

April 28, 2003: I was sitting on the couch watching TV when Margaret came downstairs and asked why I had put a chair in the middle of the breezeway. I told her that I had put it there to remind me that **a bird had got inside** the garage last evening and that I had to try to get it back outside. Just as I said that, I glanced at the TV. It was a commercial also about **a bird (stork) that had got inside** a furniture store and was scaring the employees.

May 2, 2003: This evening I turned to the 6:00 p.m. *Leherer News Hour* show and found that New Hampshire PBS station channel 11, which usually carried it, had an auction on instead. I turned to another station for news, but after a few minutes I flicked back to channel 11 to see if the auction was still going on and there was the name **Fowler** on the screen. It pertained to someone who donated an item for the auction. I then turned back to the other news station and watched until there was a commercial. At that point, I again flicked back to channel 11 to see if the auction was still on and was amazed when the screen again was showing the **Fowler** name.

June 13, 2003: While camping, we heard a bird singing. I located it, pointed it out to Margaret, and said that it was a song sparrow because of the distinctive large **dark spot** on its breast. Simultaneously with my remark, the sparrow deliberately bent its head down and touched the large **dark spot** with its beak!

July 14, 2003: I sat down on the couch, flicked the TV on, and waited for the noon news. My watchstrap had broken earlier. I took my watch out and placed it beside me. I then flicked to channel 11 to see what was on prior to going to channel 6 for news. It was almost noon, so I picked up my watch to see the actual time. Just as I touched the **watch,** the host on channel 11 said the word **watch.**

October 7, 2003: I carried a **glass of water** out of the kitchen into the living room and met Margaret carrying a **glass of water** into the living room from another direction.

October 8, 2003: I was watching the six o'clock news when it broke for commercials. Concurrently, I was day dreaming about a conversation on the telephone that I had with a TV program called *Unexplained Mysteries*. It had been about non-payment for a release that I had signed. When I had gotten to the point of the conversation where I said the words **I have received nothing** to the TV producer, I was shocked to hear someone on the TV say the words **you get nothing** at the exact instance! I glanced up and saw these same words on the screen! The words were about a commercial concerning whether or not Maine should vote to allow a casino to be built in the State. [Actually, as it worked out, my check is now in the mail.]

October 21, 2003: I walked from the kitchen into the living room where Margaret was walking television. As I entered, I held up a can of Drano to my lips (in fun to shock Margaret) **as if I were going to drink it**. As I did, I glanced at the TV. On the screen was a man holding up a glass of Metamucil to his lips **as if he were going to drink it**.

December 16, 2003: I turned on the TV and waited for the news to come on. As I waited, I was daydreaming about **downloading** some information from my computer to an acquaintance. I was startled when just as I thought the word **download,** someone on TV said, **download**!

December 31, 2003: I went out to check the mail, brought it in and sat on the couch to read it. Margaret sat beside me reading a book entitled, *The Best of James Herriot*. One of the items in the mail was the January 2004 catalog entitled *Critics Choice Video & DVD*. For years, each time such a catalog comes in the mail, I browse through it looking to see if a Video or DVD had been made of a British TV Comedy entitled **'Allo 'Allo**! I was thrilled to see it listed under *New British releases*. I excitedly turned to Margaret and told her that at last **'Allo 'Allo** was finally available. Margaret turned to me with a grin on her face. She said that she was just reading a sentence in her book about a character that said**:** "**Ellow! 'ellow! 'ellow!**" he bawled jerking upright and thrashing around him with his arms."

March 20, 2004: This morning, I was working with my Spell Check using Microsoft Word. When I clicked the mouse cursor on the word **change**, my granddaughter shouted the word **change** at the very same time.

4

Corresponding Coincidences

Events are called synchronistic, if the following three conditions are satisfied:

• *Any presumption of a causal relationship between the events is absurd or even inconceivable.*

• *The events correspond with one another by a common meaning, often expressed symbolically.*

• *Each pair of synchronistic events contains an internally produced and an externally perceived component.*

—Barron Burrow
PS: Pauli-Jung…by 50 yrs.

Corresponding coincidences are identical to *concurrent coincidences* except that synchronicity does not take place simultaneously. Some may take place nearly concurrent while others are separated by an extended passage of time. Most, but certainly not all, of the *corresponding coincidences* recorded in *SynchroFile* fall under the category *of the circumstantial kind*. These will be the first kind recorded in this chapter.

OF THE CIRCUMSTANTIAL KIND

ANGEL UNAWARE?

This example hails back to my childhood in Danvers, Massachusetts. It immediately came to mind when writing this book. One tends to remember traumatic, strange and pleasant experiences from childhood. I have always remembered the following experience with a stranger. Each time I think back on the event, I ponder his enigmatic statements. I knew nothing of synchronisms at the time. I was about eight years old [1941] when it happened.

At the time, I attended Calvary Episcopal Church in Danvers, Massachusetts. One Sunday I was very impressed with a sermon given by the minister. It was based upon a Bible verse about "entertaining angels unaware." The minister stressed that we should be kind to all those in need. He explained that sometimes we might be helping angels in disguise as human beings. The possibility of an angel visiting me was intriguing to my young mind.

On the following day, I was playing near some rarely used railroad tracks. I can still see the scene in my mind's eye. It was a very hot summer day. The sun was beating down on the oil-saturated railroad ties, causing a shimmering mirage-like effect. As I glanced down the track, I saw a lone figure appearing in the distance. His image was distorted by this shimmering effect. I stopped and watched as his form took shape. I waited by the track until a very clean-cut young man stopped opposite from where I was standing.

In retrospect, he looked as if he were in his late teens. His blonde hair was crew cut. He was wearing blue jean pants, that we called dungarees in those days. We exchanged names and in the process of conversation, he told me that he was hungry. Immediately, Sunday's sermon came to mind. I thought in my innocent childish mind, "perhaps this man is an angel in disguise and I should offer to feed him."

Since it was time to go home for lunch, I invited him to come home with me. I told him that I was sure that my mother would give him something to eat. My mother smiled when I told her my angel theory. She looked him over from the living room window and agreed to feed him.

I brought him out a plate of macaroni and some milk and we ate out in the backyard together. After we had finished eating, I asked him if he would stay for awhile. I wanted to show him one of my favorite play spots on the other side of the river that bordered our property. He agreed.

I cannot remember all of the things we did together. However, I do remember that he made me a crude but workable bow and arrow. He told me that his father had *made* the tree from which we cut the wood. I can remember being puzzled about this and asked him who his father was. He simply smiled and told me that someday I would know.

Strangely enough, I cannot remember his name. I think it was David. However, I do remember that I was very sad when he told me that he had to leave. I asked him if he would be coming back this way again. He said that perhaps he would visit me again someday. The strange thing is that later in life I had a very odd encounter with a helpful stranger of similar appearance. It occurred while I was driving to give a UFO lecture.

I suddenly got a flat tire. My station wagon was new. I was not sure where to place the jack to change the tire. I was in a panic. I did not want to be late for the lecture. As I placed the jack under the car, I felt a hand on my shoulder. I swung around. There was a young man smiling at me. His hair was blonde and crew cut. He wore what appeared to be a brand new blue jean suit. A young lady dressed in the same attire stood behind him in front of a car about fifteen feet away. I never heard a car pull up behind me and was surprised.

Before I could object, the young man took the jack out of my hand. He told me that I was putting it in the wrong place and that I could injure myself. I thanked him profusely. The next thing I knew, he was replacing the tire for me. I thanked him and tried to converse with the young lady. It was weird. She just stood staring into space as if in a dream and not responding to me. After the tire was changed, the young man handed me the jack and headed back to his car. His looks and dress brought my mind back to my childhood *angel.* This sudden intervention may have saved my arm from being crushed by the car.

I did not consistently record synchronisms until 1995. I mentioned some in my 1950 diary while stationed in England but did not call them synchronisms then. I believed that they were in answer to my prayers. This is not to say that they were not but only that they happened after prayer. The next item was of this type.

PRAYER PRESCRIPTION

Other than meeting my future wife in England, I also met a kind gentleman. He had a great influence on my life and on many friends. Prior to meeting him, I was courting Margaret. I was finding it very hard to visit her weekly in London. The bus fares, meals and hotel bills were very expensive for the likes of my salary. I was trying to save money for our future but not doing very well. We **prayed for a solution** and decided that I would have to cut my visits down considerably.

According to my diary, my next visit to London was on September 23, 1954. While waiting for Margaret to get out of work, I browsed a bookstore in London. I felt very conspicuous in my air force uniform. People coming and going stared at me as did an elderly gentleman who had just walked in the door as I was walking out. He stopped and asked what part of America I was from. When I told him I was from Danvers, Massachusetts, he smiled. He said that he had just returned from the U.S.A. and had spoken at a church less than 20 miles from Danvers. During the course of our conversation, he asked me where I was staying in London. I told him that I was staying at a hotel near Margaret's apartment. Much to my surprise [and, I must say suspicion] he offered me an open invitation to stay at his house free of charge. I could hardly believe this wonderful answer to our need.

He told me that his name was Robert Thomson and that he was a retired colonel in the British army. He said that because of his mastery of languages, he had been parachuted into Germany to assist in capturing and translating the German archives. After his discharge, he was awarded the distinguished MBE [Member of the British Empire] and became the chief foreign correspondence translator for the royal family and for Winston Churchill.

I must confess that I was wondering if this fellow was telling me the truth about himself. I also wondered if he had an ulterior motive for asking me to spend my nights in his house. The Air Force had warned us about becoming friends with anyone associated with a country other than our own. This pertained especially to the Soviet Union and its Satellites. I [and others on base] held an above top secret clearance. We were privy to information that someone might try to extract from us. A red flag really went up when he told me that he had made multiple trips to countries behind the *Iron Curtain*. He said that he smuggled Bibles, money, food and clothes to needy Christians.

I thanked him and took down his address and telephone number. As soon as I got back to my base, I reported the incident to my commanding officer. He told me to wait to see if Mr. Thomson was all he was before taking him up on his offer. Soon after, the commander told me that Colonel Thompson was who he said he was and that I was free to fraternize with him.

I began staying at his home weekly and was soon calling him Uncle Robert along with many of my friends, who also were invited to visit him. The adventures that I shared with him and others in London could be made into a small book. His wise counsel and advice continues to help me to this day. Hundreds grieved his passing in August of 1967 while on one of his missions behind the then *Iron Curtain*. The amazing result of my seemingly chance encounter with this distinguished man met a specific desired need. It is another addition to the synchronicities that haunt my life.

"I JUST READ ABOUT YOU!"

Sometimes it seemed as if someone behind the scene of reality was aiding me during my UFO investigations. The following example took place during my investigation of a UFO sighting that took place in 1967. At the time, I was serving as an Early Warning Coordinator for a USAF-contracted UFO Study.

On August 2, 1967, at 9:30 p.m., dozens of witnesses reported sighting a string of brilliant lights that appeared and disappeared in perfect sequence off the shore of Cape Ann, Massachusetts. Some believed that they saw a strange object that carried the lights. I notified the UFO Study headquarters via a special telephone hot line. Two scientists were dispatched to investigate the case with me. Witnesses were interviewed. Special reporting forms were filled out and compared. Checks with the FAA and local military services indicated that there were no aircraft in the area at that time. The USAF-contracted scientists gave me the impression that they considered the sighting to be a true unknown object.

A few weeks later, considerable excitement was caused by new sightings along the shorelines of Cape Cod, Connecticut and Rhode Island. Coincidentally, descriptions given by witnesses were the same to what witnesses on Cape Ann had reported. The phenomenon again consisted of a string of bright lights that appeared and disappeared in perfect sequence. The Air Force told the press that a B-52 bomber dropping high-intensity flares on parachutes caused them. Since this sighting was extremely similar to the Cape Ann event, I reopened my investigation. I wanted to check out the possibility that flares had been the stimulus for this incident also.

My first move was to place a telephone call to Headquarter 8th Air Force (SAC), Westover Air Force Base, Chicopee Falls, Massachusetts. I was connected with Captain William J. Ballee, Assistant Chief, Operations Division, and Directorate of Information. When I gave my name to Captain Ballee, he sounded very surprised and said, **"I just read about you!"**

In one of those uncanny coincidences that so often coincide with my UFO interests, Captain Ballee recognized my name. **He had just read about me** while reading the book *Incident at Exeter* in which I was prominently mentioned. We laughed at the coincidence and he cooperated fully with my request. I asked him to send messages to all Air Force bases that would be involved in flare drops for the month of August 1967. [Later, his superiors reported this. to higher-up in the Srategic Air Command (SAC). A TWX (teletype message) was sent to all commands that such cooperation must not be afforded to me in the future.]

However, this was after I had received the information. It *was* a B-52 that had dropped flares off Cape Ann. I immediately got on the hot line and reported my findings to the USAF UFO Study. The scientist on the other end of the call's first reaction was—"Who tipped you off?" It was apparent to me that the flare drop was an intentional test to demonstrate how UFO sightings can often be misinterpretations of man-made objects! I was glad to have discovered this. It demonstrated that true UFO sightings are those that remain unidentified *after* a thorough investigation.

THE CANTERBURY CAPER

Another surprising synchronism took place during my investigation of a UFO sighting in Canterbury, New Hampshire on May 13, 1972. I had never been to this town and was not familiar with directions given me by phone. I left early from work and headed north along route 93 until I reached the exit for Canterbury. When I reached the town limits, I stopped on a lonely road to eat a flying saucer investigator's supper—sandwiches! While munching away, I happened to glance up the road. I saw a man staring at me from the porch of a distant house. Soon, he got up and began walking down the country road toward my car. Then, one of those uncanny coincidences, encountered often during UFO investigations, occurred again. He stopped at my open car window and spoke to me.

"Hi!" he said, "Are you in trouble? Saw your car off the road and wondered if you need any help."

"No, just eating my supper," I replied "You might be able to help me out on something else though. I'm going to be visiting a Mr. James Lilley and really don't know where he lives."

The man looked shocked and said, "Why Jim Lilley works for me! I'm his boss. My name is Arthur Stavros."

It turned out that that Jim and Arthur were a two-man company in Canterbury! Arthur gave me excellent directions to Jim's house—a synchronism of the helpful kind!

This next humorous coincidence took place in 1978 during my writing of a book entitled, *The Andreasson Affair—Phase Two*.[1] The incident took place after the following synchronistic event which was *of the TV kind*:

BUGGED BY *BEAMS* AND *BUGS BUNNY*

I had just finished typing up chapter three of *The Andreasson Affair—Phase Two* which was about UFO experiences called *Close Encounters of the Third Kind*. This particular chapter described an object that approached 5 year old Bob Luca and focused a white **beam of light on him**. When the beam hit Bob, he found that he could not move a muscle. This was on my mind when the telephone rang. I picked up the phone. It was a call from a fellow employee at GTE. She told me that her son had *just* been riding a trail bike in a field when an object approached and hovered over him and **shot a beam of light** at him. As she described the incident, I felt a weird feeling of déjà vu. Her son's experience was identical to the one I had just finished writing about!

However, that was not the end of it. I went back to writing the book but stopped for several minutes to respond to a call of nature. On my way to the bathroom, I glanced at a TV program that my son, David, was watching. On the screen there was Bugs Bunny talking to a dwarf-like helmeted Martian alien entity!

I continued on to the bathroom chuckling to myself about the coincidence. I had just been writing about aliens and the Close Encounter of a Third Kind experienced by the Andreasson family. Suddenly I got a strange feeling that I had seen this same *Bugs Bunny Show* before. Then it hit me. This was the identical *Bugs Bunny Show* portrayed in the scenes of a movie. In the movie, Richard Drefyuss, a UFO abductee, suddenly awoke to the sounds of this very same TV show. He looked up and saw Bugs Bunny and the alien. The name of the movie was **Close Encounters of the Third Kind!**

The following synchronism coincided with the death of my best friend. Another one that followed several days later provided comfort:

HIS EYE IS ON THE SPARROW

It was the morning of July 25, 1981. My friend, Chet, lay dying in a hospital as I set off to keep a speaking engagement at a UFO Symposium held at the Massachusetts Institute of Technology. My mind was very much on Chet as I traveled down route 1A in Beverly, Massachusetts. The proverbial question "why?" was very much on my mind. Chet was younger than I and had a wonderful family that needed him.

I slowed to take a right turn as I reached the junction of routes 1A and 128. Suddenly, a flock of sparrows winged in front of my car. The car hit one. For a split second, it seemed to freeze in mid-air and then dropped to the ground. At that very moment I thought of Chet and a verse from the Bible: "Are not two sparrows sold for a penny? Yet not one of them will fall to the ground apart from the will of your Father." I wondered if the sparrow symbolized God's will regarding Chet's death. Later, I found that this incident took place in the *same time frame* that Chet had died.

I attended the funeral and was one of the pallbearers that carried Chet's body to its final resting-place. It was a sad week. A few days later I was driving home from Beverly on route 1A with the radio on. I was still wondering why Chet had to die at such a young age. Suddenly, at the same intersection of routes 1A and 128 [where the sparrow fell], a song began to play. It was **His Eye is on the Spar-**

row. These two incidents were comforting. I received a strong impression that Chet's passing, although terribly sad for us left behind, was nevertheless part of God's plan for him.

SYNCHRONISTIC SUPPER

As mentioned, I wrote a book entitled *The Andreasson Affair—Phase Two* published in 1982. It was a sequel to my first book, *The Andreasson Affair* [2] published in 1979. Both recorded the UFO experiences of Betty [Andreasson] Luca. Betty's experiences reportedly took place when she lived at South Ashburnham, Ashburnham, Westminster and Leominster, Massachusetts.

During the course of my research, I was able to examine her previous homes at South Ashburnham and Ashburnham. However, I was negligent in not visiting her former homes in Westminster and Leominster as part of my investigation.

On a very hot and humid summer day, I set off from work to give a slide show on *The Andreasson Affair* to the Knights of Columbus [KOC] at Leominster. I had never been to Leominster and had left plenty of time to find the KOC hall and to eat supper. I located the hall and drove around to find a shady tree to park under and eat sandwiches. I found a huge tree, parked under it and ate my supper. Then I headed back to the hall and gave my presentation.

Afterwards, a couple came up to me. They asked if I had ever seen the house where Betty had lived during her childhood experiences. I confessed that I had not and was surprised when they told me that they now lived in that very house. They offered to show it to me. I followed their car. When we stopped in front of their house, I was awestruck. **It was the same house** with the large tree in front of it **where I had stopped to eat my supper**!

NO VACATION FROM UFOs!

On October 3, 1988 [according to Margaret's diary], we arrived in the White Mountains of New Hampshire for a foliage-viewing vacation. A trip to the top of Mount Washington was first on our agenda. We decided to take a paid ride to the summit in a van rather than put strain on our car. When I purchased tickets at a counter, the person selling tickets **recognized me**. She had attended one of my UFO lectures many years ago.

Later, when we checked in at the Edencroft Manor in Littleton, the innkeeper's son **recognized m**e. He had read my book, *The Andreasson Affair*, many years ago. He then escorted us to our room upstairs in the inn. As I set down some suitcases in front of the room to open the door, I came face to face with a sign on the door. It read the **Blue Room**. The **Blue Room** is the name of the area where the United States Air Force's Project Bluebook stored material relating to UFO reports at Wright-Patterson Air Force Base!

This was not the end of the UFO-related synchronisms that took place on that date. After settling in our rooms, I went down to the lounge of the Inn. I began chatting about UFOs to the innkeeper's son. At that time, the TV was not on. However, just as I started talking about UFOs, a guest flicked it on. We glanced over at the screen. **It was a program about UFOs**!

When we returned home from vacation, I brought two roll of films into Fotomat for processing. Later, when I picked up the developed film, all the pictures of people, places, and autumn foliage came out beautifully. However, I found that a number of photos that I had taken of certain physical evidence related to an investigation of Betty [Andreasson] Luca were **completely blank**.

Amazingly, several hours later, Betty phoned to tell me that she had just received a roll of film back from processing. All but four exposures had come out perfectly. Four exposures taken of a black unmarked helicopter maneuvering near her trailer **were blank**! Later, I typed up the accounts about the blank film from **Fotomat** for my book, *The Watchers* [3] I had just typed up a sentence in *The Watchers* manuscript that mentioned my trip to pick it up the film from **Fotomat** when the telephone rang. It was **Fotomat** calling to inform me that prints for Margaret were ready to pick up!

As you have seen, incredible synchronisms take place when I am in the midst of writing books on UFOs. One day, in September of 1988, I was bombarded with uncanny coincidences while writing *The Watchers*.

WIZARD, WITNESS AND A WITCH!

On September 12, 1988, I was working on a chapter for *The Watchers*. It alluded to the book [and movie] entitled *The Wizard of Oz* by Frank **Baum**. The telephone rang. The person on the phone asked to talk to me about a UFO experience. Her last name was **Baum**! Her experience had taken place several miles from my home at a wooded area I often walked!

Then, that same day, I phoned my former employer at GTE about my retirement insurance. A person recently transferred from another plant answered the telephone in the personnel office. She was a UFO abductee whom I had interviewed years ago!

Still, later in the evening, Margaret asked me to take her to a movie. We found an interesting one playing at the **Cabot** Theater in Beverly, Massachusetts. As she was looking up the theater's number in the phone book, she came across the name Laurie **Cabot**. Governor Dukakis had proclaimed Laurie the official Witch of Salem. She often appeared on radio and TV shows and headed a coven in Salem. When Margaret mentioned Laurie's name, I laughed [thinking of the Baum incident] and exclaimed, "That's all I need after what happened today—a telephone call from the Salem Witch!" Less than a half-hour later, the telephone rang. It was Laurie **Cabot**! She called to report a UFO that she and a friend had sighted!

PERSONIFIED THOUGHT!

Less than a month later, I had another weird experience. While working on *The Watchers*, I was fascinated by reports made by witnesses that mentioned seeing tall blonde human-like entities during their UFO experiences. In particular, I was intrigued by such a being reported by a woodcutter named Travis Walton. Travis reported that the entity had **long blond hair, a fair complexion and was wearing a one-piece jumpsuit**. When Travis attempted to talk with the entity, he merely responded with a smile.

On Sunday morning, October 2, 1988, I was still wondering about the blonde human-like entity. Then, while driving Margaret and her mother to church, we had a strange experience. As I took a sharp turn onto a minor road, I gasped in amazement at the personified synchronism that confronted my eyes. There, standing on the right side of the road, was **a very tall, exceptionally fair-complexioned man with long blond hair**.

Dumbfounded, I watched as he half-stepped onto the road as if he was trying to capture our attention. He wore **an unfamiliar one-piece jumpsuit** and what looked like boots. As my eyes met his, it seemed that time stood still as he stared at me with a kind, almost childlike smile. The synchronicity was incredible. My heart pounded as I instinctively sped by in shock. The afterimage of his strange smile and piercing stare was still embedded in my mind's eye. Trying to keep my composure, I casually remarked to Margaret and her mother that the man looked completely out of place in that strange outfit. They agreed. It reminded me of a NASA flight suit without a helmet!

COINCIDENCE OR CHARADE?

The surprise encounter with the strange-suited blond person reminded me of another incident that occurred when I worked at GTE. Each day I drove the same way to work along route 128, a crowded three-lane highway. One morning, as I approached a field on my right, I noticed something silver glittering in the rising sun. To my utter amazement, a man's hand extended from some bushes beside the highway. It seemed as if he deliberately released a flat silver Mylar balloon directly in front of my oncoming car. It floated up in front of me and across the highway looking astonishingly like a fat flying saucer!

Tens of thousands travel this highway to work at numerous defense contractors. If this release were intentional, it had to be someone who knew of my work schedule and the type and color of my car. If it were not intentional, it was another one of those thought-provoking synchronisms that are part and parcel of my involvement with UFOs.

Let us now return to my *SynchroFile* where I have recorded some up-to-date amazing *corresponding coincidences of the circumstantial kind*. A cold tingling feeling still creeps up my spine when I recollect these uncanny coincidences. I am sure some may produce incredulity on the part of readers. I would not blame them. I would find many of them hard to believe myself unless I had experienced them.

My wife Margaret was responsible for bringing the following *corresponding coincidence* to a climax:

> **May 2, 1996:** Awoke at 5:55 a.m. An interesting synchronism occurred in the evening. During an interview with [a suspected UFO abductee], he told me of a **certain rural intersection**. Each time he went through it, he felt that something associated with UFOs had happened to him. He also had two other conscious recollections of things that had happened to him at that **same intersection**.
> 1. Once he saw a car stopped **at this intersection** and a man hanging out of the door seemingly unconscious. He went to a nearby college [Gordon College] and informed the police but when they arrived there was nothing there.
> 2. Another time he himself had an accident in which his car rolled over at **this intersection.**
>
> The surprising synchronism occurred when my wife returned from an errand. Margaret said she had just passed through that **same intersection.** She had come upon police cars and an accident there!
>
> **January 1995**: [I forgot to record the exact date of these two synchronisms that occurred this month.]
> 1. While talking on the telephone with Betty Luca, I mentioned that I was taking a strong antibiotic for a lung infection. She told me that I must eat yogurt because the antibiotics would kill both good and bad bacteria in my body. We had **no idea what kind of yogurt to buy**, as some types did not contain active bacteria. Margaret went to a huge supermarket to buy some. There, standing directly in front of the yogurt section, was a friend who is a professional dietitian. She was **able to show Margaret the best kind of yogurt to buy.**

2. Talking about the afterlife with Bob Luca reminded me of a conversation between Shirley MacLain and a person named David in a TV mini-series entitled *Out on a Limb*. I decided to watch it again and rented the commercial video of this movie. However, **the segment that I was interested in** had been deleted in the video edition.

I knew a former student interested in the so-called New Age movement. I telephoned him to see if he had recorded the TV version. He told me that he had done so but erased it long ago. Later he telephoned back to tell me that he had located a copy. The synchronistic circumstances behind his find were interesting. They involved his friends. Later, he and his friends brought me the tape and told me what had happened.

After my request for the tape, he called Friend #1 and asked if she had a tape of the show. She didn't have a copy but said that she would call Friend #2 to see if she had a copy of the tape.

In the meantime, unbeknown to all of us, Friend #2 had been sorting through her video collection to find the very *Out on a Limb* tape that I wanted. She did not know we were looking for it. The reason that she was looking for it was that she wanted to review **the same segment**! She lent me the tape.

May 2, 1995: I was talking on the phone with a friend about Lyme disease caused by **ticks** in our locale. I told him that the fear of Lyme disease was not going to stop me from walking in the woods. After I hung up, I picked up a piece of cardboard beside the telephone to put it in the wastebasket. There was a **tick** on it!

June 13, 1995: I was talking to Betty [Andreasson] Luca today. She mentioned that she had awakened about two weeks ago with a painful left side, arm, shoulder and neck. I too had awaked with the **exact same symptoms** two weeks ago, which lasted about a week.

September 13, 1995: In England during one of our daily hikes across extensive farmland, I wondered aloud to Margaret why we hadn't seen a **pheasant** in such a likely habitat. Soon after, as we continued walking back to her mother's house, I almost stepped upon a dead **pheasant** directly in our path!

The next entry alludes to a synchronicity similar to what I have dubbed a *clock coincidence*, which will be the subject of a later chapter in the book. I mention it here because this particular event relates better to a *corresponding coincidence*.

September 14, 1995: During our stay in England, I would sometimes get an impulse to glance at my 24-hour watch. I would find all the numbers lined up as they have so often done during the night. Many times, they were the numbers **5–5–5** and this did actually occur at **5:55** a.m. this morning. Later, when

I paid the milk deliveryman at the front door, the price came to **six pounds, 55 pence—5-5-5** again! Still later, I turned on the TV to watch a movie entitled, *Vanished without a Trace*. As the TV flicked on, the scene presented was a mother yelling at her child saying, "**5-5-5**, just cool it"!

September 29, 1995: In England, while traveling to London airport by subway, our fare came to **exactly six pounds, 20 pence**. At the airport, we had lunch at a Café. The bill for the lunch came to exactly **six pounds, 20 pence**!

September 23, 1996: [One of the several synchronisms on this date is a *corresponding coincidence*.] This morning I was talking to a friend on the phone. She told me that her daughter was in the hospital. Her daughter was very weak because of loss of blood. She had been **hemorrhaging** badly during the birth of her child. After hanging up, I read from a daily devotional booklet. I then looked up referenced Bible verses. The passage for reading today was about a **hemorrhaging** woman healed by Jesus!

April 21, 1997: Two days ago, Margaret and I were talking about various types of mischief that kids get into. I told her about a childhood neighbor in my hometown of Danvers, Massachusetts. His name was **Fred Sylvester.** One summer day in the 1940's, Fred got a gang of other kids together to make a backyard swimming pool. We dug a huge hole in the Sylvester lawn. We were going to fill it with water for swimming! When Fred's father came home, he was horrified to find the gaping hole in his lawn.

This evening, I presented a planetarium show for a grade school class. After the show, a young boy came up to me. He asked if I used to know a person named **Fred Sylvester**. Astonished, I said that I had known someone by that name as a child when I had lived in Danvers. He told me that **Fred Sylvester** was his grandfather!

April 27, 1997: Before beginning a class on UFOs, I put a flyer on the table for students. It was an advertisement for tee shirts that had an **alien face** printed on them. I did this for a friend who manufactures them. When the students arrived, one of them placed a package for me on my desk. When I opened it, there was a tee shirt with an **alien face** on it with the caption, "We are not alone"! [It was not manufactured by my friend.]

July 15, 1997: An interesting and sentimental synchronism. I was sitting at the piano waiting for the mailman to come. For some reason, a thought came to me about how my mother used to play a song entitled *The White Cliffs of Dover*. I decided to play it by ear while waiting for the mailman. When he pulled up at the mailbox, I went outside and collected the mail. I came in, sat down and began sorting through a pile of mail. One piece of mail was a music catalog featuring cassettes and CD's of old tunes of music. Half-interested, I opened it up. I was immediately confronted with a bold caption advertising a book of music from World War II. It was entitled *The White Cliffs of Dover!*

August 1, 1997: An interesting synchronism occurred today after I had scanned a page from my diary. The first item on the page was from June 19th and read, "Awoke with an elated feeling, saying to myself, '**I can hardly wait for my soul to go home.**' I could not remember what I had been dreaming. I thought this statement was very strange. I was so excited that I had almost blurted it aloud. Later, I picked up a book that I had been reviewing for Wildflower Press. It was entitled *Opening to the Infinite*. I opened it up and began reading the following statement: "**People will say they just can't wait to go home**, don't want to be here, hate living in this body!"

January 7, 1998: A **buzzing sound** caused me to awake suddenly with a start. A strange **tingling sensation** coursed through my body. When I got up, I wrote a brief note to put this in my diary. I then placed it on my computer to copy later. Later in the day, I collected mail from the mailbox and sat down in my chair at the computer to read it. I noticed that my note was still on the computer as I opened my mail. The first piece of mail was a newsletter that someone had passed on to me. I opened it up at random to page six and my eyes first fell on a sentence that read: I felt a **tingling sensation** and perceived a **buzzing sound**!

January 24, 1998: My father, another Raymond Fowler, worked at a large company called the United Shoe for 30 years. He had worked his way up the career ladder to become the assistant to the plant manager. Dad loved the company and often reminisced about his time spent there. He was very disappointed when the plant closed down. It was sad to see the vacant building and vacant parking lot deteriorating.

Dad's name had not always been Raymond Fowler. His parents died when he was still a child. He was placed in a Catholic orphanage. The church changed his name to George **Cummings**. It was only changed back to Raymond Fowler after his aunt was able to reclaim him back into the family. Dad died on February 17, 1994. Since then the plant has been purchased and completely renovated for offices and small business. Dad would have broken into a big grin if he could read what I read in the newspaper. The new building has been named The **Cummings** Center!

January 28, 1998: A creepy yet very funny synchronism happened this morning! Last evening during my class, one of my students brought me a model of a **flying saucer** with figures of little alien entities for a joke. She is an amusing individual and has often brought me little joke gifts that related to UFOs. In the past, I used them to tease Margaret. I would place little alien dolls in her teacup, cupboard, etc.

This evening, after Margaret had gone to bed, I went downstairs. I placed the model of the **flying saucer in the kitchen** along with little aliens on a counter beside the stove. I then joined Margaret in bed and wondered how she would react to the latest joke in the morning.

In the morning, I told her that I would bring her tea in bed and went downstairs to make it. I pulled a Salada tea bag out its envelope too hard and the tag ripped off. I placed the tag on the counter beside the flying saucer and proceeded to make the tea. I was about to throw the tag in the wastebasket but thought it might be fun to look at the message that was printed on it. [Something that I rarely do.] A chill went up my spine when I read: **"Flying saucers are sometimes seen in the kitchen!"** on the tag

March 11, 1998: I asked Margaret to pick up an old book from a local church library. It was first published in 1935 and then reprinted in 1984. It is entitled *Eternity in their Hearts*. She did and brought it home. Later that evening, we visited some friends. As I entered their living room, the first thing that I noticed was a copy of *Eternity in their Hearts* on their coffee table.

March 14, 1998: At a men's group breakfast, Jack Good mentioned that he had just returned from a business trip. He said that he had attended the **First Baptist Church in Biloxi**, Mississippi. I surprised everybody when I told the men that I had been baptized in **the First Baptist Church in Biloxi**. I worshiped there while attending radio schools at Keesler Air Force Base in Biloxi.

April 20, 1998: Two helpful synchronisms occurred today.

1. Margaret and I were out shopping. The first item that I needed was a pair of trousers with a **36" waist and a 30" pant length**. In the past, I have found this size hard to find. We walked into the trousers area of the department store. The first thing that we noticed was a pair of trousers hanging all by itself. I took it off the hanger to see what size it was. It had a **36" waist and a 30" pant length**!
2. The second item that I was looking for was a **certain kind of bicycle** that was now hard to come by. I wanted the kind that had the older type curved handlebars and one with less than 10 speeds. It was a tall order as most bikes that I had seen for sale had a least 10 speeds and a new type of handlebar that I did not like. So, I was shocked when we entered the main entrance of a store named Sports Authority. There, right inside the door facing us, was the **very kind of bicycle** that I was looking for, and it was on sale. It was separate from the bike section, which was at the other end of the store. We checked there as well, but the bike back at the entrance was the only one of its type. Another helpful synchronism. I bought it.

July 12–July 26, 1998: We vacationed at Pittsburg, New Hampshire with my brother Richard and his wife. Several synchronisms occurred. Some involved reading a word in a book at the precise time someone on TV said it. One very interesting one occurred after a discussion that I had with my brother. It was about the spooky radio shows that we used to listen to when we were children. Richard remarked that he and my other brother John shared a bedroom while I was away in the Air Force. He reminisced how scared he used to get when John listened to a radio program called **Captain Video**. I remarked back that I had never heard of the program. Fantastic as it might seem, the following day I picked up a book that I had brought on vacation to read. It was entitled *Project Mindshift*. I opened the book to where I had left off reading and was amazed when I turned to the next page. The author was mentioning the old radio program called **Captain Video**!

September 25, 1998: This morning I was interviewed about my planetarium and observatory by a newspaper reporter. After the interview, she surprised me. She confessed that she and members of her family all had UFO experiences. These included her own abduction experiences that dated back to childhood.

One of the benchmarks of such experiences is what is called a *screen memory*. This is when aliens cause abductees to initially think that they are seeing an animal with big black eyes rather than alien entities with big black eyes. The primary *screen memory* reported by alleged abductees is seeing a **deer with big black eyes**.

As we were talking, we were both amazed to **see a deer with big black eyes** suddenly come out of the woods. It walked up to within 40 feet of the picture window from which we were watching and then turned around and walked back to the woods. I have never seen a deer come that close to our house. They usually stay down in the orchard beside the woods. We joked afterwards that it might have been a *screen memory*!

October 17, 1998: An interesting synchronism occurred today. My brother mentioned some time ago that he was trying to find **an antique railroad lantern**. I mentioned that I had a lantern which I had found in the cellar when we moved into the house. However I did not think it fit the description of the type he wanted.

This evening he visited. He mentioned again that he had been searching flea markets for this same specific type of lantern with a red lens. He had found one but the seller wanted $50 for it and he thought it was too expensive. I quickly went down cellar, located the dust-laden lantern, and brought it up for him to see. We placed it in the light and through the dust we could see *that* **it was exactly what he had been looking for over many years.** I gave it to him.

November 27, 1998: Yesterday, Margaret was sorting out some of our audio tapes. The label on one of them indicated that it was a recording made by her now deceased father. I asked if she would like me to play it for her. She said no because **the voice of her father** upset her. Later, she came across some other old tapes. They were labeled as being made by our children when they were young. However, one did not have a label on it. We wondered what was on it. I put it in the tape recorder. Margaret [and I] were shocked. It was the **voice of her father** making his first transatlantic call to Margaret after she arrived to live in America!

December 2, 1998: A few evenings ago, Margaret and I were talking about all the old magazines that were no longer published. I asked her if ***Life*** magazine was still published, as I had not seen one for a long time. She said that she wasn't sure but that it might still be published on a monthly basis. Today when she went to the post office, a clerk gave her a copy of ***Life*** magazine for me. It had the new Hubble photograph of Saturn that he knew I would be interested in seeing. He had no prior knowledge of my conversation with Margaret.

January 26, 1999: Yesterday, I typed up the first pages of a potential new book detailing **my memoirs** as a UFO investigator. Today, I received an email from Wendy Conners encouraging me to write **my memoirs**!

February 19, 1999: A helpful synchronism. While cross-country skiing at Jackson, NH, Margaret, up ahead of me, picked up a **ski pass** that someone had ***lost***. It was dated for today. This made me glance down at my jacket to see if mine was still attached. It was gone. I must have lost my **ski pass** on another path. It was a good break for me as I would have had to purchase another one for $12 to stay on the trails!

June 2, 1999: Last evening, Margaret and I went for a walk. Afterwards, we stopped to get ice cream at The Junction in Hamilton. Just as we pulled up in the car, we saw a **strange couple**. A very tall skinny elderly man and a very thin younger girl held hands as they walked toward the take-out windows to order ice cream. We thought they were strange because of their appearance and wide difference in age.

Today, Margaret and I were in Ipswich and decided to stop and buy some doughnuts. At the exact time we pulled up to the doughnut shop parking lot, we were shocked to see **the same strange couple.** They walked hand-in-hand and up to the doughnut shop to buy doughnuts.

December 13, 1999: Last evening, I had conversation with my friend about my career with GTE Government Systems. One of the topics of conversation was about GTE Government Systems being recently bought by **General Dynamics**. This morning, while walking in the woods in Topsfield, MA, I almost stepped upon a piece of paper lying on the path. I picked it up and was surprised to see that it was a discarded memo with the heading, **General**

Dynamics! [The General Dynamics Plants are located in Needham and Taunton, MA. They are 30–60 miles away from Topsfield].

December 18, 1999: Another very interesting synchronism. My childhood friend, Dave Harris visited today. When we were teens, **he led me into the Christian faith**. Margaret and I went out to lunch with him, returned home, and chatted for a few hours. Much of the conversation was about the preponderance of personal synchronisms that I am recording in this diary. After Dave left for home, Margaret prepared supper. We read a devotional before we eat. This evening, the devotional reading ended with the following statement: "Over the years, who have been your 'stars'—**the people who led you to Christ?**"

December 21, 1999: Here is another synchronism involving the reading of the daily devotional mentioned in the last input. During the morning, I was thinking about a position that was opening **at church**. The editor of the church newspaper was resigning. He had asked if someone would volunteer to take his place. Since I was adept at using a word processor and clip art programs, I contacted him. I said that I would be interested in taking on this ministry. I explained that I could do it **at home** in the daytime, as my evenings were busy. Later, at noon, we read the following from today's devotional reading: Amazingly, it read—"Think of some specific ways to use your talents and abilities **in your church or in your home**."

January 22, 2000: I was going through my wife's diary looking for the date of a particular incident. I noticed a brief entry that noted we had spent a vacation in a housekeeping **cabin on the shore of Thomas Pond** in South Casco, Maine. The entry brought to mind a spooky thing that we both experienced in bed one night during our stay there. Unknown to her, I decided to include this scary experience in the book that I am writing.

In the evening, we babysat our grandchildren for our daughter. She and her husband were going to a dinner party. Later, when they came by to pick up the children, they mentioned that they had played a nice game at the party. It involved questions asked separately to husbands and wives to see if they would come up with the same answers. For example, they might be asked, "Where did you have your first kiss?" For fun, my daughter turned to us and asked, "Where did you spend your worse vacation?" Margaret instantly answered: **"At the cottage at Thomas Pond!"** Again, Margaret had no idea that I had just written up the frightening experience in the manuscript for my new book.

March 6, 2000: A few days ago, I went into my filing cabinet to get a file folder containing a **letter from James Oberg**. It was not there. I had no idea where it could have gone. I was very disappointed to think that I had lost or misplaced it. It was frustrating, as I needed the letter. Today I took out a file folder containing information on one of my former investigators named Fred Youngren. When I opened the manila folder, there, staring me in the face was the misfiled **letter from James Oberg**!

April 25, 2000: While waiting to be called for dinner, I was playing a number of songs from the 1950's on the piano. The last song that I played before Margaret called me was *Some Enchanted Evening*. This song always brought back memories of a traumatic teenage experience. This was when my girlfriend had broken up with me back in 1950. Right after the breakup, I went home and played this song repeatedly, especially the refrain—"Once you have found her, never let her go." It was typical teenage puppy love but at the time, I was devastated. The girl's name was **Margaret Cahoon**. [Now, Margaret Smith.]

In any event, I stopped playing the song and I sat down at the dinner table with Margaret. Before eating, Margaret brings in a bag of last year's Christmas cards to the table. She reaches in and picks one out each day. We then pray for the person who sent it. It was my turn to pray so she reached into the bag, pulled out a card, and handed it to me. I opened it up and was dumbfounded. It was from **Margaret [Cahoon] Smith**! My wife had no idea of the connection between this girl and the song. She hand randomly picked the card! Little did I know then that a similar synchronism would happen on April 9, 2001, which is recorded elsewhere in this book.

June 6, 2000: On the way to vacationing at Pittsburg, NH, we stopped to eat at a place called The Glen Junction. I noticed that the waitress had an English accent and asked what part of England she was from. During our conversation, she told us that she once lived in **Hampstead**, London. We were surprised, as **Hampstead** is where Margaret was attending secretarial school when I was courting her. Also, that is where we were married.

As the conversation continued, we were surprised again when she said that her grandfather had been a bus driver in **Hull**, England. Margaret's home had been in **Hull**. Since she often took buses in Hull at the time he drove a bus, we thought it was very possible she had ridden on his bus!

July 11, 2000: An amazing synchronism. I was sitting in the backyard reading a book entitled *The Coincidence File*. I had bought it to study the phenomenon of synchronisms that have been so much a part of my life. I had just read a section that said "reading about someone else's synchronisms could cause one to happen to the reader." I wondered if this were true and if I should expect one soon. I did not have long to wait. Margaret, who had been sick and not eating well, joined me. She told me that she was finally feeling hungry. She said that **she felt like eating a boiled egg**. However, when she went to look for eggs, there were none in the refrigerator. She also reminded me that we were going to go on a picnic tomorrow. She remarked that **it would be good to have eggs** for making sandwiches. All of these were hints that I should leave my reading and go up town to buy some eggs. I told her that I would go and buy the eggs.

However, before doing this, I told her that I was going up the street to take the mail out of Mary's [a shut-in's] mailbox and bring it to her. One of us did this on a daily basis. I went to Mary's, brought in the mail, and sat down to talk for a few minutes. When I got up to leave, **Mary asked me if we could use a dozen eggs**! I had not mentioned our need for eggs. I was amazed at the coincidence. She explained that various people had brought her eggs to help her out and that she had more than she could use. Margaret was very surprised when I arrived back home with the eggs.

[Note: A few minutes after I had written this in the *SynchroFile* manuscript, Margaret called down to me and asked if I would like a **boiled egg** for supper! Chock up another one for the diary.]

September 5, 2000: Earlier in the day, Margaret and I discussed how we had not heard from a friend named **John Oswald** for months. Later in the afternoon, when we checked our mail, there was a letter from **John Oswald**!

September 7, 2000: [In England.] Today, we met a fellow guest at a Bed and Breakfast establishment. He told us that he was a Methodist lay preacher from Wales who was visiting a church in Hull. We told him that we were going to attend the **Cottingham Baptist Church** on the upcoming Sunday. Much to our surprise, he said that he had been baptized there and that his ancestors had founded the **Cottingham Baptist Church**.

September 10, 2000: [In England.] This morning we arrived at the Cottingham Baptist Church and sat in the back row near the door. Shortly after the service started, a latecomer hurriedly entered the church and slid quickly in beside me. After the church service, we introduced ourselves. When she discovered that we were from the United States, she told us that she had a friend living there. I casually asked where her friend lived in America. She replied—**Danvers**, Massachusetts. **Danvers was my hometown!**

September 11, 2000: [In England.] When I last accompanied Margaret on her yearly visits to England in 1995, one *of* **her mother's friends** urged us to take a **Shearings Bus Tour** someday. This company conducts dozens of tours each year. Now, five years later, we remembered her advice. We booked a tour of the Lake District where we had spent our honeymoon in 1955. When we arrived at the pick-up-point for the tour bus, we literally bumped into **her mother's friend** as we boarded the **Shearings Bus** at the same time. She had booked the same tour that we had.

September 22, 2000: [In England.] Back home in Wenham, I jog or **take a walk** almost daily on a golf course at the end of Friend Court where we live. Over the course of a year, **I pick up about 1000 golf balls**. I sell them and give the proceeds to the church youth group. Margaret often teases me **when we walk** elsewhere and asks me if I am going to look for golf balls.

At this time in England, we are staying with Margaret's friends. One day while **taking a walk** with her friends, the subject of my golf ball mania came up. Much to my amazement, they told me that a golf ball had mysteriously appeared in their back yard. When we returned from **the walk**, they gave it to me.

Later that evening, the neighbor's burglar alarm went off. We all went over to their house to check and see what was going on. It was a false alarm. During our chat with the neighbors, they mentioned that **they had found five golf balls on their driveway**. They too are mystified as to where they had come from, as there are no golf courses or driving ranges nearby. The neighborhood is comprised of many closely-situated fenced houses surrounded by trees. We told them of my addiction to collecting golf balls and they gave me one to add to my collection!

November 18 & 19, 2000: This synchronism concerned two separate conversations with different participants. The first was with my friend John Oswald who was visiting us on the 18th. He told us how he liked to mountain climb at **Pawtuckaway State Park** in Raymond, NH. We asked him lots of questions about this place as we liked to hike. On the 19th, we went to a Thanksgiving worship service with my brother's wife. During our conversation, she said that earlier in the day she and my brother had driven up into NH for a scenic drive. They decided to explore a State Park that they had randomly come across—**Pawtuckaway State Park**!

December 11, 2000: I am the editor of our Church newsletter. For the January edition, I put together an astronomy page for the youth. It contained a star map with instructions how to find an open star cluster called the Pleiades and the constellation of Orion. I also included a Bible verse from **Amos 5:8**, which reads: "He who made the **Pleiades and Orion.**" This evening, before the publication of the newspaper, the church youth group visited my planetarium and observatory. After the show, we went outside to look at the stars. I pointed out the **Pleiades and Orion** to them, whereupon the youth director spoke up. He said that he had been studying the book of Amos and had recited **Amos 5:8** to the youth at their weekly meeting!

December 17, 2000: [Two of three synchronisms on this date are *corresponding coincidences*].
1. Our dog's metal license tag issued by the **Wenham Town Clerk** fell off and I placed it on the kitchen table to remind me to put it back on his collar. Today we invited a neighbor to our church to hear a Christmas cantata that I was singing in. After church, we invited her back for coffee. Afterwards, **she saw the dog tag** on the table. She reminded us that it was illegal for it not to be on the dog. She should know. She is the **Wenham Town clerk** and the last

time **she saw the dog tag** was when she issued it to me in April at the Town Hall.

2. While eating supper, Margaret mentioned that we had not received a Christmas card from our friends, **Jean and Alf**, in England. She figured it was because they probably had just returned from a trip to New Zealand and had no time to get their cards out in the mail. After supper, I checked my email. The latest email was from **Jean and Alf**! They explained that they decided to email us the season's greetings. A card would not have gotten to us in time for Christmas. [The British postal system was severely impacted by terrible flooding in England.]

January 24, 2001: Two *corresponding coincidences* took place on this date. [One was of the telephone kind and recorded elsewhere.] Before setting off for choir practice, I sat down at the piano and **played a hymn very rarely played** at church. It was entitled, "Once to Every Man and Nation." Later I went to choir practice and when I walked into the church, the organist *was* **playing the same tune**!

January 30 & 31, 2001: Another synchronism occurred similar to the one in the last entry. Yesterday [Tuesday], I listened to the news about electric power problems and blackouts in California. My mind then turned to an old movie entitled *The Day the Earth Stood Still*. I wondered if Hollywood might make a modern version of it. It could be based upon the now recognized relationship between electrical blackouts and the UFO phenomenon. Today [Wednesday], I turned the computer on and clicked onto an email that gives a summary of one of my favorite web sites. Each day, the sender's email is prefaced by a quotation. Today's quote read: "Klatu Barata Nicto"—Patricia Neal in *The Day the Earth Stood Still*. CAUSE HIGHLIGHTS: Wednesday—January 31, 2001."

February 4, 2001: During this morning's church service, the pastor asked the congregation to turn to **John, chapter 10**, in the Bible. I reached over and randomly opened the thick pew Bible to look for it and inadvertently opened it to **John, chapter 10**!

February 20, 2001: A synchronism occurred similar to the kind I had recorded in the February 4th entry. This morning I turned to the Gospel of John, which I have been reading as part of my devotionals. One of the last passages that I read was from **John 6:68, 69**. After my devotion time, I randomly opened a Greek textbook to practice translation. It opened to page 190 and exercise #454. Each exercise had a number of sentences to translate. I randomly placed my finger on #15 and began translating the sentences. I was amazed to see that it was **John 6:68, 69** in Greek!

February 28, 2001: A synchronsim occurred similar to the one recorded in the February 20th entry. My Bible reading this morning was short. It consisted of several sentences entitled, **Jesus, the light of the world**. The verses read: "When Jesus spoke to the people again, he said, "**I am the light** of the world; anyone who follows me will not be walking in **the dark**; he will have the light of life." After reading this verse, I picked up my Greek textbook to practice translation. I opened it to an exercise. I randomly placed my finger on #9 to translate the selection from Greek into English. It read: "But this is the judgment, that **the light** [i.e., **Jesus**] came into the world but men **loved the darkness**."

April 11, 2001: An amazing synchronism! Today I prepared a horseshoe pit. I cemented the stakes in small barrels. These will be buried at a proper distance from each other. Later, I dug holes at the proper distances to bury the buckets in with their embedded stakes sticking out of the ground. When digging one of the holes, my shovel hit something hard. It was the remnants of a similar bucket. It too was filled with cement. Someone had filled it with cement and buried it in the **exact measured spot** for my horseshoe pit.

April 13, 2001: Yesterday I asked Margaret if we had any sheets of **Styrofoam** left over from packing material. [I am going to build a firing range for my airguns. I needed this material for backing. This material will absorb rather than cause the fast moving pellets to ricochet.] Margaret said that she did not have any. She suggested that I try to buy some at the local shopping center. In any event, I went outside to dismantle an old doghouse that was given to us 13 years ago. Our dog had been put to sleep and there was no longer any use for it. I hit one side of it with a sledgehammer. An inner and outer layer of wood split apart to reveal panels of white **Styrofoam** sandwiched between them for insulation! Needless to say, I now **have a supply of Styrofoam** panels for my firing range.

May 14, 2001: [One of the two synchronisms mentioned in this entry is a *corresponding coincidence*.] I forgot to record that a few weeks ago. Dave Harris drove me to Topsfield to show me his **childhood home** on North Street. Later that evening, I conducted a planetarium show for a group. I was amazed to find that the host for the group lived in the house directly across the street from Dave's **childhood home**!

May 17, 2001: Weeks ago, we scheduled friends to visit this evening. They wanted to get advice from us regarding their upcoming **trip to England**. However, we had to cancel their visit. Margaret's brother John telephoned this afternoon. He urged Margaret to come see her mother in a nursing home in England. It was possible that she was dying. Margaret is taking a **trip to England** tomorrow!

May 31, 2001: This morning I checked my email. I found many messages relating to new evidence for the crash of a UFO at **Roswell**, NM in July of 1947. A few hours later, I received a telephone call from a man being sent by Home Depot to install a new storm door. He told me that his name was Steve **Roswell**!

June 19, 2001: Margaret and I have often biked along a narrow peninsula dotted with summer homes at Biddeford Pool, Maine. Last year, we were amazed to **see a fox** running along the road ahead of us. We wondered how it could get enough food to survive in that area. Today, we biked through the same area and discussed how we had seen a fox in the past. Moments later, **a fox darted out** from behind a house directly across the road in front of our bikes.

June 25, 2001: Yesterday, my son, Ray Jr., found an **embedded wood tick in the upper section of his left arm.** He had it removed at the Beverly Hospital by a physician at the Hospital's emergency room. Today, I found an **embedded wood tick in the upper section of my left arm** that Margaret was able to remove.

July 3, 2001: Our old neighbor in Danvers invited us again to watch fireworks from the hill beside my boyhood home. After we sat down to wait for them to begin, a person walked up the hill and sat down beside me. During our conversation, I found that he had graduated from Danvers High school with my sister Dorothy.

July 5, 2001: This morning, I sat down at the piano and played *America the Beautiful*. After playing it, I went to the computer to check email. There was an email from a friend with an audio attachment. I clicked on it to see what song would be played. It was *America the Beautiful*!

September 25, 2001: This morning, I went to a college to pick up astronomy course materials printed for me. As I passed an open door to a classroom, I saw **John Toby**, an old friend and a professor at the college. I would like to have stopped and talked to him, but he seemed to be having a long conversation with a student. I had many errands to do and could not wait around to see him. So I continued on my way and proceeded to do my errands. I dropped off photos for development, shopped for a gift for a friend and then went to a large Stop and Shop supermarket to buy some milk. As I rounded an aisle in the store, I came face to face with **John Toby**!

October 2, 2001: We are hiring a friend who owns a septic service company to install our new septic system. Prior to doing this, we had to have an engineer do soil testing and draw up plans for the system. We hired someone from a local office in Hamilton to do the work. We were surprised when he showed up. He was a **high school friend of my son,** Ray Jr. He now lived in Amesbury, Massachusetts. We told him that our daughter **Beth** lived in Amesbury. We were surprised when he said that he is a good friend of **Beth** and that he **attends the same church** as she does.

October 21, 2001: We see an **old friend** about once a year when we invite him for an annual dinner get-together. He had dinner with us several days ago on October 18. Today, we went for a walk on a huge tract of land. We decided to walk along a remote path that we had never tried before. As we walked down the path we saw our **old friend** walking toward us. We were shocked to see him. He apparently chose this hidden path because he was with someone else's girlfriend and did not want to be seen!

November 11, 2001: A friend phoned today and said that she knew someone who wanted to move to Wenham. She wondered if we knew of any **houses for sale**. She was amazed when we told her that we had put our **house up for sale** three days ago. She had not known this.

November 20, 2001: We are moving to Maine. An old friend that we had not seen for years somehow heard about it. She phoned and asked where we were moving to in Maine. Margaret told her that **we were moving to Kennebunk**. She was shocked, as was Margaret, when she said that **she lived in Kennebunk when a child**. Then she asked where we were going to live in Kennebunk. Margaret told her **we would live on Maguire Road**. Both were astonished when she told Margaret that **her elderly father lived on Maguire Road**, a half mile down from us on the same side of the road!

November 26, 2001: [One of the two synchronisms on this date is a *corresponding coincidence*.] Today a friend named Barry **Greenwood** came by to pick up some files. After he left, Margaret suggested that we go for a walk on an old road that a friend had mentioned. When we arrived at the road, we saw a sign at its entrance. It read **Greenwood** Avenue!

January 25, 2002: This morning a man from the John Deere company delivered my new snow blower. I told him that I had just moved to Maine from Massachusetts. He replied that he had moved to Maine from Massachusetts several years ago. He asked where I had lived in Massachusetts. I told him **we had lived in Wenham**. He was surprised and told me that his parents **had lived in Wenham**!

January 29, 2002: This morning, I was doing some paperwork at a table in the breezeway. The breezeway picture window overlooks our lawn and the country road that we live on. I was in the middle of daydreaming about the **John Deere ride-on mower** that I was going to buy next month. A moment later, I happened to glance out the window. I was shocked to see a truck go by pulling a trailer. On the trailer was a **John Deere ride-on mower** like the one I was purchasing!

February 11, 2002: This morning I visited the Kennebunk Code Enforcement Officer. I needed a permit to install a greenhouse on our new property. I was surprised that his name was **Paul Demers**. I told him that my childhood friend's name was **Paul Demers**. He chuckled and said that he had a good friend named **Paul Demers**!

March 1, 2002*:* After getting settled in our house in Kennebunk, we wanted to find a new primary care physician. Margaret's hairdresser highly recommended a Dr. Schill. Margaret made the first appointment with the doctor. When the **doctor saw our address**, he was surprised. He told her that the former owner of our house was a friend of his and that **he had been in our house** a number of times.

March 4, 2002: We had dinner guests this evening that was brought to culmination a synchronism experienced a few weeks ago. At that time, we started attending a church in Kennebunk. We discovered that the pastor (Jim) had been a missionary in Argentina. Years ago, a couple, Bob and Barbara, missionaries in Argentina, had rented an apartment across the street from us in Wenham during their furlough. We asked Jim **if he knew of Bob and Barbara**. He was very surprised. Jim told us that he and his wife were **like house parents to Bob and Barbara** when they first arrived in Argentina. We arranged their reunion at a dinner this evening.

March 10, 2002: I encountered two synchronisms today. [One involved my brother Richard. It is listed elsewhere in the book. The other is as follows.] While flicking through channels on TV, I came across a piano concert given by a person named **Tim Janis**. We liked it and decided to listen to it. We wondered if a CD of his music would be offered on the program. It was offered, but one had to make a substantial contribution to a Public Broadcasting Station in New Hampshire. In the meantime, Margaret had picked up the Yellow Pages. She was looking for discount coupons from furniture stores. When she opened it and turned a page, there, staring her in the face was an ad that read: **THE TIM JANIS ENSEMBLE**! As if that wasn't enough of a shock, she glanced at the address in the ad. His headquarters was located only 3 miles from our new home in Kennebunk. It was at 2 Main Street, Kennebunk, ME!

April 14, 2002: On Monday evening, we attended a supper at a church in Kennebunkport. The crowd was large. We remarked how pleased the **new woman pastor** at the church would be to see such a big turnout. This morning, we decided to go back to Kennebunkport and walk along a beach. Parking was limited. I had to squeeze in front of a car parked facing in the wrong direction so that it was facing us. When I pulled in to the spot and glanced out, there was the **new woman pastor** staring at us from the front window of the car in front of us!

April 22, 2002: One of Margaret's friends that she became acquainted with at the YMCA in Massachusetts came up to visit today. She had mentioned to one of her girl friends, Mrs. Ploss, that she was going to visit the Fowlers in Maine. Mrs. Ploss told her that her deceased husband, Alan, had had a very good **friend named Ray Fowler,** who worked with him at GTE. She was amazed when she was told that **I was that Ray Fowler.** She had no idea that I had moved to Maine. We were both taken aback when we discovered this connection with me.

May 13, 2002: Margaret and I put out an orange under the bird feeder to attract **Baltimore Orioles.** They arrived just as we sat down to eat and they were beautiful to watch. Before we eat, we read from a daily devotional booklet. I opened it up. The first sentence read—"In the spring of 1894, the **Baltimore Oriole** came to Boston."

May 27, 2002: [One of the two synchronisms on this date was a *corresponding coincidence.*] Yesterday, my friend David Harris visited. During our conversation, we told him that we had seen two of our favorite birds'—**Bluebirds and Baltimore Orioles.** He was very interested, as he had not seen either bird since childhood. This morning he called with a synchronism for me. He said that he had just walked into a flea market. There, staring him in the face, were matched, beautifully framed paintings of **a Bluebird and a Baltimore Oriole** which he bought for us!

June 24, 2002: I took an early Sunday morning walk on the beach with my son, a pastor. I suggested that a good Biblical account to use as a sermon example would be the **Israelites crossing the Jordan**. They had to have enough faith to start wading across the Jordan before God would part the waters. Later that morning, we attended church. The pastor used the **Israelites crossing the Jordan** example we had just discussed a few hours prior!

August 27, 2002: This afternoon we had lunch with our pastor. We were joined by a couple who had served with them as missionaries in Argentina. In the course of conversation, our pastor mentioned an Armenian pastor and his wife who had been close friends in Portland, Maine many years ago. They **wondered where these friends might be** now. Margaret and I looked at each other in astonishment. **They are now friends of ours. We know exactly where they are**. They had retired to Ipswich, Massachusetts where we used to attend church. In fact, we used to drive them to church, as they were elderly and not able to drive.

September 15, 2002: While waiting for our pastor to announce a hymn, I randomly opened the hymnbook and waited. When he announced **hymn number 517**, I glanced down at the page that I had opened. It was **hymn number 517**.

Another synchronistic event, again involving the mysterious strangely dressed blonde man that mirrored the image of a similar person seen by UFO witness, Travis Walton. If you recall, one Sunday morning I had been deep in thought about this incident. Later, while driving to church that morning, I had been shocked to see a similar personage standing by the road. Now, fourteen years later, I experienced another synchronism concerning this same incident.

September 26, 2002: Just before supper, between 4:15 and 4:55 p.m., I was typing up an account about a UFO witness named Travis Walton. It was about his **seeing a blond, fair-skinned human-like entity** during his UFO experience. After I typed up this up, I shut off the computer and went to supper. After supper, I decided to check email. I found an email from a person named Chris Aubeck. The subject of his email was **the human-like alien seen by Travis Walton**. Chris could have had no idea that I had just written about the same subject. On top of that, I noted that Chris sent the email at 4:22 p.m. This was within the same period of time that I was researching and typing the data on Travis Walton's experience. This is yet another one of those amazing synchronisms that continue to happen to me.

October 1, 2002: [Two synchronisms occurred today. One involved my brother Richard. It will be recorded in another section of the book. The other took place while on the way back from vacationing in the White Mountains.] We stopped at White Lake State Park to take a walk along a path bordering the lake. When we walked up to the Lake, we noticed a boat anchored at the far end of the lake. I remarked that they probably were anchored over the **deepest part of the lake** fishing for trout. We walked around the lake. As we passed broadside to the fishermen, one of them remarked loudly to his companion that—**"this is the deepest part of the lake, ain't it?"**

October 10, 2002: Our grandchildren are familiar with the animal characters in nature books written by naturalist Thomson Burgess. They were thrilled when we put up signs all over our woods and fields bearing the names of these animals.

Today, Margaret went outside and marked over each sign with an indelible marker as they were getting faint from weathering. One of the last signs that she wrote over was for **Happy Jack** the squirrel. She then came in the house and continued to read a book entitled, *I Love you Ronnie*[4] by Nancy Reagan. Margaret sat down and turned to page 89 and experienced yet another encounter with synchronicity. It read: "The Skipper was what we called Ron. He was such an easy-going child that we called him **Happy Jack**."

October 12, 2002: I was working on my manuscript for a new book entitled *SynchroFile*. I had just typed up a synchronism from my diary that had occurred on April 10, 1996. It involved a painting by a renaissance painter named Fra Angelica. It was entitled ***Angels***. I got up for a moment. As I passed Margaret, she asked me if I was going to watch ***Touched by an Angel*** on TV with her!

November 12, 2002: For the past several days I have been feverishly preparing to facilitate a program at church entitled **Alpha**. I have given preliminary talks about **Alpha** to the deacons and to the church. I've handed out booklets, printed, and distributed brochures and posters. Tomorrow evening I begin leading the 15-week course on **Alpha**.

Today, in the midst of being embroiled in this activity, I received a very large package. It was a book from a company unfamiliar to me. The book was mistakenly sent to me. It was supposed to have been shipped to someone in Oakland, California. The name of the Book Company was **Alpha**Craze.com!

November 26, 2002: When Margaret and I sat down to open today's mail, we experienced a fascinating coincidence. On the one hand, I opened a package and pulled out sheet music for ***White Christmas***. On the other hand, Margaret unwrapped December's issue of the Readers Digest and opened it. She laughed and said, "I've got to show you this." She had just opened the Readers Digest to an article describing the song, ***White Christmas***!

Four synchronisms occurred on the date below. Two were *corresponding coincidences* of the circumstantial kind. The others are recorded elsewhere in the book.

December 4, 2002:

1. I had not heard from **Ted Smith, though** he usually ordered books from me. When the mailman came, there was a note from **Ted Smith**.
2. My intense involvement with the Alpha course brought on yet another uncanny synchronism. When we returned from the **Alpha** course, I checked my email. One of the emails that I received referred readers to an [unrelated] organization called: The Institute for Advanced Study, **Alpha** Foundation, 11 Rutafa Street, Building H, 1165, Budapest.

January 6, 2003: I went cross-country skiing this morning along a gas line that runs behind our property. I made it my goal to ski about two miles to where the gas line crossed Highway **99**. After my return home, I turned on my computer to the *New York Times* on the Internet. The first item that came up to read was the Quote of the Day. Today's quote was from a poem about a **Highway 99**! "It's a thunka thunka thunka highway, a working-class highway." C. G. Hanzlicek, a Fresno poet, on **Highway 99**.

January 11, 2003: I received a small legacy from Margaret's mother. I wanted to buy something useful in remembrance of her. I decided to buy a **Mantis Tiller** to use in the garden. I searched many gardening catalogs but could not find one. Yesterday, I tried the gardening section at Wal-Mart but still without success. Today when I checked the mail, I was shocked to find a letter from the Mantis Company offering a temporary discount for a **Mantis Tiller**!

January 25, 2003: Margaret and I have been discussing obtaining a dog. Our former dog had to be put down and I missed him. He was an outdoor dog and any dog in the future would have to be the same as my son is allergic to dogs. I decided that we could keep a future dog in the garage. I would build it a little heated room under the garage attic stairwell. However, I mentioned that the remaining obstacle would be **training a puppy** which I was not sure how to do.

Today, when I checked email, the first email was from Amazon.com and read: "As someone who has purchased books about dog training from us in the past, you might like to know that ***Expert Obedience Training for Dogs, 4th Edition*** will hit the shelves on February 1, 2003. For the next few days, you can pre-order yours at a savings of 30% by following the link below." I never had ordered books from Amazon.com about dog training!

Later, I went outside to check the mail. When I opened the mailbox there was large picture of a **puppy** facing me on the cover of a catalog for a company that I never heard of called Care-A-Lot. The company is a pet supply warehouse! I have never ordered from any pet supply company before.

February 24, 2003: I received a surprise phone call from Frank Pechulis, a former fellow employee at GTE Government Systems. I had not talked to him by phone for over a decade although I have had several emails from him. Frank is from the small town of **Whitensville, Massachusetts**, population 6, 340. He wanted me to send a copy of my new book to his daughter. Afterwards, the mail came. One of the items was a bulletin from a religious organization. I opened it and found an article about a Pastor from **Whitinsville, Massachusetts**.

February 5, 2003: Several interesting *corresponding coincidences* occurred over a several day period that were related to each other by the number **five**.
1. On January 23, Margaret and I cashed some checks at the drive-up window of the Kennebunk Savings Bank. After we left, Margaret realized that the teller had given us **$5.00** too much in change. We went back and returned the $5.00.

2. On January 31, Margaret noticed that there was an unaccounted-for amount of **$505** in our checking account and notified the bank of their error.
3. Today, on February 5, we shopped for food at the local Food market. When we returned to the car, Margaret noticed that the checkout clerk had given her **.05 cents** too much in change. It was returned.

February 13, 2003: A few weeks ago my brother Richard brought over a large bag containing dozens of newspapers. Most of them were copies of a newspaper called *Barrons—The Dow Jones Business and Financial Weekly*. I wanted the newspapers to cut up vegetables on. This morning we needed potatoes and **carrots** for fish chowder that Margaret was going to prepare.

I went out to the garage, reached in the bag and randomly pulled out several pages from a *Barron's* newspaper. I laid them on the kitchen table and peeled and cut up **carrots** on the papers. When finished, I folded over the pages to prevent the peelings from falling off when I carried them to the garbage pail. When I folded the pages over, I was shocked by what met my eyes. It was the front page of *Barrons* dated December 23, 2002. It colorfully depicted a blue sky full of giant-sized **carrots** falling to the ground!

February 19, 2003: We are purchasing a pop-up camping tent via the Internet. I received word that a $500 deposit was required, so I went upstairs to ask Margaret to send a check to the company and to be sure to ask for a **receipt** from the company. I did not find her where I had seen her last, reading a book, but did find her in her den going over some papers. I was just about to ask her to send the check and a **receipt** but before doing so I asked what she was doing. She said, "I'm sorting out **receipts**." I wonder if my thinking about a receipt was telepathically picked up by Margaret, who during that time period decided to look up and throw away outdated receipts.

February 21, 2003: I came down to my classroom to check my email. As I turned on Outlook Express to get the email, I suddenly thought—"You are going to get **15 email messages**." Several seconds later when I switched to my inbox, I saw that I had **15 email messages**!

February 22, 2003: This afternoon I sat down with my book agent, Charles to discuss his marketing of my new book manuscript on Synchronicity. During our conversation, I kept meaning to tell him of a book that I had just read which I thought he might find fascinating. It is entitled *The Afterlife Experiments*, by Dr. Gary E.R. Schwartz. I was particularly interested in telling him about how the psychic **John Edwards** was successfully tested under strict laboratory conditions. During a break in our conversation, before I could bring the subject up, he asked me—"What do you think of **John Edwards**?" I told him that he must be a mind reader.

March 2, 2003: Two synchronisms. [One is Of the TV Kind] This morning at church I used a rarely used phrase to comfort a friend who was in pain from a shoulder operation. I told him—**"This too shall pass."** Soon after, during the morning sermon, the pastor while mentioning some parishioners who were experiencing difficulties said, **"This too shall pass."**

April 4, 2003: I sat down to read a book and mentioned to my wife that I wanted to watch the news at noon. Later, she called me from the kitchen to tell me that it was 10 minutes after twelve and that I was missing the news. I put the book down and turned on the TV. The news was about a person named **Raymond Fowler**!

April 6, 2003: We were shocked and saddened to hear the news this morning that overnight NBC David **Bloom**, an embedded journalist, had died from a pulmonary problem. We had followed his reports faithfully from day to day and were concerned for his safety. Later in the morning, I read my email. An email from my publisher's headlines read: Bonus Books Are in **Bloom** at iUniverse.

May 24, 2003: This synchronism occurred during a vacation at Pittsburg, New Hampshire. While fishing at Middle Pond with Dave Lindsay, I inadvertently remarked that sometimes the Fish and Game department will stock the pond with **trout that had been used for breeding purposes**. A few minutes later, I felt a huge tug on my line and set the hook. It was one of the 18-inch huge brook **trout that had been used for breeding**.

June 12, 2003: Today I picked up a brochure describing **Grafton** Notch at the campground office. I read it and then picked up a unrelated book that I had brought along to read. I read the first page and then turned to the second page, which was about an author named **Grafton**! [This is the second synchronism about the word Grafton in less than a week. The other occurred on June 3 and is listed under *Converging Coincidences*.]

June 16, 2003: From time to time, I have thought of an old teen friend named **David Jewitt** and wondered how to contact him. This afternoon I thought of someone who might know where he is and asked Margaret where this person lived. Later, I went on-line to find out about a number of new moons orbiting Jupiter. I found a BBC Science Editor's article about the new discoveries and read that one of the astronomers who discovered them is named **David Jewitt**!

June 24, 2003: I was looking for memo today and while searching through a pile of documents, I came across a **family photograph** taken back in the 1960's. Later, Margaret and I visited my brother, Richard, and his wife, Joan. Margaret and Joan went into the dining room to chat and I went about the house to find my brother. I found him. I then came back to the dining room to find Margaret and Joan looking at a photograph. I wandered over to see what it was. It was the same **family photograph** that I had inadvertently come across a few hours earlier!

August 18, 2003: Today we traveled to Gloucester, Massachusetts to bike. Afterwards, we decided to visit my daughter's father-in-law, who was recuperating from a knee operation in Ipswich, MA. We were surprised to find our daughter **visiting at the same time** from Dover, NH.

August 23, 2003: I was biking along the Kennebunk beaches thinking about how much trouble it would be to **train a puppy** if we decided to buy one in the spring. A split second later when riding by a group of people, I heard a man say loudly that he had just **trained his puppy** to heel!

September 22, 2003: Two synchronisms.

1) I used to teach classes on UFOs for North Shore Community College when we lived in Massachusetts. One of my former students, Toni Ramos, emailed me and asked if she could come to our home in Kennebunk, Maine to purchase a copy of one of my books on UFOs. During the visit, I asked her where she originally came from in Massachusetts. She told me that she had been brought up in Beverly. I told her that I had been brought up in Danvers, which is next door to Beverly. She asked me if I had known anybody on Liberty Street in Danvers. I said that I knew, and had graduated from High school with, a fellow named **Ray Toomey**. She laughed as said that **Ray Toomey** was her uncle!
2) Later, we all sat out on the deck conversing. I excused myself to get my high school graduation photo to show her what her uncle looked like back in 1951. On the way back, I noticed a **photograph of our family** that had been recently taken during a reunion. I thought that she might like to see it. I picked it up on the way back to the deck. As I opened the door to the deck, Margaret was coming in to get the photograph that I had in my hand. Toni had just asked to see a **photograph of our family**!

September 24, 2003: Two synchronisms.
1) I meant to record this about a week ago but kept forgetting about it. An email from an associate sent the following message to a list that included me. It read: "Aliens in the house! A video was MISSING for a whole week. As I looked for it, **it suddenly appeared on my shelf**."

Coincidentally, I too had been looking for a book entitled *Destiny of Souls* for a week or so. In an attempt to find it, I cleaned up my study and desk but still could not find it. Last evening my desk had only had a few things on it. This morning when I entered the study, a spooking feeling crept over me as I saw the book in plain sight. **It had suddenly appeared lying on my desk**. I asked Margaret if she had put it there. She said that she had also been looking for it and had not found it!

2) This evening we arrived at the church parking lot that was shared with local businesses. It was almost full, but I found a parking place and pulled into it. When I opened the car door to get out, I found myself looking at a large sign on the side panel of the pickup truck parked beside our car. It said **Danvers**, Massachusetts—**my hometown**. It was a truck owned by a construction company in Danvers that must have driven into Kennebunk, Maine on business.

February 29, 2004: This morning I am going to show a video to the adult Sunday school class about the subject of **inner peace**. Just before leaving for Church, I noticed a Billy Graham Day by Day calendar half buried in papers on my desk. Since I had not glanced at its pages for weeks, I decided to look at today's daily devotional reading. Since, because of leap year, it did not have a February 29 page, I read the reading for February 28. The reading was about **inner peace**. After Sunday school we attended the morning service. The pastor's message alluded to **inner peace**.

March 2, 2004: Today was a banner day for *corresponding coincidences*. There were three of them:

1) This morning I decided to trek through a swampy area bordered by woods to see if I could spot a **Red-winged Blackbird**. This is the approximate time of the year that they return to the area from the South. As I left our backyard, I heard the faint drumming of a woodpecker coming from far off in the woods. I thought, "Wouldn't it be great if it is a **Pileated Woodpecker** and if I could see it?" It is a very rare bird. Strangely enough, last year (October 23, 2003) I was hoping to see one when I started out to walk in woods at neighboring South Berwick and actually came across one. However, a repeat performance seemed highly unlikely.

In any event as I walked along a brook in the swamp, the sounds of the woodpecker became louder so I took my binoculars and scanned the bordering woods for its source. I did not see anything and continued on. However, later I happened to glance towards some distant dead trees and saw something dark on one of them. I took my binoculars in hand and focused on it. It was a **Pileated Woodpecker**. I then proceeded to carefully draw closer and obtained some wonderful views of it as it pecked loudly against a dead hollow tree. It did not stay there long so I was at the right place and time to see it.

When I got home told Margaret about it and said that I had not seen any Redwing Blackbirds. I had hoped to see the first one of the year in our area. Margaret was about ready to leave for a Women's Fellowship group and after she went I happened to go by a window that overlooks some bird feeders. I glanced out to see if any squirrels were on it to scare off and much to my amazement, there was one bedraggled **Red-winged Blackbird** under them feeding on seeds that had dropped from it.

2) A few weeks ago I asked someone named Chris to send me his diary re his strange experiences. It arrived this afternoon in a file entitled **ANGEL ENCOUNTERS2004**. Amazingly, this evening I start my Mystery Phenomena course. Tonight's lesson is about **Angel Encounters**! Christ had no idea that I taught courses like this.

3) This evening I conducted my Mystery Phenomena class. As mentioned, the subject was Angel encounters. One of the Angel encounters that I summarized in a handout for the class was an experience by the **daughter of Michael Landon**. Just before one my students came to class she had glanced at a TV that was on. There on TV was the **daughter of Michael Landon** describing her experience. Another experience that was discussed in class concerned **Acadia National Park**. On the way to the class, two of the students were discussing **Acadia National Park**.

March 13, 2004: A retired Army intelligence officer and friend of a retired General who headed up a Remote Viewing Project for the Defense Intelligence Agency is meeting with me on March 15 to talk about the subject. This morning I received the following advertisement in my email: **Remote Viewing Methods—Now on DVD! ESP from the Inside Out.** Price: $39.95. Needless to say, I forwarded to the intelligence officer who was totally unaware of the advertisement.

March 19: 2004: This afternoon we received a phone call telling us that our friend Ken Penney had suffered a major **stroke**. Later, when I checked the mail, there was a letter with a brochure enclosed in it. It advertised a temporary walk-in clinic for screening a visitor's likelihood for a **stroke**.

March 26, 2004: This morning while lying in bed I received a flashback to a synchronistic event that had taken place in my high school Biology class. Several days prior to the class, I had noticed a tiny strange-looking fish in a small pool of water near the Danvers River. It was only 1–2 inches in length and had spines on its back. When I next attended Biology class, I was quite surprised when the teacher gave us a lesson on animal behavior that involved a small fish like the one I had just seen. It is called a *Stickleback*. The teacher found it hard to believe that I had just seen such a fish and asked me to try to catch it. When I went back to the pool, it was still there and after many attempts, I managed to scoop it up into a container. I brought it to class where the teacher kept it in a small fish bowl until it died.

March 30, 2004: A synchronism. This morning I was sitting on the couch watching news on TV when an advertisement for heavy commercial equipment came on. It showed a **huge yellow crane** with a shovel on its end in operation. A few minutes later I happened to glance up toward a window beside the front door. I was shocked to see the top section of what appeared to be the same kind of machine that I had just seen on TV. I jumped up and looked out the window and was shocked to see a **huge yellow crane** with a shovel on its end in operation across the street from our house.

April 4, 2004: I experienced two synchronisms today.
(1) This morning, at Adult Sunday School, I had forgotten to bring envelopes to take an offering. I sent Margaret to see if she could find an **envelope** somewhere in the church. On the way, she met the pastor's wife carrying a large box of **envelopes** that she had brought to donate to the church this morning.
(2) Yesterday Margaret and I went to see our grandson act in a play called *The Orphan Train*. The play opened with a soloist who sang a sad but beautiful song that I had never heard before. It was entitled, *I am an Orphan Girl*. This morning, after church, I went out and sat in the car while Margaret was practicing with the hand bell choir. I decided to pass the time listening to music on the radio. I began tuning to various stations and abruptly stopped at one when I heard someone singing *I am an Orphan Girl*!

As in *concurrent coincidences*, radio, television, and telephones are also the means by which *corresponding coincidences* materialize. I remembered to record several of these in *SynchroFile*.

OF THE RADIO KIND

February 24, 1999: We drove to the local **dry cleaners** to pick up Margaret's slacks. The car radio was on. As we drove out of the dry cleaner parking lot, the person speaking on the radio began talking about **dry cleaners**!

June 10, 1999: I have been experiencing a number of synchronisms. These involve reading a word and hearing it said at the time on the radio or TV. Unfortunately, I usually forget to record them in the diary. However, I am recording this synchronism before I forget to do so.
I am currently teaching a course on the **Near Death Experience** on Wednesday evenings. A class is scheduled for this evening. This morning, I put on my headphone radio, which I listen to when I jog. I did not tune it but just placed it on my head and turned the power on. As I did, I was amazed to hear someone talking about their **Near Death Experience**.

April 12, 2000: Yesterday I mailed a letter to my old boss at GTE, who had suffered a stroke. His last name is **Slater**. When I awoke this morning, I was still thinking about him as I switched on the radio to hear the news. At the exact instant that the radio clicked on, a newscaster said the words—Rodney **Slater**!

January 24, 2001 [One of the two synchronisms on this date was a *corresponding coincidence* of the radio kind.] The other occurred today, during a conversation with an editor of a publishing company. We talked about the movie ***The Wizard of Oz***. Later in the evening, while returning home from choir practice, I turned on the radio. The disk jockey announced that the next song they were to play was from the sound track of **The *Wizard of Oz*!**

January 27 & 28, 2001: [Saturday] I finally found a long misplaced article entitled, ***The Theory of Alpha and Omega on Earth***. This evening I brought it upstairs to my study before going to bed. This morning [Sunday], I leaned over, turned on WBZ, and listened to the news. A commercial came on advertising **Alpha and Omega** Jewelry!

The next entry *of the radio kind* records an incident that sent shivers up and down my spine.

September 20, 2001: Margaret and I were driving to a favorite bike ride spot along the shoreline of Biddeford Pool, Maine. On the way there, we took the Maine Turnpike and **turned off onto to exit 2 to Wells, Maine**. As we entered Wells, Margaret turned the radio on to a Boston station to hear the radio announcer say: *"turn off on route 2 to Wells, Maine!"* [He was giving directions to someplace in Wells.]

April 7, 2003: I went down to my classroom to obtain a photograph of a **scoop** mark often found on UFO abductees. As I did so, I turned on WBZ Boston at 11:30 a.m. to catch up on the war news. Just as the radio clicked on, the announcer said the word **scoop** in relation to an advertisement!

The number of entries in *SynchroFile* reveals that television played a greater part in bringing *corresponding coincidences* together than radio. At times, what I saw on a television show mirrored what I myself was doing and/or thinking at that time. One would have to experience such a synchronism themselves in order to describe the eerie feeling such a sight evokes in the deepest seat of one's being. Read on. Perhaps you will experience secondary effects from my experiences of the ineffable!

OF THE TELEVISION KIND

March 4, 1995: I was working on a book [on UFOs] about Betty [Andreasson] Luca. One of Betty's most dramatic reported visions was standing before a holographic-like figure of the fabled **Phoenix**. She watched it burn to ashes and then become restored. At the time, my two grandchildren were across the room watching a Disney film. I had headphones on and was transcribing notes from a taped session. I could not hear the TV. But I got a sudden inclination to glance at the TV screen. There, to my surprise, was a cartoon of the **Phoenix**. I watched as it burned to ashes and then was restored again!

September 15, 1995: [In England.] I had just read a chapter entitled "Phantoms of the Past" in the book, *The Holographic Universe*. It dealt with reports by people who have claimed to have **seen past events occur in present time**. Later, I put the book down and watched a TV program entitled *Strange but True*. There, before my eyes, were people being interviewed who claimed to have **seen past events occur in present time**.

September 16, 1995: [In England.] Here we go again. I will read about a certain subject in the book, *The Holographic Universe*. I'll then turn on TV to see the same subject being talked about. Today I had been reading about the **wave-particle nature of light**. Sure enough, when I turned on the TV, the host was talking about the **wave-particle nature of light**.

March 14, 1997: Margaret was reading a book about the poor condition of some prison inmates. Later, as we watched TV, she remarked that perhaps prisons could have **gardens for prisoners to work in to help with their rehabilitation**. At that very moment, I switched to another channel when a commercial came on. Inexplicably, there on the screen was someone talking **about a prison program to rehabilitate prisoners by having them work in gardens**! One wonders if our mind sometimes subconsciously senses an upcoming event like this and comments on it just prior to it happening. This and other theories about synchronisms will be discussed later in the book.

The next synchronism was again related to my involvement with the UFO phenomenon. This time it concerned my being filmed for a TV documentary on UFOs.

March 24, 1997: Today, I was filmed for a TV documentary by *Greystone Communications*. It concerned my book, *The Allagash Abductions*. I talked about the mystery of a lipoma surgically removed from abductee Jack Weiner. It had been analyzed. He was told that it had been analyzed by the Center for Disease Control. However, during our investigation we obtained records stating that it was sent to the **Armed Forces Institute of Pathology** and was analyzed by a USAF Lt. Colonel. In another one of those surprising synchronisms, I switched on the TV news in the evening. Amazingly, the segment was about the **Armed Forces Institute of Pathology** doing research on a strange type of flu.

June 6, 1997: Margaret and I were sitting on the sofa. She was reading an autobiography of **Billy Graham**. Just as she was reading a sentence about **evangelism in Africa**, I happened to flick on the TV to see what was on. There on the TV screen was **Billy Graham's** son conducting an **evangelistic service in South Africa**! Neither of us knew about the airing of this program.

October 28, 1997: On Sunday, October 26, I had mentioned to my wife that I would like to obtain a Halloween mask that depicted one of the **gray alien entities reported by UFO witnesses**. It was too late to order one from a catalog as Halloween was at hand. This morning, a knock came at the door. I answered it. It was one of my students who had stopped by on the way to work. She smiled and said that she wanted to give me a present. I thanked her and off she went. I closed the door, sat down, and opened the package. Inside was a mask depicting one of the **gray alien entities reported by UFO witnesses**!

October 2, 1998: I read the newspaper story about me written by the reporter mentioned in the September 25, 1998 entry. I then wrote a note to remind myself to write her a letter of thanks for the article. Her last name is **Applegate**. I then proceeded into the living room where Margaret was watching TV. As I entered the room, a TV host was being introduced. Her last name was **Applegate**.

November 11, 1999: Today is my birthday. I decided to attend the evening Bible study. We had nothing special planned for the evening. At the study, **we had a spirited discussion on whether or not Hell existed**. Afterwards, I returned home, sat down and put on the TV. I began randomly flicking to various channels but stopped short at one. As I flicked to that channel, a woman on the screen said—**"The Vatican says that Hell does not exist!"**

February 2, 2000: I was scanning some documents when Margaret called me for lunch. The documents contained photographs of supposed alien **implants**. They had been removed from people claiming that they had been abducted by alien entities. As I arrived at the table and sat down, Margaret mentioned that she had just received a letter from her uncle. She told me he had written about an **implant** that had helped him to see well without glasses!

March 21, 2000: I have been trying for days to locate a friend [via the Internet]. He had been stationed on an Air Force installation with me in England. His name is **Ralph Carter**. This morning I turned on the TV news. The story being reported on was a fire at a Marina in Newbury, Massachusetts. As I sat back to watch, a fireman being interviewed appeared on the screen. As he spoke, a caption flicked on at the bottom of the screen. It depicted his name—**Ralph Carter!**

February 29, 2000: This morning I am mailing a book to a person named Brenda **Haddock**. I had never heard of this last name before. When I turned on this morning's *Today Show,* there before my eyes was a 90-year-old lady dubbed Grannie **Haddock**. She had just completed a walk of 3100 miles across the United States!

May 21, 2000: While walking with church friends, we discussed the **Near Death Experience** phenomenon. When I returned home, I immediately turned on the TV to see what was on. A movie was just ending that portrayed a **Near Death Experience**! [Note: The reader will recall that an identical *concurrent coincidence* took place about a year ago on June 10, 1999, except that it involved radio rather than TV.]

November 17, 2000: Another synchronistic happening. Mary came with a group to see Saturn and Jupiter at my observatory. Afterwards she came in the house for a snack. During our conversation, she wanted to know what I thought about Tuesday's Bible Study. A vigorous discussion had come up about the Biblical accounts of Jesus casting out demons. The discussion included alleged accounts of **exorcisms** being conducted in our day and age. As Mary and I discussed this subject, it led to other weird subjects. They included **communication with the dead**. After Mary left, I turned on the TV to see what was on. It was *Dateline*. The interview at that very moment was with a person who allegedly was able to **communicate with the dead**!

November 18, 2000: This synchronism was a continuation of yesterday's conversation with Mary about **exorcisms** and communication with the dead. I randomly turned on the TV and the program was about ***exorcisms***!

January 7, 2001: During the day, Margaret and I were talking about several important incidents that occurred in our childhood. We remembered exactly where we were when they occurred. Margaret is English. She told me that she clearly remembered where she was **when King George died**. Later in the evening, while watching a movie on TV, I randomly flicked to another channel during a commercial. There, staring me in the face, was an English newsreel covering **King George's death** and funeral! The scenes were a segment of a documentary about the life of Princess Margaret.

February 1 & 2, 2001: While teaching my astronomy class this evening, I randomly used the city of Indianapolis during a discussion of latitude and longitude. For some reason, I **blurted out the name Indianapolis loudly** without forethought. The following day, while watching TV news, someone mentioned Indianapolis and Margaret **blurted out the name Indianapolis loudly** in response to what was said.

Corresponding Coincidences   67

February 23, 2001: I was watching a movie entitled *Phenomenon* this evening. During commercials, I have a habit [that my wife hates!] of flicking fast through other channels to see what is being broadcast. I flicked to Channel 56. The movie *Star Wars* was being shown. Just a split second before I flicked to another station, some character in the movie shouted, "**Princess**, what is going on?" When I flicked to the next station to a different program, the word **PRINCESS** took up most of the screen.

June 23, 2001: While watching the news on TV this morning, I randomly flipped to another channel during a commercial break. There, on the screen, was a young lady answering a telephone call saying: **"It's a call from the Fowlers!"** [The show was called Critter Getters.]

October 6, 2001: While listening to the evening news, I remarked to Margaret that I was going to call **David Harris** when the news got over. Moments later, a person on the news was introduced. His name was **David Harris**!

January 28, 2002: I was in Margaret's den talking about the possibility that we might have to place some **money in escrow** for a new septic system at our home in Wenham. After this conversation, I left her room. As I passed through the living room, I wondered if there was anything interesting on TV. I stopped and turned it on. The first words from a person on the show were about putting **money in escrow**!

March 21, 2002: [One of two synchronisms recorded today was a *corresponding coincidence*.] This afternoon, I gave a talk on **the life cycle of the dragonfly** to the residents of the Caldwell Nursing Home. When I got home, I flicked on the TV. The program that came on was about **the life cycle of a dragonfly**.

October 22, 2002: Last night I was working on a talk that I am going to give on **Peter**, the apostle. One of the last sentences that I wrote before stopping for the night reads: "He was an authority in the early church headed by **James at Jerusalem**." The "He" is **Peter** and the "**James**" **is the brother of Jesus**.

This morning we turned on the 6:30 a.m. channel 8, ABC news from Portland, Maine. Other than news about the serial killer sniper, the next lead story was about an amazing archeological event. It was the discovery of an ossuary [burial box] with the inscription: "**James**, son of Joseph, **brother of Jesus**."

November 23, 2002: We had just heard from my daughter. Her mother-in-law was dying. I sat down on the couch with a heavy heart randomly flicking channels on TV to find some news. I flicked to a channel where a man was just saying the words: **"feeling like it is when time is running out."**

November 27, 2002: [Two of the TV kind occurred today.]

1. While reading a newsletter, we came across a name that sounded familiar to both of us—Eleanor **Vandervort**. Neither of us could place the name Vandervort with someone that we could remember. This evening, while watching the PBS news, someone named Grace **Vandervort** was briefly interviewed.
2. This afternoon I finished reading a book entitled *C.G. Jung's Psychology of Religion and Synchronicity*, authored by **Dr. Robert Aziz**. Several minutes after the Vandervort incident mentioned above, I switched to the NBC news telecast. I was astonished to see another person named **Dr. Robert Aziz** being interviewed*!*

February 20, 2003: I was sitting on the couch with Margaret. We both were reading. I was reading The Orvis Fly-Fishing Guide. One of the chapters that I was looking at was about the various types of knots one uses in fly fishing. I took particular interest in a knot called a **loop-to-loop knot**. At this time, Margaret decided to watch a TV program called Wildlife Journal. I put down the book and watched with her. As it switched to a segment called, "Let's go Fishing", I watched dumbfounded as an instructor demonstrated how to tie a **loop-to-loop knot!**

May 21, 2003: We are vacationing at Pittsburg, NH. When I turned on the TV to listen to the news, the lead woman reporter's name was **Vivian Lee**. Back home in Kennebunk, Maine, the lead woman reporter's name is **Vivian Leigh**!

May 22, 2003: I was eating supper. Margaret brought me a piece of pound cake made by **Sarah Lee**. When I turned on the TV to watch while eating, the person speaking on TV was a **Sarah Lee**!

May 26, 2003: I was walking from the kitchen to the living room to watch TV I was thinking about the service that was to be done on my **John Deere tractor**. I sat down to watch TV and glanced up at the screen just as an advertisement for **John Deere tractors** came on!

July 7, 2003: Margaret and I had just watched a nature program about Polar **Bears** on the PBS TV channel. Just as I left to check email, I glanced at the TV screen, which showed a Panda **Bear**. I went to the computer and happened to glance at the calendar on the wall. There, on the lower right, was an obscure logo for the World Wildlife Fund (WWF)—a tiny panda **bear**. I had never noticed it before.

November 22, 2003: This evening we were watching the musical *Oklahoma* on TV when I remembered that I wanted to check out the position of Saturn's rings. I needed to know this for my astronomy class. During a lengthy commercial requesting donations for PBS, I quickly brought a small telescope through sliding glass doors onto the back deck to view Saturn.

Several minutes later, Margaret came out to take a look. Afterwards, she turned around to go back through the glass doors. She thought that I had left the doors open. Darkness prevented her from seeing that they were closed. Margaret **crashed into the glass door** severely bumping her head in the process. She immediately went into the kitchen and placed a cold pack on her head to reduce bruising.

After helping her, I went back to viewing *Oklahoma*. Since PBS was still making requests for contributions, I flicked to another channel. There was a commercial on. I was just about to flick back to the PBS channel when I experienced an amazing sight during this commercial. It showed a woman shopper with Christmas packages walk out of a department store toward a closed glass door. She **crashed into the glass door** just as Margaret had done a few minutes ago!

March 19, 2004: Two synchronisms occurred today. One was of the television kind and is recorded below. The other is recorded elsewhere in the book. This morning I wrote an email to my publisher's editor in response to his following request pasted from his email to me: "Text graphics should be **embedded** in the document and also sent as individual TIFF files." I in turn sent the following email to him this morning: "Here is the other half of the text graphics to **embed** with the other half sent yesterday." I would note that the words embedded and embed are not words that are often used. This makes the synchronism that follows that much more remarkable. In any event, while the text file graphics was being uploaded and sent to the publisher, I decided to go upstairs to watch the Today Show. Just as the TV came on I heard the Today Show's hostess, Campbell Brown, say and repeat the word **embedded**. Listening further, I realized that she was talking about **embedded** reporters in the war with Iraq.

There are fewer entries in *SynchroFile* concerning *corresponding coincidences* via telephones. Those that follow continue to reflect the same high level of strangeness embodied within the radio and TV kind:

OF THE TELEPHONE KIND

January 28, 1997: Today I started to scan my out-of-print novel entitled, *The Melchizedek Connection.* While doing so, I received telephone calls and a letter requesting copies of *The Melchizedek Connection.* I also talked on the telephone with someone who mentioned a **mutual friend** whom I had not talked to for years. Soon after I hung up, I received a telephone call from this **same mutual friend!**

April 3, 1999: During my UFO class last Wednesday, a student who has the benchmarks of a UFO abduction experience approached me after class. He said that he has been hearing **someone calling his name.** This evening, I got a phone call from the Lucas. Betty said that she; Bob and Becky have been hearing **their names being called**. They knew nothing about my conversation with the student that was experiencing the same phenomenon.

October 2, 2000: Margaret's mother introduced us to her favorite nurse, who had become close friends with her. Afterwards, we commented upon her unusual last name—**Jemma**. Today, two days after returning home from England, I received a phone call from a TV station desiring an interview. The surname of the woman that called was **Gemma**!

October 9, 2000: Last night I flicked on the TV and unexpectedly came upon a documentary on the *Crop Circle* phenomenon. The person being interviewed was a fellow researcher and Emmy-winning television documentary producer named **Linda Moulton Howe**. The next day I dialed a telephone number for [I thought] David Harris but somehow dialed another number on the same page. The person who answered the phone was **Linda Moulton Howe**!

December 2, 2000: I have opened the observatory for public viewing of Saturn and Jupiter by appointment on Friday and Saturday evenings. Today I received a telephone call from a man called **Dominic** to make an appointment for his family. The next call was from a woman named **Dominque**, who arranged to bring her child. When they arrived, it was fun to introduce Dominic to Dominque!

December 15, 2000: Margaret and I are in the process of **renovating her office**. This morning, when we were just about to nail up a piece of paneling, the telephone rang. It was a sales person asking if we were interested in **home improvements**!

August 20, 2002: Synchronism/Telepathy? This morning, I decided to phone John Oswald to help in editing a manuscript. I had been **thinking about John all morning** long and had had no personal contact with him for over a year. When I phoned him, he was quite surprised. He said that **he had been thinking of me off and on all** *morning* and that it must be ESP!

October 20, 2002: [Two synchronisms occurred on this date. One involved my son, David. It will be recorded elsewhere in the book.]The other occurred when Margaret and I watched the 6:30 p.m. NBC news. One of the lead news items was **Billy Graham's** Crusade. At 8:30 p.m., I received a telephone call from a friend. He told me that he had just bought an original drawing of **Billy**

Graham from an artist at a flea market. [He had no idea that Billy Graham had just been on the evening news.]

December 4, 2002:
1. Margaret and I were sitting at the kitchen table going over a calendar. We were discussing the dates we had planned for a visit by **David Harris**. I was going to phone him and give him some suggested visit dates. Just as we were discussing this, the telephone rang. It was a totally unexpected phone call from **David Harris**.

2. Margaret also was bemoaning the fact that her brother **John rarely** wrote or **telephoned her**. Just as we were about to leave for church, her brother **John phoned her**.

April 8, 2003: Last night I was teaching a course entitled *Mystery Phenomena* at the adult education program in Kennebunk. The evening's subject was *The UFO Abduction Phenomena*. During the class, I showed students a number of photos of scoop marks located on the shins of abductees, which appear to be punch biopsies. While doing this, I decided to inject some humor into the discussion. I told them of a woman who had read my books who phoned to tell me that she had the same kind of scoop mark on her shin. I told her that I would like to see it sometime. One day a knock came at the door. My wife, Margaret, answered and asked this same woman what she wanted. Needless to say, Margaret was shocked when the woman said: "Your husband wants to examine my leg!" I told the student that the woman's name was Judy but from then on (in fun) I called her **legs** when she attended my classes on UFOs.

Early this morning I received a telephone call. I answered the phone and heard a woman say, "Hi Ray, this is Judy—**Legs**!" I had only heard from her once, over a year ago, when we first moved to Maine in December 2001.

5

Converging Coincidences

Synchronistic events...serve to nurture, support, protect and enhance human life and spiritual growth.

—M. Scott Peck.
The Road Less Traveled.

This chapter will deal with coincidences that do not materialize until sometime in the future and at that point of time are verifiable. The time that exists before a *converging coincidence* materializes may be minutes, hours, days, months or even years. In addition, persons on either end of the time period would acknowledge the coincidence as being inexplicable. My earliest remembered converging coincidence took place during a fall foliage trip in the 1980's.

NEAR MISS

In 1951 I was a counselor at the Massachusetts Conservation Camp in Western, Massachusetts. I met a girl named **Betty** at church and she became my girlfriend over the two months spent at camp. She lived on the same country road on Bear Mountain as the camp. Her house was within easy walking distance from the camp. Afterwards, I maintained correspondence with her when I was in the Air Force. This ceased when I shipped overseas and met and married Margaret.

In the 1980's Margaret and I were in Western Massachusetts, so I suggested that we go to see the camp. Only the lodge remained. The former field where we pitched tents was all grown over with trees. However, I was amazed to meet the same grounds keeper that worked at the camp back in the 50's. He was very elderly but still watched over the place. I reminisced to him about my camping days and inadvertently mentioned **Betty**. He looked surprised and said that **Betty** had just visited the camp from her home in California! Strange that we both should have returned to visit the camp within a week of each other!

My next remembered coincidence in this category began shortly after enlisting in the United States Air force in 1952.

AU REVOIR

I took basic training at Sampson Air Force Base in Geneva, New York. The old drafty barracks on the Base were originally used by the United States Navy. The Air Force took over the naval facility for a training base between 1950 and 1956 during the Korean War. During this period, it also was the home of the largest USAF Hospital. I was only one of over a quarter million men and women stationed there during its operation.

None of us were prepared for the rigors, discipline and weather encountered during Basic Training. The Base [now a State Park] was located in Seneca County in the Finger Lakes of New York. The winter there is harsh and long. We marched everywhere, day or night. Snow and icy temperatures kept morale at a low key. In addition, we faced new challenges every day. These included arduous physical training, weaponry, mock battles and going through painful tests with gas masks. Thanks to my shooting experience with the Junior National Rifle Association, I was graded Expert.

Other than sleep, another oasis in the midst of this turmoil was the brush-up classes in English and math. The instructor, Sergeant **Frank Stowell** was several years older than I. Friendliness literally exuded from him, in contrast to my seemingly sadistic Flight Chiefs! I enjoyed chatting with him and missed being in his classes when they were over. Unknown to me, he would become part of the hundreds of synchronistic events that interface the core experiences my life. Amazingly, eight years later, I joined and attended a small Church in Danvers, Massachusetts. Who should walk in the church door one Sunday?—you guessed it. It was **Frank Stowell**! He had moved to Danvers. He became a Church member and one of my closest friends!

DEJA VU

Another valuable *converging coincidence* took place several months later. Before enlisting, I had studied for and received two amateur radio licenses. I hoped to become involved with radio in the Air Force. The coincidence involved a textbook entitled ***Elements of Radio***. An electrical engineer had given it to me when I was in my late teens. He strongly encouraged me to study it. Although difficult, I studied and mastered its contents.

After basic training and a several months wait at Lockbourne Air Force Base, Columbus, Ohio, I was sent to Keesler Air Force Base, Biloxi, Mississippi. I was enrolled in the General Radio Operator School. You can only imagine my astonishment and delight on my first day of class. The textbook used for the course was **Elements of Radio**! My familiarity with the text resulted in high marks and assignment to an advanced radio school. Graduates from this school came under the auspices of the National Security Agency.

BEYOND FORTUITY

The next notable *converging coincidence* took place after graduating from Radio School. My high marks earned a choice of Alaska, the Far East or Europe for permanent assignment. I chose Europe. **I wanted to be stationed in England.** However, I was sent to Germany with no hope of transfer to England. On the way to Germany, we docked at South Hampton, England to let airmen embark. Afterward, we left port for Bremerhaven, Germany. I prayed that somehow I could return and be stationed in England. Incredibly, several weeks after arriving in Germany my prayer was answered. I was called into an office and abruptly given orders to replace an airman in England. I had to leave in several days! **I spent the rest of my enlistment in England!**

DOUBLE-SHIFT DUMAS

The beginning of this *converging coincidence* took place in England while in the USAF between 1953–1955. It involved Jerry Dumas, a fellow Radio Intercept Operator. He was nicknamed **double-shift Dumas**, as he would work an extra shift for money so others could have a day off. I hired him so that I could spend more time in London courting my wife-to-be. Jerry was discharged before me and I missed his friendship and services.

In August 1960, we visited my parents in Surrey, Maine. According to Margaret's diary, we attended the LaMoine Baptist Church on August 21. The church has a circular driveway. After church, I drove out of the exit of the driveway and prepared to turn right onto the highway. I waited as a car approached from my right. However, it turned into the entrance of the church driveway to my right. I glanced at the driver and he glanced at me. Both of us were shocked. It was **double-shift Dumas**! Needless to say, it was a renewal of an old friendship.

SAMARITAN SYNCHRONISM

The event that caused this synchronism on December 14, 1974 converged 26 years later in 1990. The initial event was published in my book, *Casebook of a UFO Investigator*.[1]

At 7:30 a.m., Mr. and Mrs. Herbert Lower of Townshend, Vermont discovered a strange circular impression in the snow. It appeared as if something had landed and taken off. This prompted the Lowers to report these events to the widow of a local UFO investigator. She also reported the event to the *Brattleboro Reformer*. Reporter Greg Wordon responded. Greg arrived about 10:00 a.m. He interviewed the Lowers and photographed the supposed landing marks. The following week, he wrote a front-page story in the *Brattleboro Reformer* on the incident.[2]

In the meantime, the widow of the local UFO investigator phoned another UFO investigator who had worked with her husband. His name was Bob Jackson. Bob phoned me about the incident. I assigned Mutual UFO Network [MUFON] New Hampshire investigator, John Meloney, to investigate the case. I then phoned the Lowers to inform them of our investigation plans.

John arrived at the Lowers' home at 2:30 p.m. He photographed the area, secured soil samples, and took temperature readings at various soil depths. A check for radiation gave negative results. Mr. Lower told John that a man had phoned and asked him to put up a Keep Out sign at the site. John assumed that I had called and continued his tasks. John was puzzled when Mr. Lower later mentioned that the man was sending a helicopter to examine the site. He wondered how and why I had secured helicopter services to investigate what he was already investigating.

Who was the caller? How did he know about the event on the Lower property? [An unmarked helicopter did appear the following day. It circled low over the mark in the snow but did not land.] In the meantime, it started to snow. When the snowfall became intense, John decided he had better get home fast. He left the Lowers' property at 4:00 p.m. Shortly afterwards, his car skidded and hit a tree.

Bleeding and in shock, John stumbled down the country road looking for help. It seemed like an eternity before a pickup truck slid to a halt beside him. The kind driver helped John into the passenger's seat and took him to Townshend's Grace Hospital. There, John stayed for weeks for treatment of multiple fractures. During this time, he received visits from the kind driver.

Nine years later, I investigated a UFO incident that occurred on the Allagash Waterway in Maine. It resulted in my book entitled *The Allagash Abductions*.[3] One afternoon, I sat interrogating the witnesses. One named Chuck mentioned to me that I was the second UFO investigator that he had met in his lifetime. Curious, I asked him who the first one was. Chuck said that he had come upon a bleeding man staggering along the road during a snowstorm and had brought him to the local hospital. The man told him that he was investigating a possible UFO incident in Townshend, Vermont. (Chuck lived in Wardsboro, Vermont, a neighboring town of Townshend, Vermont.) Chuck happened to be on his way home from work when he had come across John. Weird as it may seem, **Chuck was the Good Samaritan who rescued John—my investigator**! Later, I phoned John to share this amazing coincidence with him.

The *converging coincidences* discussed thus far were recorded from memory. Let us now return to those in my diary dubbed *SynchroFile*. The entry below involved what might be called a precognitive vision. Whatever it was, it may have saved me from being injured or killed.

> **May 4, 1995:** I was riding a bicycle in Rockport, Massachusetts and approaching a steep hill, which has a sharp left turn near the bottom. Suddenly, I mentally **pictured a truck backing out in front of me** as I turned the corner at the bottom of the hill at high speed. In my mind's eye I could see that the driver didn't know which way to turn as he was blocking the road.
>
> Incredible as it may seem, when I turned the corner, I actually could see a truck in a driveway. Because of my mental vision, I instinctively knew that it was going to back out in front of me. It did, and the driver suddenly noticed me coming right at him. It looked like he did not know which way I would try to avoid him. I decided to swerve to my right. He moved forward just in time to get out of my way. **It was just as I had imagined it** less than a minute before it happened!

The next entry describes a *converging coincidence* that took place during a mini-vacation. We were visiting Margaret's mother in England. In this case, a friend was the mediator between the coinciding factors.

> **September 22 1995:** [In England.] Margaret and I are vacationing at a bed and breakfast establishment in a tiny village called Thorpe. Last week, September 15, we hired bicycles and explored the countryside. Fred and Shirley were coming to take us out for dinner in a week's time. We decided to bike to a nearby village named Ashbourne to look for a place to eat with them on Sep-

tember 22 [today]. Thorpe only had one restaurant and we wanted to eat at another place for a change.

As we biked into Ashbourne, we came across an English pub called **The Bowling Green**. We decided to have dinner there with our friends who were coming from their home in Sheffield. They arrived this afternoon. Later, in the evening, we had dinner with Fred and Shirley at **The Bowling Green**.

It was then that Fred grinned at me and asked if I knew where I was eating. I thought this a strange question and asked him what he meant. He smiled and told us that this was the first English Pub that I had ever visited. He reminded us that we had visited him and his former wife [deceased] in Sheffield back in 1990. He had taken us for a long ride into the countryside. During the ride, Fred had driven us around the Ashbourne area We had stopped there to have lunch at **The Bowling Green**, about 40 miles from his home in Sheffield! I was amazed. We had forgotten that we had been there before with him. By some quirk of fate, we had picked the same pub. [Later, when we returned home in the USA, I glanced through my wife's diary to see if this were really so. It was. We had eaten at The Bowling Green with Fred and Shirley on October 15, 1990.]

October 19, 1998: Two synchronisms occurred today. One had to do with Amelia Earhart and is recorded elsewhere. The other was a converging coincidence. Yesterday, I received a phone call from someone name **Gavin** Macleod to order my books. While riding my bike today, I found that the name Gavin was not so unique. I rode by a street called **Gavin** Circle.

Sometimes synchronisms have a mysterious way of bringing long forgotten, but significant, relationships of one's past together once again without warning. This was so when the following coincidence converged:

October 31, 2000: This evening, Margaret and I were dinner guests at a church that we do not attend. Other friends were there as well, but since we were last in the buffet line we were not able to sit with them. We looked around for a place to sit and decided to sit beside two women who were sitting apart from everyone. They had prepared the meal.

I talked to the woman beside me. She told me that her name was Pat and that she had been living in Vermont. When her husband died, she moved back to her hometown in Massachusetts. I continued to make polite talk and asked about her hometown. Surprisingly, her **hometown was the same as mine**—Danvers. She looked about my age so I asked if she had attended Danvers High school. When she replied yes, I told her that I had graduated from there in 1951.

She looked amazed and said that she had graduated in 1951. She asked me for my last name. When I told her that it was **Fowler**, she looked shocked. I, in turn, asked for her last name. She said her maiden name was **Brown**. We looked at each other in total amazement. **Patricia Brown was my old girlfriend**! We used to rendezvous and snuggle at a movie theater in Danvers when we were about 12 years old. I had not seen her for almost four decades.

The following synchronism requires a little background information in order to fully understand its import. I had recently [after many attempts] contacted and become re-acquainted with a dear friend, David Harris, whom I knew as a teenager. He had been a temporary foster child in our home and had shared my bedroom.

Dave and I had been members of the junior division of the Danvers Fish and Game Club in 1950. Adult members taught us gun safety, marksmanship and fly-tying. They also brought us on fishing trips. After I enlisted in the Air Force, David Harris became a great friend with a mutual acquaintance named David Lindsay. Now re-united, David Harris and I began talking about rejoining the Danvers Fish and Game Club. We discussed buying guns to go target shooting and perhaps hunting again. He also asked after our teenage friends. He especially asked about David Lindsay's whereabouts. I replied that I had lost track of our friends and had not seen David Lindsay for many years.

Now, let us discover how the above information applies to the following *converging coincidence* extracted from *SynchroFile*:

November 9, 2000: Two more synchronisms:

1) Margaret and I were on our way to take a walk at West Beach in Beverly. Along the way, **on a sudden impulse**, I decided instead to walk in the woods on the property of my alma mater, Gordon College. The college owned 1000 acres and the woods were laced with paths for hiking and cross-country skiing.

While walking deep in the woods, we came down a hill to a junction of three paths. We converged at this junction at the exact time another person walking his dog did. As he passed us, I thought he looked familiar. The person looked like an old friend from our teen years whom David Harris and I had been talking about recently. I felt embarrassed doing so but shouted after him—"Are you David Lindsay?" He swung around, stared at me with a puzzled look on his face, and shouted back—"Yes"!

David did not recognize me and I had hardly recognized him. As mentioned, he had been a close friend with Dave Harris and me back in the 1950's. When I introduced myself, the first words that came out of his mouth were "Have you been in contact with David Harris?" Dave Harris had also been asking about him!

We talked for awhile and during our conversation, he asked me if I still did any shooting. He said that he still had his guns but no place to shoot them.

He said that he would like to join a club so he could do some target shooting! Of course, I told him that I recently had found and become reacquainted with David Harris. I told him that we were planning to join the Danvers Fish and Game club together.

To make a very long story short, we three did join and are now meeting periodically to target shoot and talk about the happy days of the 1950's that we shared together. I would add that the timing for meeting David Lindsay in the 1000 acres of woodland had to be perfect. We were about to head off to our right at the junction where we met to take another path. We would have missed him completely in less than a minute. But, there is more. There was a second coincidence of the *corresponding* type awaiting me when I returned home from the walk.

2. After we got home, I turned on the computer to check my email. The first email was dated 11/09/2000. It was addressed to a large list of UFO researchers. Nevertheless, the two words to the right of its subject heading were highlighted in blue. They read: **Another coincidence**?

As we have seen, some *converging coincidences* appear to be telepathic or precognitive in nature. The following two synchronisms are similar to my precognitive biking experience involving a truck:

> **October 30, 1996:** I had had a synchronistic, realistic precognitive dream about being outside in **rain mixed with some sleet and snow**. I could actually feel it hitting my face. I got up this morning, had breakfast and turned on the local weather on TV. The weatherman said that we had had a surprise **mixture of rain, sleet and snow** during the night! I would add that in the evening while watching the TV news, the newscaster stated that there had been a fire in New Hampshire. Instantly, the thought that the fire was at **Exeter Academy** popped into my mind just before he stated that it was at **Exeter Academy**. This was the first time I would have heard the news about it.

Why did I dream about something that was actually occurring during my sleep? How did I know where the fire was before it was announced? Examples like these plagued Carl Jung. They still frustrate others in their attempts to come to terms with the seemingly unknowable something or someone behind synchronistic events involving precognition.

The *Encarta Dictionary* defines *precognition* as knowledge of something before it occurs and *telepathy* as communication through means other that the senses. Sometimes it is difficult to ascertain whether a *converging coincidence* involves precognition or telepathy. The distinction between these phenomena is sometimes blurred as in the following incident:

January 17 & 18, 1997: On the evening of Friday the 17th, for some unknown reason, I began thinking about our neighbor, Jean Wallace. She had taken a **photograph of our grandchildren on Halloween** last year. However, she never followed through in giving us a copy of it as promised. The next day, Saturday afternoon the 18th, I checked our mail and found an envelope in our mailbox from the neighbor. It contained the **photograph of our grandchildren that she had taken last Halloween**!

The question is: did Jean forget to send the picture but then remembered when she telepathically picked up my thoughts? Alternatively, did I pick up her thoughts of remembering the photo and planning to put it in my mailbox? In either case, this is *a converging coincidence* separated by less than 24 hours.

The next six synchronisms of this type concern my thoughts manifesting themselves physically in the future. I would think of a certain bird and shortly afterward see the exact kind of bird. The first example of this kind took place prior to my keeping records in SynchroFile.

I was working for GTE Government Systems at Westboro, Massachusetts. We had just moved into a brand new, state of the art building located in a rural area. During lunch breaks, I began exploring the fields and woods surrounding the plant. I also had taken up the hobby of birding. I had just finished reading about a heron named the **American Bittern** before embarking on one of my lunch hour explorations. I had read that the Bittern is a secretive bird. It preferred to freeze and trust its concealing coloration when approached rather than flush like other herons. I was particularly fascinated when I read about its technique of camouflage. When an observer is nearby, the Bittern will raise its head, point its bill skyward, and wave it slowly from side to side. In doing this, it imitates the waving reeds that conceal it. However, it will fly up uttering a low barking call if the observer gets very close to it.

On that day, we had been temporarily transferred to another rural location. After lunch, I set out to explore a dirt road. It seemed to lead to nowhere in particular through fields and woodland. During my walk, I came across a small pond with reeds along the shoreline. As I gazed at the reeds, I noticed that one stalk was swaying back and forth while the others stood straight. I was puzzled, as there was no wind of any consequence.

This surrealistic-like scene instantly reminded me of the Bittern's method of concealment. So, I approached the bed of reeds slowly, half-wondering if a Bittern would suddenly fly out of them. No sooner had I done this when an **American Bittern** rose out of the reeds. I watched in utter wonder as it flew off making the low barking call that I had just read about. The following events are synchronistic *echoes* of that extraordinary experience of the past:

> **February 21, 1998:** I went for a walk in woods and fields to do some bird watching. Most of the interesting birds had migrated south, but **I thought** it would be nice to see a **Red-tailed Hawk**. About halfway through my walk, I crossed a field. A movement above caused me to glance overhead. There, flying low and circling me were two **Red-tailed Hawks**!
>
> **April 25, 1998:** One of the men attending the men's breakfast at church this morning mentioned how excited his wife had been to see **a Bluebird**. They were rarely seen. I remarked that **I would love to see a Bluebird**, as I had not seen one since my childhood. Later, in the afternoon, we brought one of our grandchildren for a walk. We walked at a green space that bordered a Catholic retreat center named Don Bosco. As we strolled along a path, I noticed a bird up ahead of us. It was perched on a low tree branch that was directly over our path. I looked at it through my binoculars and was astonished. **It was a Bluebird**. It remained on the branch until we walked under it and then flew away.
>
> **May 29, 1998**: Several days ago, I mentioned to a friend that I had not seen a bird called a **Cedar Waxwing** for years and that I would like to see one. Today, while walking at Laudholm Farm at Wells, Maine, I **saw a tree-full of Cedar Waxwings**! This synchronism is similar to those involving the Red-tailed Hawk and Bluebird incidents recorded recently!

I was curious about when I had last seen a Cedar Waxwing. It was at a place called Spruce Meadows in Maine that we visited during a vacation. I searched through Margaret's diary and found that we had visited there on August 18, 1982. Thus, I had not seen this kind of bird for about 16 years!

The next three synchronisms involving animals took place on the same day and again concerned birds. The first two took place on the same day while camping in Bethel, Maine.

> **June 14, 2003:**
> 1) Our campsite is located beside a huge open grassy field. I thought to myself that this was an ideal environment for **Bobolinks** and wished that I could see one. Several minutes later, I saw a distant bird and looked at it through my binoculars to identify it. Amazed, I watched it fly directly at me growing larger and larger until it almost filled the binoculars' field of view. I removed the binoculars from my eyes. There, about six feet away from me perched on a post looking at me, was a **Bobolink**!

2) Margaret and I were walking along a paved walk called the Bethel Parkway, which ran alongside the Androscoggin River near our campsite. As we passed by a small marsh with bull rushes, I casually remarked to Margaret that this was an excellent environment for **Red-winged Blackbirds**. No sooner had I made this statement when a beautiful **Red-winged Blackbird** flew out of the marsh towards us, landed on a branch about six feet away and stared at us!

October 31, 2003: Last evening Margaret and I were talking about a rarely seen bird called the **Pileated Woodpecker**. I had seen one in the past and hoped that I would see one again. This morning we decided to go for a walk in woods in nearby South Berwick, Maine. We had only been walking for about 10 minutes when I heard a loud knocking sound among some trees off the path. I investigated. It was a **Pileated Woodpecker** pecking a tree!

Are my improbable synchronistic experiences with animals related to chance? Conversely, is there some unknown cause operating behind our limited perception of reality? Dr. Robert Aziz makes notes of this type of coincidence from the works of Jung. Aziz relates it to what he calls *the synchronistic patterning of events* wherein meaningful interdependence supersedes space, time, and causality as the determining factor. He states that Jung's case is an example of such a synchronistic patterning of events. He quotes Jung's comments about it as follows:

> It [the archetype] manifests itself therefore not only in human beings but also at the same time in animals and even physical circumstances....I call these latter phenomena the synchronicity of archetypal events. For instance, I walk with a woman patient in a wood. She tells me about the first dream in her life that had made an everlasting impression upon her. She had seen a spectral fox coming down the stairs in her parental home. At this moment a real fox comes out of the trees not 40 yards away and walks quietly on the path ahead of us for several minutes. The animal behaves as if it were a partner in the human situation.[4]

Aziz comments that:

> With this example, there are three meaningfully related events appearing in the psychophysical, synchronistic pattern. They are (1) the woman's dream of the spectral fox (2) the woman's description of this dream to Jung as they walked through a wooded area and (3) the appearance of a real fox as this description was being given. Here, then, we have a synchronistic patterning of events—events which are not linked collectively by space, time, or causality—events whose import can only be properly established through an investi-

gation of their roles in relationship to the psychophysical pattern as a whole....Jung's description of the activity of the fox is certainly apt, for its timely appearance and subsequent behavior suggest that indeed it was there to contribute something to their discussion....The fox, therefore, clearly was a partner in the human situation, for it was a compensatory synchronistic partner in the struggle to bring the central archetypal pattern of the woman's individuation [her hidden psychological problem with guilt] into consciousness [for Jung to deal with]. [5]

Obviously, psychologists such as Jung and Aziz are more interested in theorizing about how the mental meanings of such synchronisms aid in psychoanalysis and healing of their patients. This book, for the most part, avoids the psychoanalytic aspects of synchronicity. My hope is that readers will also share the same some of sense of wonder that synchronisms have evoked in me. I trust also that such examples of synchroncity will cause readers to ponder deeply about their meaning and perhaps even expand their own views of reality.

The next two converging coincidences of a precognitive kind concerned dreams of my teenage activities. One of my hobbies was building various types of fireworks and even bombs. Today, a teen doing these things would be considered a juvenile delinquent!

> **March 1, 2000:** Last night I dreamed about my boyhood hobby of making small gunpowder-powered rockets called **bottle rockets**. Today I went for a walk in one of areas that I frequented as a teen. I brought binoculars to do some birding. While walking by a field, I noticed something strange sticking up out of the grass. I focused my binoculars on it. It was an upright plastic bottle with a blackened top. I walked into the field and up to the bottle. All around the bottle were spent, and a few unfired, **bottle rockets** that someone had been shooting off in the field!

Making bombs and rockets was just one of many teen interests in my happy days of the 1950s. Back then I had an almost fanatical interest in hunting and fishing. Therefore, it is no wonder that sometime I go back to those days in my dreams such as the one recorded below.

> **June 15, 2000:** During the night, I dreamt about going to a small farm [as a teen] in Danvers, Massachusetts to ask permission to hunt on its property. I often really did this when I was in my late teens. It was named **Conners Farm**. This morning, when jogging and listening to my headset radio, a short commercial break came on. It was an announcement that **Conners Farm** in Danvers, Massachusetts was hosting a strawberry festival. [This was the first time

that I heard this commercial or any other kind of reference to Conners Farm since my teens!]

Sometimes I experience a *converging coincidence* of the television kind such as the one that follows:

August 24, 2003: Yesterday Margaret and I were talking about blueberries and some bears that were knocking down birdfeeders along our street. I mentioned that my father had once been picking blueberries with a bear nearby doing the same thing. Margaret asked me **how the bears picked blueberries**. I told her that they probably licked them off the bushes but really did not know.

This morning we got up and turned on the TV to a program called *Backpacker*. On the show, two men were shown walking a trail in Alaska where there were a lot of black bears. They came across some blueberry bushes and one of the men asked the other man **"How do bears pick blueberries?"** The other man said that they are able to pick the blueberries off the bushes with their paws.

The next three entries again record how my thoughts or dreams later converged with reality. The first is not a diary entry as I had no idea that my thought would converge into reality about a year later. Sharon and her family had moved to Dover, New Hampshire on January 1, 1998 to be near Portsmouth Christian Academy where her husband teaches history. At that time, the school was in a crisis. The lease for the building that they were using was coming to an end. A search for another building had not been successful.

Almost a year later, we visited Sharon on January 23, 1999 and she took us for a ride around the area. The school's desperate need for a building was still the topic of conversation. We had only driven a few minutes when I noticed a building set way back to our left up on a hill. I asked her what it was. She thought it was a hospital. I suggested that we drive up the hill to look at it.

We found that it had been a hospital but was closed now. The building was on many acres of rolling fields that bordered a salt-water river. I suggested to Sharon that she tell the superintendent of Portsmouth Christian Academy about it as the building and grounds would make a great location for the academy.

To make a long story short, my statement later coincided with the purchase of the building by the academy. It was completely refurbished. New educational buildings have now have been added to the property. My thinking that the old hospital would become the academy's building materialized in the culmination of a *converging coincidence*.

The next converging coincidence concerned my somehow sensing a past traumatic event during a stroll with Margaret.

> **February 3, 2001:** Margaret and I were returning from a walk along a minor road that ran parallel to a runway of Beverly Airport. I glanced over at it and for some reason began thinking about a **plane crash**. When we got home and turned on the evening news, the reporter described **a plane crash** that had taken place at Beverly Airport that very day!

The next entry is unique in my experience. For several moments during the night, my mind melded with the mind of my wife. Our thoughts converged and became one as the unknown process behind synchronicity again manifested itself.

> **January 29, 2002:** Upon waking, Margaret told me about a dream she had of being such a fast swimmer that it amazed onlookers how fast she could swim using her rather unorthodox dog-paddle method. I was shocked. In my dream, I was watching her swim. I remarked to others that I could not understand how she could swim so fast using her unorthodox method. Somehow, **we both shared a dream** in which she was the fast swimmer and I, along with the crowd, was amazed at how fast she could swim using her own unique swimming method!

> **February 2, 2002:** This morning I dug the snow out of the driveway. I also took great pains to do a good job digging out around the mailbox so the woman who delivered the mail could deliver it easily. For some reason, **a thought** came to me that she might **write a note to thank me** for digging out the mailbox. This afternoon, when I checked the mail, **I found a note thanking me** for the nice job of shoveling that I had done for her!

Did some psychic part of me wander out of my body? Did it enter an already predetermined future? Did it telegraph back to me that the mail carrier was going to write me a note? Such a process certainly could explain incidents like this and the one below. Especially, perhaps future death and extreme danger are catalysts for initiating and bringing such precognitive thoughts and dreams to us. This seems to be the case in the following incident that involved a good friend of mine.

My friend was named Alan. He carpooled with me to GTE. We took walks together during our lunch breaks. At a certain time, he began talking about death over a period of several weeks. At first, he just casually mentioned to me that his father had died young. He wondered if he too would follow his father's fate. Another time, Alan told me that he had talked with his wife about death. They concluded that if one of them died they could still be thankful for the good life that they had together. Time went by. Then one day he mentioned that he had taken out extra life insurance beyond the generous insurance provided by GTE.

Because of these incidents, we talked about the afterlife. I, at that time, had just begun to do research into near death experiences. I described in detail what people reported after they were resuscitated from clinical death. He showed great interest.

One day, while walking, Alan told me that he was very nervous about going on a business trip the following day. He did not want to go but felt obligated. He was needed at a site where an experimental lithium battery was being tested for use at Minuteman Missile facilities. Alan was so upset about it that I suggested he refuse to go. However, he would not hear of it. On the following morning, he handed me a sealed envelope. He made me promise that if anything happened to him on the trip that I would give it to his wife. I thought this strange but told him that I would. We went to work and he later flew out to the test site. The following morning while I was getting ready to leave for work, the telephone rang. It was Alan's wife. She told me that her husband had been killed. An experimental battery that he was carrying had blown up.

I visited her in the evening and brought her the memo. It contained information about the program that would help her in a lawsuit against the company. She tearfully told me that the night before the accident Alan had laid out all of the insurance policies on her bureau. He told her that if anything happened to him on the trip that she would be a "rich widow."

I have heard of other incidents of this same nature. This was one of several that I have been involved with at close hand. Again, did Alan's psychic *essence* somehow have access to the future? Was it trying futilely to keep him from going on that trip? If it were just a warning, perhaps he could have taken heed and refused to go on the trip. However, if his death was predetermined, there was nothing he could have done to save himself.

Incidents like these make one wonder if the future is determined. Perhaps it already is *happening* in another dimension. If this were the case, it would mean that time in a linear sense is an illusion. Perhaps reality just *IS*. Perhaps what we experience as past, present and future are all *NOW*. I will discuss this in more detail in chapter 11.

The next incident involved personal prescience of danger lurking ahead for Margaret and me as we set out to drive on the Maine turnpike. Thankfully, it just presaged danger. I would like to be a physical inhabitant of earth for many more years to come!

May 16, 2002: This morning as we pulled out of the driveway to take a trip down the Maine Turnpike to Massachusetts, a sudden thought came to mind. I thought of a **side collision** with another car rather than a head-on or rear-end type. I felt strongly that this was something to watch out for.

Sure enough, when underway on the pike, a red sports car raced out from an entrance to the highway on our right hand side. It headed right for the right hand **side of our car**. Margaret ducked and yelled, "She's going to hit us!" I glanced over to see that the car had swerved just in time. It was only inches from scraping us on the right hand side of our car.

When Margaret yelled, I kept our car going straight. There was no time to look to my left to see if cars were in the lane to the left of me. The driver, a young woman, dropped back and around us. She sped off at a speed well over the 65 mile-per-hour limit. After it was over, I told Margaret of my sudden premonition. She asked me if I had "second sight!"

The following *converging coincidence* was quite comical at the time. It started with an off-hand humorous question by a friend. It literally [well, almost] came to fruition a half-hour later:

November 22, 2002: A funny precognitive synchronism. John Oswald, a former UFO investigator, visited today. One of the activities I planned for the day was to introduce him to a hike along the trails at Laudholm Farm in Wells, Maine. When we set out he jokingly said, "I hope **aliens** aren't **in the bushes** where we will be walking."

Later, we had a good laugh. As we walked along one of the paths, we came to a sign **in the bushes** that read: **Aliens have invaded!** There, on the sign, was a picture of a flying saucer with an alien peeking through its transparent dome! [The sign referred to alien Barberry bushes invading the forest and choking out other vegetation.]

A triple series of synchronisms occurred on the date below. Two were *corresponding coincidences*. They are recorded elsewhere. The other was a *converging coincidence* and is as follows:

November 27, 2002: This morning I was thinking about Corinne Comly. She is the daughter of some good friends, Lee and Sandi Comly. In the past, Corinne faithfully sent us **a newsletter** about her activities in Children's Haven. This is an organization that works with street kids to which we contributed money. I felt badly that she had no idea we had moved to our new home in Kennebunk, Maine. This afternoon, I checked the mail and was surprised to see Corinne's **newsletter**. We had not received it for over a year. Somehow, she had found out our new address.

The experiences above were examples of precognitive *converging coincidences*. However, precognition is only one type of this kind of coincidence. As strange as this type may be, other types are even more bizarre.

Over the years, I have had a number of experiences where my presence appeared to have a converging coincidental effect on electrical devices. Some of these incidents converged with thoughts about my books about UFOs or persons associated with the books. Others were coincidental with other strange phenomena. Researchers call this *electrical sensitivity*. For some unknown reason, some peoples' windup wristwatches become magnetized. Televisions, radios, lights and other electrical devices turn on and off in their presence.

On January 2 & 3, 1996 and November 17, 1999, I had *converging coincidences* that involved such electrical sensitivity. Before recording these entries, I will provide some background information. I will list a number of entries from my diary to demonstrate that this coincidence was not an isolated happening but part of a larger phenomenon.

A number of events associated with electrical sensitivity happened before I kept the *SynchroFile* diary. I remember a dental assistant being shocked when she turned a spotlight to focus on my face. When the light hit my face, it suddenly flashed brightly, blinked out and came on again.

I remember an incident when a nurse hooked me up to an electrocardiogram during an annual physical exam. When she turned on the machine, it went haywire. This sent her literally screaming out of the room for help. However, the machine quickly calmed down. There was nothing wrong with it.

The following are other incidents that exhibited electric sensitivity! The advent of 1993 heralded the first entry. Again, I include them as background information before moving on to the next *converging coincidence*, which also was of an electrical nature:

> **January 1, 1993:** I was sitting beside my computer. It, and both printers, came on and off for a moment. This was repeated in the evening. Later, while sitting beside the computer watching a TV program, the TV set shut itself off. I turned it on again with my hand-held control. There were no power cuts.
>
> **March 31, 1993:** [My computer came on by itself.] The circuit breaker clicked on and off very fast. I pulled the plug to stop it. Later, when I plugged it in, things were normal.

April 3, 1993: Again, I was in the room sitting directly below the computer in my classroom upstairs when I heard the printer come on and off. I dashed up to pull the plug but when I entered the room, it stopped. I started downstairs and it started again so I pulled the plug. Later, when I plugged it in, it operated normally.

April 12, 1993: Again, while in the room directly below the room where my computer is located, I heard the system come on by itself for several seconds and then go off

April 19, 1993: I was sitting in the room under the computer room. I had just opened an envelope from Betty Luca with data for a new book, [*The Watchers II*]. [6] Suddenly, the computer and printers came on by themselves for a moment and then shut off

May 9, 1993: I went to the telephone recorder and listened to a recorded message from UFO abductee Jack W. As I listened, all the lights suddenly dimmed and the computer and printers came on and off for a moment.

May 21, 1993: The computer/printers came on for a second and then shut off. The circuit breaker had to be reset.

June 30, 1993: I was in my study when the computer equipment came on and went off for a few seconds.

December 30, 1995: A few seconds before my alarm watch went off at 6:45 this morning, I was awakened by a high [female] voice that called "Ray." This same type of voice has called me before. It was the voice that first called, "Ray, look at the clock" when the **numbers all-lined-up on the digital clock phenomenon** started. Strangely, as I wrote the words, "Ray look at the clock" in my diary, **I watched them fade to near invisibility** on the computer's monitor. This lasted for perhaps 15 seconds before brightening back to normal! This has never happened before!

A repeat performance took place just as I lay down to sleep in the evening. I again heard the same voice call "Ray." Again, later, as I was writing about this incident in my diary, the **screen faded in and out for a second**.

September 16, 1996: I was sitting on a couch writing a letter. Then, I got up and walked by the TV to enter another room. As I did so, the TV came on by itself.

September 23, 1996: Around noon, I got up to do something and the TV set in front of me went on by itself. I tried duplicating my movements and other movements to see if I could make it come on again but failed to do so.

July 11, 1996: I was sitting beside my computer reading my daily devotional material when suddenly it came on all by itself. [Also, both printers came on as they are interconnected to go on when the computer comes on.]

July 15, 1996: As I was leaving my computer, it started up by itself again.

December 22, 1999: The following synchronism and apparent electrical sensitivity phenomenon is reminiscent of similar events that took place several years ago. I was in the bathroom shaving. The faucet was running and making noise. I was thinking that I would be able to spend time writing my new book on UFOs entitled *The Andreasson Legacy* [7] after my daughter's visit this morning.

Concurrent with this thought was my noticing a new background noise coming from the adjoining room. I turned off the water and glanced out of the door. I was amazed to see that both my computer and monitor were on. I do not remember turning them on! My memory could easily trace my steps up until that point. I came back from jogging all sweaty. I came upstairs and went into the bedroom to remove my clothes. I put on my bathrobe and placed the sweaty clothes in the laundry basket. I went into the bathroom and began shaving before taking a shower.

At no time do I remember turning on the computer and the monitor. As fantastic as it would seem, they must have come on all by themselves. They had done this on a number of occasions several years ago. At that time, I had a different computer. It was rigged so that when turned on, the monitor and printer would come on at the same time. My present computer monitor and printer need to be switched on individually. It is interesting to note that **they came on at exactly the time I was thinking of continuing to write my book** this morning. [Note: I had the **same thought** at the outset of a similar event on April 19, 1993.]

Another reason why I think it came on by itself was the fact that I do not remember hearing its hum before turning the faucet on. Yet, I suddenly noticed it above the noise of the faucet.

I should add before continuing that a surge protector manufactured by Tandy protected my computer, printer and monitor. I wondered if a surge of electricity could somehow have been responsible for the phenomenon. So, I contacted local and national Tandy technicians. They told me that what I described could not happen. They insisted that the surge protector would protect my equipment from an electrical surge. They said that nobody else had complained to them about such a thing. In fact, they essentially said that what I described was impossible!

A concurrent coincidence occurred several seconds before the next onslaught of electrical sensitivity.

May 29, 2003: I was about to scan some pages from the May 20, 1979 *New York Times* Book Review. I noticed that the front page had a picture of **Billy Graham** and a review of a book about him. It was entitled *Billy Graham—A Parable of American Righteousness*. This occurred just as I had been looking at my **Billy Graham** devotional calendar beside my scanner. Almost simultaneously, **my computer shut off by itself and then re-started by itself!** I had to run scandisk to get back to my scanning program. I had not begun to scan nor did I touch the computer on and off switch.

The entries just discussed were background for the following *converging coincidences* involving electrical sensitivity. These concerned the seeming effect of my person upon the digital message counter on my telephone answering machine. The first coincidences were only a day apart. However, they were harbingers of a *concurrent coincidence* that took place almost three years later.

January 2, 1996: Around 11:30 at night, my answering machine telephone **read zero messages**. As I passed by and **glanced at it**, there was a "click" and the glowing LCD display **flicked to seven messages**. When I moved away, it clicked back to zero but back to seven when I moved beside the telephone, then back to zero as I moved away. After this, it no longer repeated itself. I checked the message tape. It was rewound to zero messages. This reminds me of my computer coming off and on by itself and the time my TV came on by itself.

Then, on the next day, January 3, it happened again seemingly in response to my thoughts.

January 3, 1996: An incredible repeat performance of last night. As I wandered by the telephone at 10:23 p.m., I **stopped to look at it. It read zero messages**. I thought to myself that what happened last night probably would never happen again. **Just as I thought this**, there was a click and the LCD display **flicked from zero to seven** and then flicked back to zero. At that very time, I had *a ringing sound* in my left ear that stopped few minutes after the event.

Then, three years later, the same thing occurred.

November 17, 1999: An interesting thing happened this morning. I looked for something near my telephone and answering machine. **As I glanced around it**, I heard a whirring sound come from it. Suddenly, the **message**

counter flicked to one. The telephone did not ring nor was there any message on the tape. Similar things have happened before in the past.

October 17, 2002: I am in the midst of writing a book about *Synchronicity* and have been wondering what **agent** to send it to. This evening, when teaching an introductory course on UFOs at the Kennebunk Adult Education Program, one of the students attending was a local literary **agent** who mentioned that he was looking for manuscripts. I will contact him later.

January 16, 2003: While searching for information on the term *numinosity* on the Internet, I clicked on a site with **a photograph of a solar eclipse**. It looked very familiar to me. On the following day, I happened to look at an outdated December 2002 calendar above my computer. It was the **same picture**! All I had to have done was to look up and see the calendar but for some reason did not.

January 24, 2003: The following is my fourth panic attack that coincided with an attempt to tell others about one of my abduction experiences. While conversing with a book agent today regarding my new book on synchronicity, he asked me if I had seen a UFO. I told him about my teen sighting on a Danvers farm and others that I had seen consciously. He asked me about my abduction experiences and if I had undergone hypnotic regression to retrieve details. I said that I had undergone hypnosis three times and had relived some of these experiences but had to stop because of Margaret's protests. He then asked if I could relate these experiences to him. I agreed and tried to do so but was suddenly hit with the same type of panic attack experienced in the past when I tried to tell my former Pastor, Mark Coleman and another person about my experiences. I found that I could not talk and that I found it hard to breathe. It took a few minutes to come back to normal.

March 15, 2003: Last March, Margaret and I were sitting in the living room watching TV when all of a sudden **a mouse appeared running around the front hall**. I went down cellar and got a trap. I set it just inside the clothes closet in the front hall. A few hours later, I had caught the mouse.

A few days later Margaret got up in the morning and went to use the bathroom. I heard her shriek and went to see why. There was **another mouse**. It was **in the toilet!**

Today, a year later, on Wednesday, March 15, 2003, Margaret and I again were again sitting watching TV in the evening when all of a sudden we saw **a mouse running around in the front hall**. We were amazed because the same thing happened last year in March. Like last year, I went down to the cellar, obtained a trap and set it just inside the clothes closet in the front hall. A few hours later, the mouse was caught.

The next day we told painters who had arrived to paint the living room about the weird coincidence. However, the synchronism did not end there.

This morning, two days after catching the mouse, I went to use the bathroom. There, in **the same toilet**, again was **a dead mouse**!

March 28, 2003: Last evening I was discussing the asteroid belt with my class on astronomy. I was asked what the chances were of a populated area being hit by debris **from the asteroid belt**. I answered that the chances were astronomically slim.

This morning I received news via email that yesterday a meteor flashed over Illinois, Indiana, Ohio and Wisconsin and broke up into pieces that covered a path about 80 by 20 miles wide. Police were deluged with reports of falling meteorites striking homes and cars. One home suffered damage when a ten pound meteorite crashed through their roof into their living room. Experts estimate the original meteor was about the size of a Volkswagen and that it originated **from the asteroid belt**!

May 1, 2003: An incredible synchronism. I glanced out the sliding glass doors to our outside deck and saw a large beautiful fox prancing around the backyard. I called to Margy to look. As we watched, the fox stopped, approached and **sat in front of the deck steps and began scratching himself**. I ran upstairs and grabbed a camera, but when I looked out the upstairs window, he was running around the yard again. I took some pictures through the window before he ran off but was disappointed not to photograph him sitting still and scratching himself in front of the deck steps.

Several hours later I happened to glance out the sliding glass doors and was amazed to see the fox running around the yard as he did before. I grabbed the camera to take a picture and was **shocked to see him come to the exact spot in front of the deck steps, sit down and scratch himself again**. Needless to say, I took the picture that I had missed before.

June 6, 2003: [Recorded at home after vacation trip.] On May 21, on the way to Pittsburg, NH to vacation, we stopped in Bethel, Maine to check out a campground. We liked it and booked a site for June 11–14. We noticed that it was near a State Park called **Grafton Notch**. We wondered if there were hiking trails in the Park. Last night I found a website on the computer about Grafton Notch and found out that the park did have hiking trails, so I printed out a map of the trails. This morning I turned on TV channel 8 from Portland, Maine. I was shocked to see a segment appear on the hiking trails at **Grafton Notch** State Park!

June 11, 2003: I have been trying to find **a breeder of English Setters in the State of Maine**. Both my granddaughter and I have searched and searched for one via the Internet without success. Today, while on a camping trip, Margaret met a fellow camper who had an English Setter puppy. She asked him where he had bought it. He told her that he bought it from **a breeder of**

English Setters in Buxton, Maine not very far from our home in Kennebunk!

December 17, 2003: This morning, Margaret tried to make an appointment for my haircut but was told that there were no openings. Later on when the phone rang, I somehow immediately knew that it was the barber calling to say that one of her clients had cancelled and that there was now an opening for me.

February 5, 2004: Today was the culmination of a *converging coincidence* that started in June 2002. One day during that month I decided to go brook trout fishing in Day Brook which borders our property. I hiked along its banks until I found a pool which looked promising and began fishing. I caught several trout and released some of the smaller ones. While fishing, I heard some voices looked around to see where they were coming from. In a few minutes time I saw and elderly man hobbling alongside the brook accompanied by a woman. He was complaining that he hadn't caught any trout and that he had always caught trout in this brook. I stopped fishing and shouted to them that I had been catching trout out of the pool in front of me. The woman approached and I told her to tell the old man I would leave and let him catch some trout in the pool. The woman was very grateful and shouted the offer back to her father. I quickly left the area hoping that he would catch some trout.

We had moved to Maine in December of 2001 and began worshipping at the First Baptist church in town. It took a while to get to know people but we got to know a 95 year old lady named Lillian very well. When she found out that I enjoyed fishing, she introduced me to her brother-in-law, Ken, who loved trout fishing but had not been able to fish because of his weak legs. I had lots of frozen trout that I had caught in our freezer and began giving him some to eat from time to time.

Today, Margaret and I took Lillian and Ken out to lunch. We brought them back to the house for dessert and to watch some of my trout-fishing videos. I offered to take him fishing in the spring. He told me that his daughter had taken him a few years ago but that she no longer wanted to take the responsibility for him because he had trouble walking. He told me that he fished Day Brook and was surprised that the brook ran by our property. I told him that I too fished the brook and it was then that I realized the possibility of an amazing coincidence. I asked him if he and his daughter had fished Day Brook a few years ago. He said that his daughter brought him to fish one day at that very Brook. I then asked if he remembered meeting a man at the brook who gave up a nice pool that he had been fishing so he could fish in it. A surprised look came over his face and he smiled broadly as he recognized that I was the one who had helped him to find trout that day.

February 24, 2004: About six months ago I purchased a number of videos to use for Sunday school. Two days ago, I showed a video to the adult Sunday school concerning a young man's heroic sacrificial efforts to bring international attention to the terrible persecution of an ethnic group in Burma called the **Karen** that had been going on since the end of World War II. Today we received the latest edition of the journal, Christianity Today. One of its lead stories was about the persecution of the **Karen.**

This ends the chapter on *converging coincidences*. The majority of synchronisms that I experience are the *concurrent* and *corresponding types*. If you thought them incredible, wait until you encounter my *counter coincidences* in chapter eight. These appear to be supernatural! However, these will be discussed later. The next chapter deals with what I have dubbed the *clock coincidence*. It is yet another type of synchronism that haunts my life.

6

Clock Coincidences

Synchronicity experiences, even if shrouded in mystery and separated from us by a chasm of time, usually hold extreme importance for us. Although the unreliable bridge of memory is our primary connection to them, they continue to shape our lives long after they occur.

—Victor Mansfield
The Challenge of Synchronicity

I purposely reserved this chapter for a synchronism that I call a *clock coincidence*. It is the act of inadvertently observing the line-up of *identical* numbers on a clock. This phenomenon is manifest in all three categories of coincidences. I will not always highlight the specific type of categories in the following incidents. By now the reader should be familiar with the three kinds covered in the preceding chapters.

As far as I can remember, this phenomenon began in the late 1980's. One night I was awakened with a start by a voice that simply said: "Ray, look at the clock." When I sat up in bed and glanced over at the digital clock, it read 5:55 a.m.

At first, I dismissed the incident as a weird coincidence but the strange phenomenon continued. At times, I would be awakened by a voice. Sometimes it would be by sounds like a wind chime, a bell or an electronic-like beep. At other times, it would be by a buzzing noise, a fire alarm or dogs barking. Once, it was a loud bump against the side of the house. Most of the time, I would awake with a start for no known reason at all. In all of these scenarios, identical numbers would be lined up on a digital clock.

This began to disturb my sleep pattern. I would stay awake to see if vehicles were making noise at these precise times and waking me up. This did not seem to be the case. So, one evening I half-in-jest asked the phenomenon to wake me up at 1:11, 2:22, 3:33, 4:44 and 5:55. It obliged—I woke up with a start at each of these times. Whatever it was coincidence or real—it repeated this again for me on another night. Now I took the phenomenon seriously, especially because of other strange things that coincided with these strange wake-up calls.

Sometimes it would be an overpowering vibrating, tingling sensation coursing through my body. At other times, I would awake after a *flying dream* and a sensation *of floating out ofk my body*. What really disturbed me was that I would find strange cuts, scratches and bruises on my body. In the morning, there would be blood on my pillow. Many times these physical effects reflected things that had happened to me in my dreams.

During my research, I have come across others who are experiencing this same phenomenon. They are called UFO abductees. The *clock coincidence* is considered one of benchmarks of a UFO abduction experience.

Such incidents prompted me to begin entering these enigmatic incidents into my diary. I kept a diary of *clock coincidences* between 1992 and 1996. Finally, I stopped recording every incident because of their preponderance. After 1996, I recorded only those that coincided with other anomalies. I have summarized these on charts.

You will note that the following charts [for the most part] deal only with clock number line-ups that occurred during the early morning hours. I should add that this same phenomenon occurs during the day. Most coincide with an innate urge to glance at a clock. When I do, the numbers are lined up. This often occurs when I am just beginning or finishing a task.

I should also mention that similar coincidences with non-clock-numbers also occur. These are not recorded in *SynchroFile*. They involve numbers lined-up on a mailbox, in a book, a newspaper or on some other physical object that I inadvertently glance at.

The nighttime incidents are the most interesting. In most instances, the stimulus to awake is not apparent. I simply awake with a start. However, there are times when varieties of stimuli are the cause. Many are incidents of high strangeness. I will highlight examples on the following charts. These charts provide a quick-look summary of the *clock coincidence phenomenon* that occurred between 1992 and a portion of 1996. The phenomenon continues. This morning [November 1, 2002], I awoke with a start at 3:33 and 5:55 a.m.

1992

| JUN | 9 | | 3:33 |
| SEP | 27 | | 2:22 |

1992 (Continued)

OCT	7	1:11			
OCT	10				5:55
OCT	27			4:44	
NOV	4		3:33		
NOV	10			4:44	
NOV	18		3:33		
NOV	27		3:33		
NOV	28			4:44	
NOV	29			4:44	
DEC	2		3:33	4:44	
DEC	5				5:55
DEC	6				5:55
DEC	11				5:55
DEC	18				5:55

On a number of these occasions, I awake from a dream of being in a strange place where I am being tested with unfamiliar instruments. Sometimes when I wake, I am lying in a strange position. At other times I awake when commanded by what I, for want of a better description, call an inaudible voice.

> **October 7, 1992:** I woke up in the middle of the night and lay in bed with my eyes closed. I received **an inaudible voice-like-thought** to open my eyes and look at the clock. I did and again the numbers were all lined up—3:33.

At other times, I am awake when I receive these telepathic-like impressions

> **October 10, 1992:** I got up to go to the bathroom during the night. Between the bathroom and the bedroom, I again received **an inaudible voice-like thought** that said: "when you go back to sleep and wake up again, the clock will read 5:55." I thought—"Come on now, this is getting silly"—and went back to bed. Later, I awoke with a start and glanced at the clock. It read 5:55.

As mentioned, many times, I also awake to a *clock coincidence* while concurrently experiencing an electric-like tingling sensation coursing through my body.

November 27, 1992: At 1:00 a.m., I woke up with the "feeling"—**a tingling sensation**—feeling up-tight—like something was about to happen. I got out of bed and went to the bathroom. The next thing I knew, I was waking up with a start [and a tingling sensation]. I glanced at the clock. It read 3:33. The tingling sensation was very strong. I found it hard to sleep and kept waking up.

November 18, 1992: Shortly after retiring to bed, I got a feeling that something was going to happen. It was a feeling of apprehension. I dozed, woke up, and looked around the room to see if anyone was there. I could see nothing. I dropped off to sleep but later, woke up with a start. I glanced at the LCD numbers on the clock. They read 3:33. I was experiencing **the tingling feeling** all through my body. It continued through the morning hours and I found it hard to sleep. It finally dissipated shortly after I got up.

Another curious thing was that when we woke up, my wife told me about *a scary dream.* It involved *two scary looking wolves looking through a window at us.* I got up and brought them. in I told her that I could tame them and not to be afraid, but she was terrified. [Later], I sat down in front of the computer at about 8:00 a.m. to have my devotions. The printers and computer came on by themselves for a moment!

What is even stranger is that sometimes I wake up after *clock coincidences* with fresh scabbed-over cuts. One puncture-like cut appeared quite often in the upper back part of my neck. It would scab over and begin to heal, only to be cut again after waking up to numbers lined up on the clock.

December 18, 1992: [I awoke] with a start to glance at the clock—it read 5:55 a.m. Shortly after getting up in the morning, my hand suddenly unconsciously reached around to the uppermost back of my neck to touch it. My finger landed on a **new fresh scab** in the same area where similar scabs have appeared in the past.

1993

JAN	8		4:44
JAN	14	2:22	4:44
JAN	21			5:55
JAN	22			5:55
JAN	23	2:22	

1993 (Continued)

JAN	25				4:44	
JAN	31					5:55
FEB	5			3:33		
FEB	7		2:22	3:33		
FEB	8		2:22			
FEB	12				4:44	5:55
FEB	13				4:44	
FEB	14		2:22			
FEB	16			3:33		
FEB	19		2:22			
FEB	20					5:55
FEB	21				4:44	5:55
MAR	4				4:44	5:55
MAR	7					5:55
MAR	12			3:33		
MAR	15				4:44	5:55
MAR	20				4:44	
MAR	21			3:33		
MAR	22			3:33		
MAR	28	1:11				
APR	2					5:55
APR	7					5:55
APR	9					5:55
APR	10					5:55
APR	13					5:55
APR	16					5:55
APR	24					5:55

1993 (Continued)

APR	28				5:55
APR	30				5:55
MAY	1		3:33		5:55
JUN	15				5:55
JUN	16				5:55
JUL	18	2:22			
OCT	21		3:33		
OCT	22			4:44	5:55
OCT	26		3:33		5:55
OCT	28		3:33	4:44	
OCT	29		3:33		
OCT	30				5:55
NOV	8			4:44	5:55
NOV	10				5:55
NOV	11				5:55
NOV	14		3:33	4:44	5:55
NOV	16		3:33	4:44	5:55
NOV	20			4:44	5:55
NOV	21				5:55
NOV	23		3:33		
NOV	30				5:55
DEC	2				5:55
DEC	12				5:55

Periodically, I will awaken and find strange gouges on my body after *clock coincidences*. Sometimes there will be blood on the pillow where my nose touches the pillowcase.

January 14, 1993: I woke up twice to see the clock read 3:33 and 5:55. During the day, I felt pain behind my left shoulder. There were **three gouge marks** with heavy scabs of blood, which looked fresh. Two marks are about three quarters of and inch and the other about one eighth of an inch. I remembered noticing similar marks some time ago in the same location. I went back to check my 1992 diary entries. I found that almost exactly one year ago, on January 13, 1992, I felt and discovered the same type of gouges in the same place.

February 5, 1993: Awoke at 3:33. When I got up later, I found **blood and a grayish stain on the pillowcase**.

Sometimes I awake to a *clock coincidence* from what appear to be normal stimuli such as the few examples recorded below. Why do these mundane things happen when the clock numbers are lined up?

January 31, 1993: Awoke at 5:55 when **the fire whistle blew**.

April 28, 1993: Margaret **poked me** to stop me from snoring. I glanced at the clock. It read 5:55.

April 30, 1993: I awoke when the **fire whistle blew** and glanced at the clock, which read 5:55.

October 22, 1993: I awoke suddenly to windows making a **rattling sound** at 4:44.

November 10, 1993: Dogs barking loudly in neighborhood woke me up. I glanced at the clock, which read 5:55.

At other times, I hear what appear to be musical tones and telepathic-like voices that awake me to the *clock coincidence*.

March 4, 1993: A short **musical tone** caused me to wake up at 4:44. I woke up again. The clock read 5:55.

March 8, 1993: I awoke with the words **death mission** in my head. When I looked at the clock, it read 5:56 but was probably 5:55 when these words stirred me to awake.

April 2, 1993: I awoke with a **soft tone** in my ear. I thought that my alarm watch had gone off. The clock read 5:55. I have been experiencing synchronisms. I will be reading or typing a certain word while listening to the radio or

TV. Just as I read or type the word, the same word will be said on the radio or TV.

June 15, 1993: An **inaudible voice said, "It is 5:55"** and woke me up. The clock read 5:55. Such *clock coincidences* sometimes occur several times a week.

The phenomenon continues. [Today, as I write this book on November 1, 2002, I awoke with a start at 4:44 and 5:55.]

1994

JAN	2				4:44	
JAN	4				4:44	
JAN	11				4:44	
FEB	2			3:33	4:44	
FEB	4		2:22			5:55
FEB	7		2:22	3:33		
FEB	9		2:22			
FEB	10			3:33		5:55
FEB	12				4:44	5:55
FEB	21			3:33	4:44	5:55
FEB	22				4:44	
FEB	26			3:33		5:55
FEB	28					5:55
MAR	3			3:33		5:55
MAR	8	1:11				
MAR	9		2:22			
MAR	10		2:22	3:33	4:44	5:55
MAR	11				4:44	
MAR	17		2:22			
MAR	20				4:44	5:55
APR	6				4:44	

1994 (Continued)

APR	9		2:22			
APR	15			3:33		
APR	16			3:33		5:55
APR	28				4:44	
MAY	7			3:33	4:44	
MAY	13				4:44	
MAY	30			3:33		
JUN	14			3:33		
JUL	10				4:44	
AUG	18				4:44	
AUG	19			3:33		
SEP	5				4:44	
SEP	18					5:55
SEP	21					5:55
SEP	24	1:11				5:55
SEP	27			3:33		5:55
OCT	21			3:33		5:55
OCT	22					5:55
OCT	25		2:22			
OCT	28			3:33		
NOV	7				4:44	
NOV	10			3:33	4:44	
NOV	12				4:44	5:55
NOV	16			3:33		5:55
NOV	18			3:33	4:44	
NOV	23			3:33	4:44	5:55
NOV	25					5:55

1994 (Continued)

NOV	26		3:33	5:55
NOV	28		4:44	5:55
DEC	9 [Note: Awakened at 11: 11 p.m. after a "flying dream".]			
DEC	12			5:55
DEC	15		3:33	4:44	5:55
DEC	16	1:11		
DEC	20		4:44	
DEC	21		4:44	
DEC	22		3:33	

February 2, 1994: I was awakened by two hard blows to my buttocks. [Same as an incident on November 23, 1994.] I glanced at the clock, which read 3:33! Later, I again woke up with a start at 5:55! Later during the day, I felt a new scab on the upper back of my neck.

February 12, 1994: I awoke at 4:44. Later, I awoke and felt I should look at the clock. When I gave in to curiosity, the clock turned from 5:55 to 5:56. The following day, we **noticed four spots of blood** across the face of my pillow as if they had dripped from the head area. I found no cuts on my face. My right nostril is lined with dried mucus but no dried blood.

March 3, 1994: Awoke to wind-chime-like sounds at 3:33 and 5:55.

March 10, 1994: I heard **a bell** like a telephone, which woke me up at 1:11. I awoke again at 2:22 and again at 3:33. Later, I heard **a buzzing sound**. I turned over to see the clock flick from 4:44 to 4:45. Later, I awoke facing the clock. It read 5:55!

I should mention that often, after experiencing a *clock coincidence*, I feel as if I were two selves. I will awake from a flying dream and my body is lying in a strange position.

February 9, 1994: I awoke went to the bathroom and returned to the bedroom at 2:22. All that night, I was in a half-sleep/half-awake state until about 5:30 when I experienced a weird phenomenon. It felt like a more alert me suddenly slipped into my body through my head like a hand being thrust into a glove!

> **March 11, 1994:** I awoke and glanced at the clock, which read 4:44. I remained in a half-sleep/half-awake state until 5:51 when I again experienced what I had before on 2/9/94. It felt like a more alert me suddenly was thrust into my body through my head like a hand being thrust into a glove. [This was violent and caused a whiplash. I had to wear a neck collar for several days.] I awoke again at 5:55, felt very relaxed and fell into a sound sleep.
>
> **March 20, 1994:** I awoke at 4:44, again at 5:54 and watched the clock turn to 5:55. I was lying in the same position that I had been in the past when paralyzed. My legs were crossed tightly at the ankles. My arms were raised up and crossed at my chest. My wrists were crossed tightly together. Later, during the day, I received a flashback to a dream that I had last night. In the dream, I was flying and saw buildings and streetlights below. At daylight, I saw a desert area below.

I began to wonder if these out-of-the-body feelings were connected with *clock coincidences*. I knew another person who experienced similar experiences that coincided with clock numbers being lined up.

> **July 19, 1994:** While vacationing friends at Colebrook, New Hampshire, one woman named Robin told me of a reoccurring experience of leaving her body and floating through the wall to a light outside. She said that she too awakes quite often when the **hands of her clock are lined up**.

Since this book is primarily about synchronisms, I will not delve further into this out-of-the-body experience aspect of *clock coincidences*. I have mentioned it for the benefit of others who may be having the same kind of experiences. They may like to know that they are not alone in their experiences. Nevertheless, later we shall examine their possible linkage to other forms of synchronicity.

The following entry dissolved doubts that ordinary disturbances might be waking me at these precise times. I had essentially ruled this out but still wondered. because what happened on a camping trip proved that its cause was not limited to my home surroundings! The phenomenon again coincided with a flying dream and seeming out-of-the-body-experiences (OBE). It also tallied with Robin's experiences. It indicated that these clock times might be related to out-of-the-body experiences!

> **August 8, 1994:** While camping in Maine on Mt. Dessert Island, I awoke in the tent and glanced at my watch, which read 3:33. I remembered a vivid dream of being at 4 Dodge Court, Danvers where I had experienced child-

hood visitation/abductions. I was showing an Air Force buddy around the house. I brought him to a set of drawers located in my bedroom and opened one. Inside were sculptures of alien *gray* heads. I then showed him that I could float and floated around the house.

Then the dream suddenly changed. I was inside the tent and floating out through the zippered tent flap. That is all I could remember of the dream. I cannot help but wonder if the onset of an OBE caused my flying dream. Then, when I left my body, I had a fleeting memory of actually floating out the tent. Am I, like my father, being taken somewhere for some purpose while my physical body lies back in bed? Unlike my father, I cannot remember what has occurred during the apparent OBEs.

The following are actually *corresponding coincidences* and are recorded out of place in this chapter to acquaint the reader with my encounters with electrical sensitivity:

September 5, 1994: I woke with a start at 4:44. Later, I noticed a slight pain when I sat down. I didn't think further about it until evening when I undressed and glanced in the mirror. There on my buttocks was the now familiar circular pattern of scabs.

September 12, 1994: A **whistling sound** woke me up at 12:12 a.m. It **lasted about 20-30 seconds**. Strangely, instead of getting up and glancing out the window, I simply got up to use the bathroom. Later I met UFO abductee, Charlie Foltz, and MUFON hypnotherapist, Tony Constantino, for lunch. Charlie told us that he had been doing some photography in a remote area earlier in the morning. He said that he had heard a **whistling sound for about 30 seconds** but could not determine its source.

October 28, 1994: Margaret awoke and jolted upright in **bed pulling the covers off** me at 3:33. My right nostril is still sore

November 23, 1994: I was awakened with a start at 3:33 by **a hard blow** to my buttocks. I awoke later with a start at 4:44 and 5:55.

December 9, 1994: I was awakened by the **Town's fire whistle**, which sounded at 11:11 p.m. I went to sleep and had a flying dream. I recollect flying over a battlefield.

December 15, 1994: I awoke out of a deep sleep and thought to myself—"They floated me back to bed." I then got up to go to the bathroom. When I started out the door, **something told me** to look at the clock on the bureau. I did. It read 3:33! I went back to sleep but awoke again at 4:44. Later, I awoke and watched the clock flick from 5:54 to 5:55!

December 20, 1994: Margaret and I awoke at the same time with a start at 4:44.

1995

JAN	1	1:11				5:55
JAN	2	1:11		3:33	4:44	5:55
JAN	5		2:22			
JAN	7					5:55
JAN	6				4:44	5:55
JAN	18					5:55
JAN	20					5:55
JAN	25					5:55
JAN	26					5:55
FEB	1					5:55
FEB	3				4:44	
FEB	5				4:44	
FEB	6	1:11				
FEB	8				4:44	5:55
FEB	9				4:44	
FEB	11		2:22			5:55
FEB	15		2:22			
FEB	17		2:22		4:44	
FEB	18					5:55
FEB	22		2:22			5:55
FEB	23		2:22		4:44	
FEB	25					5:55
FEB	27					5:55
MAR	2				4:44	5:55
MAR	18					5:55

1995 (Continued)

MAR	22		3:33	4:44		
MAR	26		3:33			
MAR	29				5:55	
MAR	31			4:44	5:55	
APR	2			4:44		
APR	8				5:55	
APR	9			4:44		
APR	11			4:44	5:55	
APR	14		3:33		5:55	
APR	17	1:11				
APR	19				5:55	
APR	21				5:55	
APR	24		3:33		5:55	
APR	25		3:33			
APR	26				5:55	
APR	29				5:55	
MAY	6		3:33			
MAY	8			4:44		
MAY	10				5:55	
MAY	17	2:22				
MAY	18	2:22			5:55	
MAY	19			4:44		
MAY	21	2:22	3:33	4:44	5:55	
MAY	22		3:33			
MAY	23			4:44		[Awoke 1:11 p.m. from a nap.]
MAY	26		3:33			
MAY	27			4:44		

110   SynchroFile

1995 (Continued)

MAY	30	1:11					
JUN	5		2:22				
JUN	15				4:44		
JUN	18				4:44		
JUN	29					5:55	
JUN	30			3:33			
JUL	1				4:44		
JUL	4				4:44		
JUL	8					5:55	
JUL	9					5:55	
JUL	19		2:22			5:55	
AUG	12					5:55	
AUG	13			3:33	4:44		
AUG	16				4:44	5:55	

[Note: Visited England. I cannot see the clock at night, but I have glanced at my digital watch many times during the day when its numbers were lined up.]

| SEP | 17 | | | 3:33 [On my watch when I went to the bathroom.] |

[Note: Returned home. Can now see illuminated clock numbers in bedroom.]

SEP	30			3:33		5:55	
OCT	5				4:44		
OCT	12		2:22				
OCT	13					5:55	
OCT	27					5:55	[Awoke from a nap at 1:11 p.m.]
OCT	28					5:55	
OCT	31					5:55	
NOV	1			3:33			
NOV	14		2:22	3:33			

1995 (Continued)

NOV	18		4:44	5:55
NOV	26		4:44	
DEC	6			5:55
DEC	10	1:11		
DEC	14		4:44	5:55
DEC	15			5:55
DEC	17		4:44	5:55
DEC	22		4:44	[Awoke 11:11 p.m.]
DEC	28	2:22	4:44	

The year 1995 revealed the same types of incidents that coincided with *clock coincidences* that had occurred in previous years. The concurrent numbers coincided with anomalous physical effects on my body. At times, I felt as if I had returned from floating outside of my body. [Such effects and feelings sometimes occur without a *clock coincidence*.]

> **January 25, 1995:** I woke up in the early morning hours with the remnants of, or the beginning of, the **tingling, uptight feeling** experienced in the past. I could not stay asleep and kept waking up with this feeling. I do remember thinking at one point that I should look at the clock when it turned 5:55. I remember doing this and then going to sleep. I felt worn out and had a severe headache during the day.
>
> **February 22, 1995:** I awoke at 5:55 with what **sounded like my wife's alarm clock** going off. Later, when we got up, I asked her to make sure that she pushed the alarm button in as her alarm had woken me up. She told me that the clock was not wound. We checked. It read 7:20. It was unwound and not running. The alarm clock downstairs was running. However, the alarm had been set for 3:45 in the afternoon. The button was all the way in.

I remembered another time that this had happened before but forgot to record it. In addition, a number of times I have been awakened by a beeping sound. I thought it was my alarm watch going off, but it was not.

> **March 22, 1995:** I awoke with a **feeling that I was floating and entering my body.** I opened my eyes and glanced at the clock, which read 3:33. Later,

I again awoke. The 3:33 experience must have been on my mind because I said to myself—"This is confirmatory that OBEs and the *clock phenomenon* are related." I then glanced at the clock. It read 4:44!

May 6, 1995: I woke up at 3:33. I had a **dream of floating** in a blimp. The operators of the blimp let me take control of it and I put it through a number of acrobatic-like maneuvers.

May 18, 1995: I awoke at 2:22 and 5:55. A smear of **blood was on the sheet**.

May 19, 1995: I awoke hearing **a bell ringing** softly. I glanced at the clock. It read 4:44.

May 30, 1995: I awoke and glanced at clock. It read 1:11. Later I felt that I slipped into myself through my head as if I were **returning from an OBE**.

August 16, 1995: Awoke at 4:43 and 5:53. Both times, I felt that I must look at the clock until they changed to 4:44 and 5:55, but think I fell asleep. My **pillow had bloodstains** on it in the morning, apparently from the nose area. Yet, I felt no soreness and had no visible cuts on my face. My right inner thigh had a cluster of **three small bruises**.

November 14, 1995: I turned over and awoke to see the clock, which read 2:22. Later, I awoke with a start to see the clock reading 3:33. I was anxious and experienced the ***tingling sensation*** felt in the past. I went to the bathroom and then found it hard to sleep because of the tingling and anxiety. When I awoke, my wife had left to go swimming. I tried to get up, but each time I tried to move [**paralysis**], there was an equal and opposite tingling force that matched whatever movement I wanted to make. It also affected my will. Each time I desired to move, a desire not to move immediately counteracted it. It took fifteen minutes for this paralysis-like phenomenon to subsist. Later in the day, I discovered the **usual scab on the upper part of my neck**.

November 18, 1995: I awoke to see the clock change from 4:43 to 4:44. I awoke again to see the clock read 5:55. During the day, I noticed a **thin one-half inch long hairline scar** scabbed over on the outside lower part of my forefinger.

The following chart reflects my last efforts to record all instances of my awaking to *clock coincidences*:

1996

JAN	4		3:33			
JAN	7	2:22			5:55	
JAN	9				5:55	
JAN	10				5:55	
JAN	28			4:44		
FEB	2		3:33			
FEB	3			4:44		
FEB	11			4:44		
FEB	25			4:44		
MAR	25	1:11				
MAR	26	1:11	3:33			
APR	8				5:55	
APR	11				5:55	
APR	12				5:55	
MAY	1				5:55	
MAY	2				5:55	
MAY	4			4:44		
MAY	9				5:55	
MAY	10		3:33			
JUN	2				5:55	[Awoke 11:11 p.m.]
JUN	3			4:44		
JUN	6	2:22			5:55	
JUN	7			4:44		
JUN	8				5:55	
JUN	9				5:55	
JUN	11		3:33			
JUN	20				5:55	

1996 (Continued)

JUN	21	2:22
JUN	29	2:22

February 3, 1996: A **snowplow passing by on the street woke me up**. I glanced at clock numbers as they moved from 4:43 to 4:44. When I got up, I found an irregular dark blob of **hardened blood** soaked into the pillowcase in an area about three quarters of and inch by one-half inch in size with three small round lighter surface drops of blood directly under this blob. These three drips looked as if they had fallen onto the pillow from above. The larger blob looked like where my nose would have touched the pillow when I slept. My nose showed no sign of bleeding nor was it sore. I had no cuts on my face that would have caused bleeding. This same thing has happened periodically in the past.

June 29, 1996: I found it hard to get to sleep. I tossed and turned. I finally got to sleep sometime after 11:00. The next thing that I remember is a **hazy dream of being put back in bed** from somewhere else then saying to myself—"Oh my God, how did they do that?"—And waking up abruptly to see the clock reading 2:22. My using God's name in vain is completely out of character for me because of my Christian background. Whatever I saw in my dream must have totally shocked me to use this expression.

Although I stopped specifically recording the *Clock Phenomenon* after 1996, it continues as I was bringing this book to an end. I thought it worthwhile to record the following incident from my diary because of its uniqueness.

March 25, 2004: As mentioned earlier in my diary series, I have experienced what I have dubbed the clock phenomenon. I wake up suddenly, glance at the clock, and see identical numbers lined up on the digital clock. Sometimes I just wake up for no apparent reason. Other times I am awakened sounds like a bell, a buzz, a clicking sound, dogs barking, a thump against the house, a fire whistle blowing, etc. However, this time I was awakened by the alarm on my wrist watch. I woke up and glanced at a digital clock and then at my digital watch. **They both read 1:11**. I never set the alarm on my watch.

7
Family Coincidences

Although we may not be able to make synchronicities happen, we can create environments that foster their occurrence. We can create an inner environment of wholeness and an openness to intention; and in our outer lives we can go and engage ourselves fully in the world, mix with the social field, go out and play.

—Peter Russell
How to be a Wizard

Members of my family have also experienced several strange synchronistic experiences. I turn first to some examples from my children's lives:

AUTHOR'S SONS

The following are extraordinary *corresponding coincidences* that involve my youngest son. The first two involve the location of the house that he recently moved to in Plaistow, New Hampshire:

> **September 24, 2001:** [A double synchronism.] My son David and family have been searching for affordable property in Southern New Hampshire for a long time. However, each time they found a place to their liking, someone would beat them to it. Finally, they got to a house first in Plaistow and put their down payment on it. When they were introduced to the elderly owner, David was shocked to find that **his name also was Fowler**! Another surprise was that his neighbor across the street is the **Town Clerk of Plaistow**. Our next door neighbor in Wenham is the **Town Clerk of Wenham**.
>
> **October 19, 2002:** Another incredible synchronism. When we lived in Wenham, Massachusetts, Margaret met a woman named Marion while swimming at the YMCA. Coincidentally [another one!] Margaret then found out that she

had worked for Dad at the United Shoe! She has become a good friend. However, the coincidence involving my son David took place today.

Today we visited friends in Massachusetts and Margaret had lunch with Marion. During the conversation, Marion mentioned that her cousin, Tom Jones, lived in Plaistow, New Hampshire. Since our son lived in Plaistow, New Hampshire [Population: 7664], Margaret asked where Tom lived in Plaistow. Margaret was amazed when Marion told her that Tom lived on **Autumn Drive**. David lives on **Autumn Drive**! Marion did not know his street number so I got on the Internet. I checked the assessor's records at the Plaistow Town Hall's web site. The coincidence took on even greater dimensions of incredulity. I found that her cousin lives at **21** Autumn Drive. Amazingly, my son, David, lives across the street from him at **20** Autumn Drive!

The next one is of interest as it involved my mouthing a term that I am not accustomed to using. This term just happened to be in David's mind and mouth a moment before I said it.

>**October 20, 2002:** I received a call from my son David's wife, Lisa, that they would be late coming to dinner with us. I asked when they would be able to arrive by using a term I rarely use. I asked Lisa what their **ETA** [estimated time of arrival] would be. She laughed and said, "You Fowlers are all alike. David just said to tell Dad what our **ETA** would be!"

So much for David, we now turn to my son, Ray Jr. I have only four entries for him but they are extraordinary. The first one was a *converging coincidence* and involved a young lady named Rose.

During his high school years, Ray worshiped with us at North Shore Community Baptist Church. He became great friends with a married couple at the church, Fred and Sherry Hartley. Fred attended nearby Gordon Conwell Seminary. **Fred and Sherry took a great interest in Ray and became Ray's mentors**. Later, Fred graduated and left the area to become pastor of the Christian Missionary Alliance Church [CMA} at Homestead, Florida

A young lady named Rose, at that time, lived in Homestead, Florida. Prior to moving to Massachusetts to attend Gordon College, she attended the local CMA Church where Fred was the pastor. **Fred and Sherry took a great interest in Rose and became Rose's mentors**.

During this time, Ray graduated from Berklee College of Music where he majored in audio engineering. He moved to California and was employed at an audio recording studio.

Rose left Florida and enrolled at Gordon College located in our then hometown of Wenham, Massachusetts. Rose attended North Shore Community Baptist Church and joined the choir. I sang in the choir and became acquainted with Rose. Since she had no car, I sometimes drove her home. After graduation, she obtained employment in the Boston area. **Rose rented an apartment and attended the CMA Church in Jamaica Plain.**

In the meantime, Ray felt called to the Christian ministry. He returned home from California and enrolled at Gordon-Conwell Seminary. Ray moved to the Boston area to take specialized off-campus courses. **Ray rented an apartment and attended the CMA in Jamaica Plain.**

Now you know *the rest of the story*. Ray, mentored by the Hartleys in Beverly Farms, Massachusetts met Rose who was mentored by the Hartleys in Homestead, Florida. They fell in love and got married! Little did I know that the young lady in the choir for whom I provided transportation was to become my daughter-in-law. Little did Ray and Rose know that both of them had been mentored by the same family at different times and places separated by over a thousand miles. I should add that neither Ray nor Rose knew of each other until they met in Church at Jamaica Plain.

The next synchronism experienced by Ray was a corresponding coincidence. At the time, Ray was staying with us at our former home in Wenham. He had traveled up from Florida to take courses towards a Doctor of Ministry degree at Gordon-Conwell Seminary in Wenham. My daughter, Beth, experienced a *converging coincidence* on the same day, which will be mentioned later.

> **June 12, 1997**: Our son Ray, a Christian pastor, arrived today from Florida with his family for a surprise visit. He told us about an interesting synchronism. They had wanted to visit, as we had not seen each other for several years. However, their car was too small for his family to make a long trip and it was in poor condition. Ray said that they had been praying that someday they could afford a van large enough to accommodate his family for a long trip.
>
> Ray had purchased a CD recording of a music group called the *Bee-Gee's*. A week or so ago he decided to listen to it. The first song that came on was entitled: **Coming Back to Massachusetts**. He laughed and half in jest told his wife Rose that it was a sign that they would soon be able to visit us in Wenham, Massachusetts.
>
> Shortly after they played the CD, the phone rang. A man from his church congregation was calling. He told Ray that he was buying a new van and would sell Ray his older van for one dollar! Ray bought and registered it and soon was **coming back to Massachusetts!**

Ray again visited from his home in Florida and shared an interesting *converging coincidence* of the TV kind with me.

> **November 11, 1999:** During my son's visit from **Fort Lauderdale**, Florida, another synchronism occurred. I was sitting in the living room flicking through different channels on the TV when Ray came in and sat down to watch. Just as he sat down, I flicked to a station that displayed in large words—**FORT LAUDERDALE**! It was a lead-in to a newscast of a Veteran's Day celebration in that city.

At the time of the next incident, Ray was again staying at our home in Wenham. One Afternoon he mentioned the following episode regarding coinciding birth dates:

> **June 22, 2001:** My son, Ray Jr., who is visiting while taking a course at a nearby seminary, told me of an amazing coincidence. One of his fellow students has been jokingly calling Ray "Timothy McVeigh" because of a similarity in appearance. Today, this student remarked that he just discovered that his own birthday was the same as that of Timothy McVeigh. He said that perhaps Ray should be calling *him* by that name.
>
> Ray asked him what the date was for Timothy McVeigh's birthday. The student replied that it was **April 23**. Ray laughed and told him that his birthday also was **April 23**. Another student listening to the conversation chimed in and said that his birthday was **April 23** as well!

Ray's fourth coincidence was of the *converging type*. It took place a year later when Ray again traveled from Florida to continue taking courses at the seminary. Since then, we had moved to Kennebunk, Maine. This coincidence involved wishful thoughts in Plantation, Florida that later converged and became reality in Sanford, Maine.

> **June 29, 2002:** My son, a pastor, is still visiting and experienced a synchronism today. Before leaving Florida, he and his wife **had hoped to purchase a Cocker Spaniel** but the cost was prohibitive. This morning, he remembered that he had an old friend named Jeff that had moved to a town [Sanford]. It is located next to where we now live in Kennebunk.
>
> Ray looked up Jeff's name in the phone book and called to arrange for a visit. Incredibly, just a few minutes into the phone conversation, Jeff inadvertently asked Ray **if he would like a Cocker Spaniel**! Jeff's dog had nine 12-week-old puppies. He had no idea that Ray and his family wanted one. He

had not seen Ray for many years. Ray brought one of the puppies home to Florida with him!

AUTHOR'S DAUGHTERS

I have asked my daughters, Sharon and Beth, for interesting coincidences that have happened in their lives. Beth could not remember anything significant except a *converging coincidence* that involved their son Johnny and her husband Steve. It had taken place on the same day that Ray Jr. had experienced the Cocker Spaniel synchronism. I thanked Beth and recorded the following in my diary:

> **June 22, 2002:** Yesterday was the **first day of school vacation** for my grandson, Johnny, **age six**. Today he **fell out of a tree** and broke his wrist. When his father came home from work and found out, he was surprised. When he was **age six**, he too **fell out a tree** and broke his arm **on the first day of school vacation**!

Sharon did not care to share any personal extraordinary coincidences but did inadvertently mention one to Margaret and me, which is recorded below:

> **November 8, 2003:** Sharon was the MC for a symposium this afternoon and wanted to buy gifts for 20 leaders. Since the lighthouse was the motif for the symposium, she thought it would be nice if she could buy **20 lighthouse models** for them. However, she only had time enough to go to just one store. She went to the store and found 1 lighthouse model on the shelf. She asked if there were any more. The clerk found some more. Sharon asked for 20. The clerk counted up what she had. There were exactly only **20 lighthouse models** left in the store.

AUTHOR'S DAUGHTER-IN-LAW

Two synchronisms occurred on the date below. One had to do with my coincidences involving the name of Amelia Earhart. These will be recorded elsewhere in the book. The other concerned my son David's wife and is as follows:

> **June 26, 2000:** My daughter-in-law is a home nurse. Her adopted children's names are **Matthew and Sarah**. She works part-time and was assigned two children. Their names are **Matthew and Sarah**.

AUTHOR'S SIBLINGS

When I queried my three brothers about interesting personal coincidences, only my brothers Richard and John could remember anything of circumstance. Some of John's [and others of Richard's] will be discussed later in the book under another subject. The following entries record *corresponding coincidences* experienced by Richard and an amazing converging coincidence by John:

July 25, 2000: My brother, Richard, and his wife are vacationing with us at Pittsburg, New Hampshire. Today we arranged to meet at a beach on a nearby lake. I put on **a short-sleeve shirt that had German writing on the face of it**. My daughter had sent it to me when she lived in Germany with her husband, who was in the army. When I showed up at the beach with Margaret, we were shocked to see that Richard was also wearing **a short-sleeve shirt that had German writing on the face of it**. It spelled out *OSRAM*. This German company had bought GTE Lighting Division where Richard was employed.

July 26, 2000: Another synchronism occurred regarding my brother and me. In the morning, I had jogged to a **bridge over Perry Stream** and then back to the cabin. It was about a mile each way. My brother and his wife had rented a cabin about five miles from us. Unknown to me at the time, he had also used the **bridge over Perry Stream** as the terminus for a long walk he had taken.

October 13, 2001: A few months ago, I donated several copies of my book, *The Andreasson Legacy*, to an organization that was running a dance and a raffle to raise funds for research into fibromyalgia. Several hundred attended the function. My brother Richard attended. He took a chance on the raffle and won a copy of my book, *The Andreasson Legacy*.

December 19, 2001: [Two synchronisms occurred today.]

1. My brother, Richard, and I were driving up to Maine on the Maine Turnpike to deliver some items to our new house in Kennebunk. I told him that a prospective buyer of our house in Wenham was concerned that the older part of the house was not insulated. I asked if he knew how this type of wall could be insulated. Richard replied that a company called **The Jones Boys** drilled holes in the sides of the house and blew fiberglass insulation into the walls. Moments later, a truck passed by us on my right. We glanced at it when it was broadside to us. The sign emblazoned on its side read: **The Jones Boys!** Apparently, they also do business outside of Massachusetts.

2. During our drive to Maine described above we somehow got talking about cookies. I mentioned to Richard that I used to like a **very thin molasses cookie** that our mother used to make when we were kids. We arrived,

unloaded the items and sat down to eat a lunch that Richard's wife had prepared. When I opened a bag containing our dessert, there were the same **very thin molasses cookies** that Mom used to bake! Richard was unaware of the kind of cookies his wife had baked.

March 10, 2002: My brother Richard visited today. He told me of an amazing synchronism. He called his former company to change his address. His address was no longer **1 Arrowhead Trail**, Ipswich, Massachusetts. The clerk was amazed at the contents of his letter. She once lived on **Arrowhead Trail** in Ipswich! The woman located a few desks down from her had lived at **1 Arrowhead Trail** many years ago!

April 5, 2002: My brother, Richard, and I were working on our shared garden. A man pulled up and got of a truck with a clipboard in this hand. He was from the town and checking to see if my greenhouse had been installed according to the building permit.

When the greenhouse passed muster, I asked him if the permit for my observatory had been approved. When I said the word "observatory", he glanced back at his paper work and looked at my name on it. He said: "Observatory? Are you Ray Fowler?" I nodded yes. He then said that **he used to live in Danvers**, Massachusetts. He asked if I were from that area. Richard told him that **Danvers was our hometown**. He then asked if I had a planetarium and an observatory near Danvers. I told him that I operated **Woodside Planetarium and Observatory** on my previous property in Wenham. He and I were taken aback when he said that as a youth he had attended **Woodside Planetarium and Observatory** with a Danvers Boy Scout Troop.

May 11, 2002: My brother Richard said that while chatting to his wife recently, he wondered out loud when the bank would have his order for a deposit box filled. A few minutes later, the bank telephoned to tell him that it was ready.

October 1, 2002: A synchronism occurred at the motel where we were staying. When we arrived, we were assigned room #16. We were told that my brother Richard, and his wife, Joan would be in #19. When they arrived later, **I kidded them** that **I had told the proprietor** to keep us **two rooms apart** so that I would not hear Joan talking. (Joan is quite a talker!) I really had not said anything of the sort to the proprietor but was just kidding her. Joan looked strangely at me and said that when they arrived, the **proprietor kidded them** and **told them that I had told him to put them two rooms apart**!

March 6, 2004: My brother John and his wife Kathy told me about an incredible synchronism that had come to light today while traveling to our home today for a family reunion. On the way here in Kennebunk, Maine, from Lynn, Massachusetts, they had passed Dayton Street in our home town of Danvers, Massachusetts. Cathy told Johnny that she had lived on Dayton Street for a short time until her family had found a permanent house in Ipswich, Massachusetts.

Cathy related to Johnny that when they moved to Dayton Street that she was very unhappy. Her father worked nearby at the Danvers State Hospital and mentioned Cathy's unhappiness to one of the volunteer women who worked there. She told him that she would help cheer up **the little girl** by giving her some dolls dressed in clothes worn by different nationalities. Cathy said that later, the kind woman and her son delivered the dolls to her at the Dayton Street home which did indeed make her very happy.

Johnny (10 years older than Cathy) was shocked to the core. He told Cathy that the lady was none other than his (our) mother and that he was the son that she brought along with her! One of our mother's hobbies was buying dolls and dressing them in the clothes of various nations to use as gifts to others. Twenty years after Mom and Johnny gave the little girl the dolls, Johnny unknowingly (until today) met and married **that little girl**!

Once in a while, Margaret will admit to experiencing remarkable coincidences.

AUTHOR'S WIFE

September 8, 2003: Margaret stopped to buy gas and asked the attendant to fill the tank. She then went to get some money out of her handbag and found that she only **had $23 left**. She panicked as gas was expensive and she thought it might come to more than $23. Just then the attendant came around to the car and told her that the cost of the gas **was exactly $23**!

Apart from those recorded above, members of my family, including my brothers John and Richard, have also experienced some extremely *unusual* synchronicities. These incidents appear on the surface to be paranormal in nature. I have recorded them in the next chapter entitled—*Supernatural Synchronisms?*

8
Supernatural Synchronisms?

Should synchronicity be a part of parapsychology or are parapsychological phenomena merely different manifestations of synchronicity? For example, precognition (the ability to see the future) can be imagined both as the ability to sense and predict the universal event patterns and to project them forward in time. But the same precognition can also be seen as having caused or triggered the predicted event. The association of the predicted event with the actual occurrence has no logical connection because of our concept of time. Nevertheless, the two events are somehow linked.

—Stephen J. Davis
Synchronicity: Trick or Treat?

OF THE PERSONAL KIND

It is at this juncture in the book that I will introduce *counter coincidences*. This is a term that I invented to describe instances where *two events that should naturally coincide do not*. They involve circumstances in a given event that appear to be opposite to what natural law dictates.

A *counter coincidence* may appear supernatural to the percipient, although there may be a yet-to-be recognized rational explanation for them. The observer believes that such an event should coincide with the dictates of natural law, but they do not! They appear to operate outside of the boundaries of reality that we normally experience. My earliest *counter coincidences* were not recorded in *SynchroFile*. They occurred many years prior to my keeping a diary about such events. The following example happened in 1957.

I was driving through a section of Danvers, Massachusetts called the Port. It was foggy. Visibility was limited to about twenty feet. Suddenly, an old woman appeared ahead to my left. She glided, not walked, directly in front of my car. She appeared to be floating in a straight line barely a few inches above the road.

This happened so fast that I could not brake in time not to hit her. Amazed, I saw her still mobile to my left. It seemed as if she passed right through the front of my car. I watched her disappear into the fog to my right. My heart was pounding as I continued driving warily through the fog.

What I saw certainly *did not coincide* with known reality. People walk, they do not move by floating above the ground. I should have hit her, but somehow I did not. It has been suggested that I had seen a wisp of fog blow by and imagined it to a woman. I disagree. She came so close that I could see sharply defined physical features.

The next experience of this kind and the ones following are similar to the one above. Because of their similarity with those recorded years later in *SynchroFile*, I will discuss them together in the following paragraphs.

I believe that this event took place around 1957 or 1958. Margaret and I were sitting in a small restaurant chatting over a meal when I looked up to see a man staring at us. I did not see him come in but he was just standing near the door motionless with his eyes fixed upon us. This was spooky. He looked familiar to me but I could not place him in my memory. At some point, when I glanced up, he was no longer standing there. It was only later that I realized that the man was Herb Cooper. The problem was that Herb had passed away just before Christmas of that particular year!

The next event occurred at my place of employment. My career was with GTE Government Systems, previously known as GTE Sylvania. I worked in the Minuteman Program Office. My manager's name at the time was Jerry. My desk was opposite his office door. I could easily see him moving around or sitting at his desk. It was only about fifteen feet from me.

One day, I glanced over and saw him sitting at his desk. I looked away for a moment and glanced back. Jerry was not there. There was no way he could have left his desk without walking by me. In fact, I found that he had been elsewhere at that time! Again, his location *did not coincide* with what I was plainly seeing fifteen feet away. It was counter to what I was plainly seeing.

The next example is even stranger. It occurred at my former home in Wenham, Massachusetts. It was May 5, 1979, a day after a three-week book publicity tour for Prentice-Hall and Bantam Books. In the past, I always guessed at when this event occurred. However, while writing this book it dawned on me that Margaret keeps a diary. Her diary entries have helped me retrieve dates for events that occurred before maintaining *SynchroFile*.

It was a Saturday morning. I ducked as I entered our half-cellar. I glanced ahead to the full cellar, which lay ahead of me down two steps. There, to my disbelieving eyes, I saw a person about fifteen feet away. He had my build. His body had a misty appearance to it. I could not make out facial features. The person walked out from behind the furnace where our upright freezer was located. He wore black dress pants and a white dress shirt, minus a tie.

A chill rippled through my body and I literally froze in my tracks as if time stood still. I watched the person casually walk around from the back of the furnace. He turned slowly to the left toward the cellar stairs and disappeared from my view.

Abruptly coming to my senses, I rushed into the full cellar to the stairs that led to our dining room. No one was there. I did not hear the upstairs cellar door open and close. I yelled up to Margaret and asked if she had been down in the cellar. She had not and she was not wearing black pants and a white shirt.

The person was there, but a moment later there was no sign of him. The experience was counter to what my eyes had registered. It was an instance where two events should have naturally coincided but did not. It was a *counter coincidence*! However, the full significance of this experience did not come to fruition until later.

One day, I went down cellar to get a frozen vegetable from the freezer behind the furnace. I was wearing a pair of **dress black pants and a white shirt without a tie. I followed the exact path of the apparition**. It suddenly dawned on me that what I had seen in the past was myself in the future! I can think of no other explanation. At the time I saw the apparition, the cellar was well lighted by sunshine streaming through a window near the furnace. I was not hallucinating. I saw the figure with my build distinctly. I was wearing the same color clothes. I had just had taken the exact same path as the apparition had taken.

One might say, after reading the accounts above, that I am prone to hallucinating. However, the next event of this nature included another eyewitness—my daughter Sharon. It took place in the early 1980's.

Sharon was married in February 1979 and no longer living at home. When she came for a visit in January of 1981 [according to Margaret's diary], we thought it would be nice to go cross-country skiing together for a father-daughter time. We decided to ski on the golf course at the end of our dead-end street. We used to do this when she was a youngster.

It was a beautiful sunny day. The snow was deep and relatively untouched by others. We had a good time. On the way home, as we skied along a level section of the golf course, we *both* saw a strange-looking man. He was standing under a tree ahead of us and to our right. His presence puzzled us for two reasons. He was dressed in a long black overcoat and had on a tall old-fashioned black brimmed hat. He also was standing in deep snow, which would make walking difficult.

We continued to head toward the tree because it was near our normal route home. We glanced up briefly several times and commented about him. However, when we glanced up next, he was nowhere to be seen. This seemed impossible because there was a wide-open area all around the tree. No one could have moved that fast in the deep snow.

Curious, we skied over to the tree. We were astonished to see that there were no footprints in the snow where he had stood. The snow lay pristine all around the tree and the surrounding area except for our ski tracks and little indentations caused by melting ice falling from the tree. Like the cellar experience, a man was seen but further examination revealed no trace of him. Our seeing him should have naturally coincided with continuing to see him a moment later but did not. It was counter to what should have been a concurrent event but was not. His disappearance certainly did not correspond with natural law. Both of us felt very strange about the matter. I was glad that she had seen him too. This anomalous experience would be similar to my next *counter* coincidence. It would take place eight months later in August of that same year.

In August 1981, our family vacationed by Lake Wallace in Canaan, Vermont. One evening, at dusk, Margaret and I walked down to a public boat landing on the lake. Our route took us along a road that led to a sparely populated area. On our way back to the cottage, I saw a short, stout woman ahead of us on the road. She was dressed in old-fashioned clothes and shuffled down our side of the road towards us. She wore a heavy shawl pulled up around her head like a scarf and carried a large wicker basket.

When she passed within several feet of us, I wondered where she could be going as it was getting dark. I commented about this to Margaret. She gave me a puzzled look and asked, "What lady?" I was shocked that she had not seen her and even more shocked when we both turned around and found the road empty. The strangely dressed woman had just passed within a few arms length of us a moment ago but was nowhere in sight!

One year later, in 1982, I experienced another *counter coincidence.* It had all the hallmarks of the paranormal. It took place on a Sunday morning at North Shore Community Baptist Church in Beverly Farms, Massachusetts. A group of retarded children in Brownie Scout uniforms was attending morning service. After the service, church members were greeting them in the lobby. While I stood watching, one of the little girls came up to me. She looked up, smiled, and puckered her lips, making a kissing sound. It was obvious that she wanted me to bend down and kiss her.

I smiled down at her but was reluctant to kiss her on the lips. I felt that it might appear improper to the scout troop leaders who were in the room. At that very point, something totally incomprehensible occurred. I felt two strong hands grasp each of my shoulders from behind. They applied a firm downward pressure pushing my head down toward the little girl's face. For some unknown reason, I thought that it was her Scout leader encouraging me to kiss her. So, I obediently bent down, with the hands still pressing down on my shoulders, and kissed her.

I then felt the hands release my shoulders. I straightened up and turned to see who had done this. There was no one there. In fact, my back was only a foot from a wall. There was no room for a person to stand behind me! Here was an *anomalous* situation that coincided with the little girl's desires. However, it was exactly counter to my firm decision not to kiss the little girl and counter to known reality.

Still later, I became the catalyst for another *counter coincidence* in that same church lobby. One Sunday morning I noticed an elderly lady [a stranger] walk into the church. She had arrived early for the morning service, so she sat down in the lobby to wait for it to begin. I went up to her, introduced myself and asked if I could be of help. She told me that she had forgotten to bring her Bible with her. That was no problem. The church had ample Bibles for visitors to use so I proceeded to get one for her. When I leaned over to give her the Bible, her face broke out into a radiant smile. At the time, I thought it reflected her pleasure at being given a Bible. I found out later that the smile was for someone else!

I found this out later when Margaret and I became good friends with her and other members of her family. We found out that her younger son had died from exposure to a defoliant used in Vietnam. One day, while talking to her older son, he told me a startling story. It concerned why his mother's face beamed all over when I gave her a Bible. When I had leaned down and passed his mother the Bible, her dead son suddenly appeared directly behind me. He smiled at her and vanished as quickly as he had appeared!

Was this my imagination? Was it a Ghost? Who really knows for sure? In any event, the next event recorded in *SynchroFile* was similar in nature to the one above. It was another *counter coincidence* of the apparition kind. This time the ghost-like image that I observed was my wife!

April 4, 1995: I awoke when Margaret got up to go swimming early in the morning. I talked to her briefly as she sat on the edge of the bed, her back facing me. Then, I went back to sleep. Later, I woke up and she was still sitting there as plain as day but did not respond to me when I talked to her. I reached over to touch her and she disappeared.

Was this a naturally induced afterimage? Is what we call time an illusion? Did I momentarily experience another dimension where past events are still happening? There are many reports, including one from my father that you will read about later, where past events reportedly have been witnessed as still happening.

Again, the above event is counter to what would normally be expected. My observation did not coincide with Margaret's physical presence. At the time that I saw Margaret, she had left the house and was probably swimming at the YMCA! A similar incident of later vintage took place during the writing of this book. This time the elusive apparition was an automobile in the yard of a house that my brother, Richard, had recently moved into from Ipswich, Massachusetts.

October 27, 2002: While about to drive into my brother Richard's driveway, Margaret mentioned that there was someone else's black car in it. I glanced up and saw **two** extra black cars. One was parked in the driveway. The other was on the lawn to the right of his garage. I remarked that the latter looked like the Jeep Cherokee that my son had because it had a tire attached to its rear. For some reason, Margaret did not respond to my remark. She may have had other things on her mind and did not hear me. When we stopped and walked up the driveway, there was only the one black sedan in the driveway. There was no car on the lawn where I had seen it clearly less than one minutes ago. Margaret had not seen it. Why would I hallucinate such a thing? This reminds me of other incidents that I have experienced of the same nature, such as the following *counter coincidence*.

April 29, 2003: This is another incident where I may have seen the past or the future in the present. I arrived to go fishing at the Merriland River in Wells, Maine. I found 3 cars parked at the river. I hoped that whoever was fishing was not at some of my favorite fishing spots. I figured that there were at least 3 fishermen, so I decided to count them as I made my way along the stream. I saw the first one and continued walking along the path. I then came across number 2 standing in the water about 70–100 feet from me. I stopped to watch him and counted 2. I then started to walk away but glanced back quickly again to see what he was doing. **There was no fisherman in sight**! The area was wide open. There was nowhere he could have gone in several seconds. I kept looking and looking up and down the river, but there was no one there and yet several seconds earlier I saw him clearly!

Supernatural Synchronisms? 129

The next events are reminiscent of Margaret's *counter coincidence* with the falling ladder mentioned earlier in the book. They implied that some unnatural presence or power was providing protection. In Jungian terminology, that kind of a response would reflect what I took subjectively to be the *meaning* behind this acausal coincidence. The next *counter coincidence* produced the same subjective feeling of *meaningfulness* to me. It could have saved our house from catching afire.

> **January 2, 1999:** This morning I checked the heater in the cellar that we use to keep the dog warm. Somehow it had become unplugged. Puzzled, I plugged it in again and retired to bed. The heater was on when I left it. Later, after getting up from bed in the morning, I checked it and found that it had been unplugged again! But, this time I saw that the dog I had covered with a blanket had gotten up from lying down. In doing so, he had pushed the blanket up and over the heater! It would have caught on fire if the heater had not become unplugged. It is important to add that the plug fits very *tightly* into the extension cord. There was no tension between the extension cord and the heater cord! One really has to exert pressure to unplug it. There is no way the dog could have unplugged it. Perhaps someone out there is looking out for us!

Whatever or whoever pulled the plug out of the extension cord saved our house from possible fire. My finding the plug out of its socket for no known reason is counter to what I naturally should have found that morning. Once again [and in the incident that follows] we have events that should logically coincide but do not. The next entry also describes an enigmatic incident that runs directly counter to what naturally should have occurred, that is—a *counter coincidence*! Again, it seemed as if something or someone provided protection against grave harm.

> **September 2, 2000:** An unexplainable event happened this morning. I got up early to make cups of tea and coffee to drink while listening to the news in bed with Margaret. I left the kitchen to use the bathroom. When I returned, the kettle was boiling violently and it was almost time for the news to begin. I shut off the gas and hurriedly tried to pour the boiling water into one of the cups. I somehow missed the cup and poured boiling water over my left hand. I immediately put the kettle and cup down and instinctively rushed to the sink. I put my hand under cold water. Amazingly enough, my hand felt no pain nor was there any blistering. I looked at my hand in disbelief and wiped off the remaining, now cool water, with a towel. I have no explanation for this. Fresh bubbling boiling water over my bare hand should have coincided with a pain-

ful burn and blistering. This experience was certainly counter to what we understand natural law to be.

April 22, 2001: A weird event. The past few days I have been thinking about my father and the strange experiences that he had during his life. For some reason I wondered if he would be able to contact me from where he is now. I actually asked him mentally to show me a sign if he was all right. Afterwards, something inexplicable happened this morning. When Margaret turned up the thermostat, the furnace would not come on. She thought that the furnace had malfunctioned. Then she happened to notice that the emergency shut-off switch in the kitchen was off. Neither she nor I ever touch this switch except when the furnace needs to be shut off. This would be in an emergency or when a repair man needed it off. How did it get placed in the off position? Neither of us did this. It certainly could not do it by itself. Was it Dad responding to my request?

February 15, 2003: Yesterday, I was thinking about the appearance of my deceased mother who woke me up one night and told me that I had stopped breathing. [This event is recorded later on in the book.] I have also on occasion been awakened by her voice. I often wondered if Dad were also watching over me. He had many OBEs and had experienced a variety of paranormal experiences. I even asked him mentally why he was not making himself known. The last time that I did this, we found the furnace emergency switch turned off. Neither of us touch that switch unless there is an emergency. In any event, last night I had opened my top bureau drawer to get some things out and saw **nothing unusual**. But, this morning when I opened the same bureau drawer, there was a **photograph of my father** staring me in the face. It was on top of everything else. I did not even know that this particular photo was in the drawer and had not seen in last night. It did not seem possible that I could have missed seeing it then. Did Dad somehow place it in this position in answer to my thoughts about him?

February 20, 2004: Margaret and I decided to take a walk on Blueberry Plain this afternoon. As we approached the tiny parking lot, I noticed that a car was already parked there. I turned my eyes away for a moment and then looked ahead again. There was no car parked there although I had seen it as plain as day a moment ago. Margaret had not noticed the car and in fact insisted there could not have been and that I must have imagined it. This has happened before and I wonder if the car had been there sometime in the past and that somehow I momentarily had a glimpse into the past. Perhaps this happens more often than people think but they usually do not have a reference point notice.

March 14. 2004: On Tuesday evening, March 9, I told my class about some strange events in the past that coincided with my thoughts about asking my

deceased father to contact me from beyond the grave. The first time coincided with my finding the emergency switch to the furnace shut off during the night. The second time coincided with my finding my father's photograph facing upright in my bureau drawer which had previously been buried under things for some time. This week either Margaret or I were awakened for several nights by what sounded like her alarm clock going off **at 12:00 a.m.** However, when we checked her clock, it was set for 6:30 a.m.
Last night, Margaret was awakened again by the clock and woke me to tell me about it.

Concurrently, I heard the last notes of **our doorbell sounding** faintly from downstairs. It is operated by radio frequency and sometimes goes off when a cell phone is being used by a passing motorist. Again, it was **exactly midnight**. This time she noticed that the sound was coming from my study. I checked the clock in the study and found that the alarm had been set for **midnight** and that the alarm switch had been turned on. Neither Margaret nor I had set the clock for midnight nor had either of us pushed the alarm switch from off to on. Again, something strange coincided with my thinking about contact with my Dad.

March 15, 2004: The mystery deepens. Last night Margaret woke me up from a sound sleep. She heard my wrist watch alarm going off at **12:00 a.m.** I never set the alarm for **midnight.** Who or what is setting clock and watch alarms to go off at midnight? Is it Dad or something else just as strange?

I must add that I am not the only on in my family who has encountered what appear on the surface to be supernatural synchronisms. Other family members have shared the few that they remember with me.

AUTHOR'S FATHER

I often ask family members if they have experienced *exceptionally* strange coincidences over their lifetime. Most reply that they cannot remember any. Several told me a few that they remember. Some of the ones that they do recall are bizarre, even psychic in nature. I will start with my father [now deceased].

While serving in the Navy as a radio operator, Dad was struck by lightning. By all accounts, this should have coincided with his death, but it did not. What happened was counter to what should have happened. It was a *counter coincidence.* It certainly did not correspond with the reality that we are familiar with on a day-to-day basis. It appeared supernatural. Dad, after being hit by the lightning bolt, began experiencing paranormal phenomena. When he was struck by the lightning, he had what is now called a *near death experience.* It would be best to start with an account of this experience before describing other of his apparent *supernatural synchronisms*. The lightning incident appears to have been the catalyst for them. The following was transcribed from a taped interview with Dad. Be warned! You are now about to enter the *Twilight Zone*!

Near Death Experience at Otter Cliffs

In 1923, at the age of 22, I was a radioman in charge of a U.S. Naval Radio Compass Station atop Otter Cliffs on the beautiful island of Mount Desert, in Maine. My watch was from 4:00 p.m. to 4:00 a.m.

One late autumn day, a violent electrical storm was in progress when I reached the station to relieve the day man. He left for the main transatlantic station a quarter of a mile away wishing me luck. I would need it, for static was terrific. The storm winds were near hurricane strength and had spread out over the North Atlantic shipping lanes. The ships were constantly calling in for bearings [by Morse code].

At 11:00 p.m., the S.S. George Washington started testing for bearings. A violent lightning bolt hit the cable outside the building. In seeking a ground, it went through the transmitting key, jumped through the air space and landed right inside my abdomen. It lodged behind my solar plexus where it remained and revolved like a fiery sun inside of me! Amazed, I sat in the operator's chair transfixed. I could only watch it wonderingly as it whirled inside of me. It was eight inches in diameter.

By this time I should be dead, I thought. It was pulsating resonantly with my heartbeat in a slow and steady rhythm. When I looked up, I was more amazed than ever. There was a soft light that went *through* the compass station roof, through the storm and darkness of the night, up to what appeared to be a radiant star.

I tried to move—to get out of my chair—but found that I could not move even an eyelid. However, I was conscious of a pulsating in the ray that was turning that ball of fire within me in perfect time with my heartbeat. I looked down and saw that the ray went *through* the floor of the compass station deep into the rocks that formed Otter Cliffs. I sat quietly in an eternity of silence, the peace of which was beyond description. It seemed that in these rays of light, neither time nor space existed.

Suddenly the rays expanded about seven feet in all directions. Three distinct flashes of light unfolded into three majestic-looking smiling men in shining robes of light. Although they did not speak, my thoughts and theirs were in perfect attunement, making verbal speech unnecessary. My thoughts formed many questions concerning them: the light rays, the electronic fire inside of me, and what manner of star it was that projected such rays. However, the thought-questions remained unanswered.

These three beings were fine-featured and had light cream-textured complexions. Their eyes were so bright it was difficult to see their color, but I thought they were blue. The brilliant aura surrounding them made it impossible for me to determine the color of their hair, for they wore strange velvety-looking hats that were like three tiers of rolls upon their heads. Like their robes, the headdresses were rich blue in color. They wore soft doe-skin-like form-fitting boots.

Next began the strangest ball game anyone has ever witnessed. The being on my left pointed his finger at the ball of fire still revolving within me. In a flash of light, it leaped into his open hand. He held it for an instant, during which the ball was reduced to six inches in diameter. Then he tossed it to the open hand of the one in front of me. He held it for an instant, reducing it to four inches or thereabouts. Whereupon, he threw it to the one on my right who held it and reduced it to two inches. He then threw it to the one on my left who tossed it into the copper mesh screening of the station where it disappeared in a shower of sparks. All three smiled, bowed, and disappeared in three flashes of light!

After this experience abruptly terminated, Dad was able to move about. Upon checking the equipment, he found burned-out transformers and pools of melted rubber insulation all over the operating table. The power cables and their internal solenoids were burned out. He was covered with some kind of oil residue. Its smell was so fragrant that he could taste it. As he sat recuperating, a number of naval personnel, including a medical corpsman, burst into the smoldering radio room. They were amazed to find Dad alive and perfectly well. This experience was etched in Dad's memory and each time he told it to us from childhood to adulthood, the details never varied.

Many of Dad's follow-on experiences were impossible for me to verify. They were just as strange, or stranger, than the one recorded above. However, I was able to verify three very strange incidents that fall under the category of *converging coincidences*. I heard the first one many times during my childhood and adult years. My mother, Dad's constant skeptic, told me that it was true.

Dad had tried to find answers for the paranormal experiences in his life. He shared them with local religious leaders but was rebuffed. He studied religions and cults, but the results fell short of satisfactory explanations. However, he did have an empathetic friend at the United Shoe where Dad was employed as assistant to the plant manager. His name was Charlie Furbush. [I have childhood memories of our family visiting the Furbush family.] Dad told me that he shared many a strange experience with Charlie. One involved Dad in an unbelievable, yet verified out-of-the-body experience (OBE). It made me wonder if his other OBE tales corresponded to reality.

During World War II, Charlie's son Bud was drafted into the army and shipped overseas. This *converging coincidence* revolves around Bud and my father. Two weeks passed before his OBE experience was verified. Dad wrote out this amazing experience, which I have copied and recorded as follows:

Out-of-the-Body-Travel?

When I arrived at work, a friend of mine of many years, who worked at the factory, came to me with tears in his eyes.

"Neither my wife nor myself have been able to eat or sleep properly for worrying about our youngest son in the Infantry who is somewhere in the European battlefield."

"I'll see what I can do," I said and tried to comfort him. "I will ask our Father [i.e., he would pray] tonight if it is His will and let you know about him first thing in the morning," I said.

When I arrived home that evening, tired, I was told that dinner would be late, so I dropped onto the couch and said, "Don't disturb me if I'm asleep when supper is ready," but then decided to go to my room where I would not be disturbed.

I kicked off my shoes and lay down saying: "Father, if it be Thy will for me to find this friend's son"—immediately there was a flash of light and I was spirit (out of my physical body) and traveling so fast that it was only a second before I landed upright on my feet on top of the brow of a hill beside a winding road amid howling winds and slashing rain in the night. The place was lit up brightly from time to time by flashes of light from bursting shells and flares throughout the area.

Beneath the hill and at one of its sides lay a river with gunboats steaming back and forth upon it, laying down a steady barrage of fire upon sections of a pontoon bridge that American engineers were vainly trying to set in place for the crossing of the river.

As I waited, wondering whether to descend [i.e. from the top of the hill] through the atmospheres into those companies to find my friend's son, or to stay where I was, the call for retreat came and the American engineering units, with their equipment that they could move, went by where I stood [unseen].

This equipment was followed by company after company of the Infantrymen whose faces I scanned through the darkness as they went sloshing by me in the ankle-deep mud and water-soaked road beside me. They were retreating in an orderly manner, and I had plenty of time to check every detail of their units as they went by me.

Finally, there was my friend's son [Bud Furbush], coming up the road with his unit, walking determinedly with his rifle over one shoulder and of all things, cuddled beneath his freed arm, a puppy dog under his raincoat, whose little face was sticking out above the coat, his eyes half closed in the rain that was pelting down.

As the boy passed me last in the file, I could have reached out and touched him. From what I saw, he was in good physical condition. What perplexed me was what he, or anyone, would be doing with a dog upon a battlefield!

My mission was complete and with another flash of light, I was back through the atmospheres across the Atlantic and safely deposited again in my physical body as I heard: "supper's ready."

[The next day], I told him [Charlie] about finding his son and the battle that he had been in. The question was, where did he get the dog? and why was he allowed to have it?

A couple of weeks later, my friend had the answer in a letter received from his son. He had picked up the dog in the shell-torn rubble of a village, which had been deserted. He asked his captain if he could keep the dog for a mascot and permission was granted if the youth would personally take care of it and that doing so would in no way interfere with any of his duties, otherwise, he and the company would be minus one dog.

A few months before Dad's death, Margaret and I picked up Dad [age ninety-two] at the nursing home. We brought him to our home for lunch. His mind was still sharp. He loved to play cards and beat Margaret at chess! If it were not for crippling arthritis and emphysema, he would have still been living with us.

As a test of his memory, I asked Dad to repeat the account that you have just read. I was particularly interested to see if he still remembered it in detail. Amazingly, Dad retold the story accurately. It was as if he were back there again seeing every detail. He did add more about the dog. He told me that Bud was only eighteen and very distraught about the horrors of war. His captain felt some sympathy about this. He told Bud that he could keep the dog and share his rations with it as long as it did not interfere with their mission. He warned Bud that if it did, the dog would be killed. In fact, the captain said that he personally would shoot it.

Sadly, when Charlie found that Bud's story matched Dad's experience, he distanced himself from Dad. It was something beyond his understanding and probably frightened him. This caused Dad to think twice about mentioning such things to friends again.

Cosmic Coincidence

My father's next *converging coincidence* took several months to converge with its verification. Dad shared his experiences with me and Margaret if he could catch our ears long enough. No one in the family, especially my mother, wanted to hear about them. One day he hounded us about a life-like dream that he had experienced. We sighed and decided to be polite and listen to what he had to say about it.

Dad related how in the dream he had entered a huge empty theater. He sat down and watched as the light dimmed. Curtains on the stage swept back to reveal a huge white screen. Suddenly, trumpets sounded and the screen lit up. A calendar date appeared in bold black letters accompanied by a thunderous voice that reverberated through the theater. The voice literally roared: "**On this day the Cosmic Age will be ushered in**!" Then, the screen dimmed, the curtains closed, the lights in the theater came on, and Dad walked out of the theater.

Margaret and I rolled our eyes and mentally sighed, "Here we go again!" However, as a test, I scribbled the date on a scrap of paper and placed it on my bureau for future reference. I thought to myself, with a somewhat devilish glee, that I was going to call his bluff on the date he saw on the screen. I would prove that it was a nonsensical nightmare. I, because of religious reasons at that time, did not believe that such things could be true.

Well, by the time the date arrived, the slip of paper had collected dust. It was almost forgotten until—**October 4, 1957!** On this date newspapers all over the world headlined civilization's once in a lifetime event. **Russia had ushered in the Space Age** with the launch of the first artificial satellite—Sputnik! I excitedly showed Dad the slip of paper with the date on it. Can you believe it? He had forgotten all about the dream!

Dad also made other predictions that later coincided with reality. They involved forecasting when and where UFOs would be seen. He told me about them not too long before he died. They occurred so long ago that I had no way to verify them. I will take my father's word at face value and include them here. They also are examples of *converging coincidences*.

Dad usually only confided in the family about his experiences. He had learned his lesson well after losing his close relationship with Charlie Furbush. However, a telepathic-like communication he had received was so strong that he decided to notify the local newspaper. It concerned a visit of UFOs to our capitol at Washington, D.C. He did this despite the possibility of injuring his reputation in town. The following are transcripts from a taped recording of our conversations about them:

Capitol Coincidence

Ray: You said that you sent a letter to the Salem News about UFOs?

Dad: Yes, I did.

Ray: What was that about?

Dad: And, ah, the guy at the Salem News, the editor or whatever he was, I told him that I'd sent a message to Washington, that I had listened to this [telepathic] message that they were going to send five spaceships over Washington on a goodwill mission that they shouldn't fire on them or do anything to harm them and I said I didn't get a reply back. I sent it to some senator. I can't remember his name.

Ray: How did the Salem News get involved?

Dad: Because I told him [in the letter] that I didn't get any reply from Washington and I thought that it was very important that they didn't get fired upon because these ships were far superior to anything that they had or had ever seen. And, the editor was mad. He figured I was trying to play some kind of a joke or something on him. That if he published it, he'd be the laughing stock. That's what I heard from the chief of police. But, anyway, the editor—I had put in the letter—"If this is not acceptable to the Salem News or you for the Salem News, enclosed is a self-addressed envelope to be returned to me"—that was the usual thing.

Well, he didn't do it. And, I'm eating my supper and a policeman comes to the door and your mother answers the door. And he says, "Is Mr. Fowler at home?" And she says, "Yes." He says, "Tell him I want to see him. The chief wants to see him right away." Well, [she says], "He's eating his supper. Can you wait until after he's through eating?" And he said, "No, it's very important. The chief told me not to wait for anything. He wants to get this cleared up." So, he says, "I'm to take him to the police station."

Ray: Mom must have wondered what was going on.

Dad: I thought to myself, all I've done for the town and everything else. They're going to take me like a common criminal and drag me away from supper. I get to the chief of police. He says, "You know, Mr. Fowler," he says, "the whole department is upset and I'm upset too" he says. But they told me that was my orders. I have your letter here and so forth and so on, something about spaceships. We know that you are in your right mind. You've always got a raise for us and the fire department. You've always voted in the warrant for us and you've taken good care of us." He says, "But I have to follow orders."

Ray: Who gave him the orders? The Salem News?

Dad: No, they got the letter from the Postmaster. Anyway, he says, "We have your letter here." And he read it off. I says, "You notice I sent a self-addressed envelope and advised him to send it back if not interested?" "Yes," he says.

"We know that now. We didn't take that into consideration until you mentioned it." He says, "They should have returned it to you." He says, "It's a misdemeanor," or something. He says, "You can go home and finish your supper now."

Dad told me that after the fiasco, UFOs were seen over Washington and made national headlines. He also said that they were seen and photographed over the local Coast Guard station in Salem, Massachusetts. I knew that both of these events had occurred. The Washington, D.C. incidents took place on July 19 and 26, 1952. The UFOs over Washington were headline news. They were also the reason for the largest press conference since World War II.

Years later I was able to interview Harry Barnes. He was the chief radar operator at Washington National Airport during the radar/visual sightings over the capitol. Harry told me that Air Force officers were in the control tower. They helped him direct fighter aircraft to intercept the UFOs. He said that as the fighters approached the objects, they would outdistance them or drop down to a low altitude where the jets could not follow.

I had also interviewed coast guard personnel during my lecture on UFOs at the station in Salem, Massachusetts. They remembered the incident mentioned by Dad very well. The objects had been photographed from inside the station and witnessed by personnel outside the station and by workers outside at the New England Power Station.

Partial Prophecy

Dad also made another prediction that was verifiable because it concerned both Margaret and me. He casually mentioned to us that we were both going to see a UFO within two weeks. We laughed, and I hoped he was right and made a note of it. However, when the date arrived, we had forgotten about it.

About two weeks later, on June 24, 1961, Margaret and I were driving through the countryside on the way to Salem, New Hampshire. At the time, I was a church youth director at Salem's First Baptist Church. It was raining lightly. Distant thunder rumbled as the sun began to filter through dissipating clouds. As we passed a large field on the outskirts of Haverhill, Massachusetts, Margaret cried out in alarm: "Ray, what is that thing over the field!" Since she often teased me about *flying saucers*, I refused to look. I quipped back, "You can't fool me, it's just the sun coming out from behind the clouds!" Then she grabbed me by my shoulders and shouted, "Look now before you miss it! I'm not kidding!"

It was too late. The field was now behind us. By the time I turned the car around and rushed back, the object was no where to be seen. Margaret described what she saw as a cylindrical object with a fat midsection hovering at treetop level over the field. It was silver and facing sideways to the road. A short, stubby, swept-back wing jutted out from its side. It had no rudder or vertical stabilizer. We reported it to the Air Force. I am still mentally kicking myself for not looking. Later, we remembered Dad's prediction. It was only half-true, but that was my fault!

The following *counter coincidence* involved Dad seeing a traumatic past event occurring in the present:

Spectral Synchronism

Dad retired from the United Shoe in 1964. He and Mom moved to Surrey, Maine close to her birthplace in Bar Harbor. One bright sunny day, Dad had to drive to Ellsworth, which bordered Surrey. He decided to take an old back road rather than the highway. While on the way, the clear blue sky suddenly darkened. He instantly found himself in the middle of a terrible thunderstorm. The rain was coming down so hard that he could barely see the road. Then, suddenly, coming right at him was an old model car. It was swerving back and forth as if it were out of control. He could see a look of panic on the driver's face. Then it was as if the storm had never happened. The sky was blue again. The sun was shining. There was no sign of rain on his car or on the road.

Dad did not know what to make of it. He told my Uncle Oscar about his weird experience. Oscar told him that others had had the same type of experience on that road. People attributed it to a terrible car accident that occurred there years ago. Apparently, the incident projected itself forward in time on several occasions. Incidents like this have fantastic implications that will be discussed later in chapter 11.

AUTHOR'S MOTHER

Precognitive Vision

My mother was not exempt from strange experiences. However, she was reticent to talk about them, especially because she criticized Dad for talking about his weird experiences. In fact, I found out after her death that she had not told Dad about them. He was surprised and somewhat hurt that she had not shared them with him. One of her experiences falls under the category of a *converging coincidence*. Again, it was precognitive in nature.

The experience occurred shortly before her heart attack. At the time, she was working in her flower garden. Mom told me that just before she had the heart attack she experienced a vision-like daydream. She saw herself having the heart attack and the ambulance arriving at the hospital minutes before these things actually happened. During her recovery in a critical care unit, she said that her long-dead mother suddenly appeared. Her mother gave her a reassuring smile and then faded away.

AUTHOR'S BROTHERS

Two of my brothers, Richard and John, also have had vivid precognitive thoughts and dreams. These fall under the category of *converging coincidences*.

Richard's Recalls

My brother, Richard, has experienced vivid dreams of future happenings. His engineering background and scientific mindset rebel against these weird events. Such dreams are unnerving to him. He does not want to accept the possibility of seeing future events as they portend that we do not have *free will*. Yet, when dreamed events begin to take place, he knows exactly what is going to happen next. Even more disturbing to him was that he did not have control of the events. They played out his part in them including the exact words of his and other's conversations.

When he first confided with me about this phenomenon, he would not discuss the content of the dreams. However, when pressed, he began sharing some with me. Once he dreamed about entering a doctor's office. He was sitting in the waiting room listening to conversations between the receptionist and others. Later, when he actually went to the doctor's office, he sat down to wait for his appointment. Then everything that he had dreamed about uncannily unfolded before his eyes.

Richard said that he makes a mental note to record such dreams. They drift rapidly from his memory. However, most of the time he forgets to do so. I urged him to write them down immediately each time that they occur. The next entry from *SynchroFile* records such a time as well as the incident being a synchronism in and of itself!

March 16, 2000: Another synchronism. This one actually coincided with the announcement of a precognitive dream by my brother, Richard. This evening, Margaret and I went out for dinner and a movie with my brother, Richard. As we sat at the table, I casually asked him if he had had any more precognitive dreams. His jaw dropped and his face registered surprise. He said that it was strange that I should ask, as he had had one come true this very day. [This is a *converging coincidence* in and of itself!]

Several days ago, he dreamed that his fellow-workers played a joke on another worker by **writing something in German** to him. Today, when he went to work, he noticed some fellows laughing. He asked them what happened. They told him that they had played a joke on another worker by **writing something in German** to him!

The next entry records yet another *converging coincidence* that was precognitive in nature.

On October 27, 2002, I had a spirited discussion with Richard about his precognitive dreams. He believes that there has to be a rational explanation for them as they imply that humans have no free will and if the future is fixed. However, he agreed to write out the following description of one precognitive incident that bothered him most. He said that it is still is riveted in his memory, whereas he has forgotten the details of others.

> I had a dream that you and I were walking in the woods, presumed to be the old Burley Woods in Danvers, [Massachusetts]. In the dream, we came across a clearing in which there was **a fire ring made of a rock circle and to one side sat a wooden box**. The box was unlocked but did have a metal hasp that was made to secure it with a pad-lock. The box was closed. There was a bottle—hard alcoholic beverage—but it was on the ground next to the fire-ring. In the dream we did not open the box and the dream ended.
>
> Shortly after experiencing this dream I went for a walk, alone, on Folly Hill in Danvers to see how much it might have changed in the forty years since I'd last been there. I walked to the top of the hill and was somewhat dismayed to see that you could no longer see Blackbird Pond any longer (it had essentially filled to become a bog).
>
> To the east of where the pond was located, there had been a cleared rise that topped at a rock outcropping. This spot had become overgrown with a rather thick 'woods' of trees. I decided to investigate. I entered the somewhat tight quarters of trees and came upon a small clearing. In this clearing was a small rock fire ring. I walked past this and turned at the opposite end of the clearing to look it over.
>
> To my amazement, there in front of me was the scene from my previous dream. The **placement and appearance of the fire-ring and a wooden box** and **the bottle on the ground next to the fire-ring** [that I had not noticed

when I first walked into the clearing] was identical to those in the dream. I stood for what seemed several minutes contemplating what was before me. I opened the box out of curiosity. It was empty.

Richard rarely went to the Burley Woods with me. He was a small child at the time I hunted and fished there. Later in his teens, our parents moved to a house bordering Folly Hill in the 1950's. His dream most likely took place in the woods that we walked in on and around Folly Hill. Soon after, it became true to reality as a *converging coincidence.*

Another brother, John, confided that he has had dramatic precognitive dreams. He said that he also had psychic impressions of future happenings. He will never forget the next two that I transcribed from a taped interview with him. The first experience involved the son of his boss who had a terrible motorcycle accident.

Death Dreams

John: Bill and his wife got into a motorcycle accident. **I dreamt about that** almost two nights before it happened or maybe the night that it happened. *I felt like I was there* when it happened.

Ray: This was two days before that?

John: Maybe the night before it happened I went to work the next day and his father told me that they were both in the hospital dying at the time. They both recovered. The motorcycle had just tipped over and they left the motorcycle and hit a pole. I was dreaming that.

The second incident weighs heavily on John's mind. It involved foreseeing a terrible tragedy that he might have prevented. I will let him tell the story as we continue with the above-recorded session.

John: And another time, this kid that was down at the Park Hotel in Beverly: I had this feeling that—some ways it just come to my mind—that he was going **to get his head shot off**. And I was going to tell him. I was sitting there and I said [to myself], "You'd better go tell him to stay away from anyone who has a gun." I was just sitting there drinking a beer. Then I said [to myself], "No, that's crazy."

So, about a week later I'm in Connecticut and I heard that someone in Salem [Massachusetts] had got shot with a shotgun. His head was decapitated. It was he! He was working in a junkyard in Salem and he went into this kid's room that worked, that lived there, the son of the owner, to wake him up. And the kid had a gun in bed and woke up startled and **shot him and blew his head off**. And I remember sitting there thinking about this, and saying, "Go and say this" [i.e., warn him]. But, I didn't know him that well. But, I envisioned that he was going to get his head blown off. And it didn't come back to me until I heard it on the radio and I said [to myself], "This is crazy!"

On October 8, 2002, John visited to go on a twenty-mile bike ride with me. During a rest stop, he told me of two other incidents that are *converging coincidences*. The first concerned a weird dream. If it were not a dream, we are talking about a different kind of paranormal phenomenon—a ghost!

John told me that he once had a serious relationship with a woman. She was heartbroken when John broke off the relationship. Years later, John had a vivid dream. It was so realistic that it did not seem to be a dream. In the dream, the young lady appeared and asked John to come with her. She seemed so real that John believed that she was real. He carried on a conversation with her. John told her that it was not time for him to come yet. He told her that he had other things to do in this life. She disappeared and the dream ended. However, a few days later while shopping, John was surprised to meet this woman's mother. He was shocked by what she told him. Her daughter had died on the same date John had dreamed about her!

The second incident also took place many years ago. One day John was driving his car through Lynn, Massachusetts. As he passed by the **Boyd's Potato Chip Company**, the car started shaking and handling differently. It suddenly felt like he was driving a large truck. Coincidentally, years later he applied for and got a job at **Boyd's Potato Chip Company** to drive a huge truck! John's prior eerie experience converged with the exact feelings of driving a large truck for **Boyd's Potato Chips**. He spent many years with this company and recently retired.

Another brother, Fred, cannot remember any amazing coincidences in his life. Richard and John could not remember any others. However, before moving on to the next chapter, I feel that I should make mention of a pertinent weird *counter coincidence* experienced by Margaret's English niece named Carolyn. During a visit in November 1979, she shared this scary experience with us. It was similar to my Dad's experience of witnessing the specter of a car accident that had happened in the past in the present.

Carolyn told us that an elderly couple used to live a few houses up the street from them. Old age had prevented the husband from driving any distance. However, he had a habit of polishing his car and driving it up and down the street. It was a familiar sound to hear him start the old car up and appear on the street with his polished car.

Time went by and the couple died, leaving the house vacant for an extended period. During that period, Carolyn was working in her garden one day when she was startled to hear the old man's car starting up. She dismissed the sound as someone else's car and continued working. However, when she heard the car coming down the street, she glanced over the fence. She froze in her tracks, horrified at what she saw. It was the old man in his car coming down the street! She watched in utter disbelief as he passed by in front of her! That was enough for her. Carolyn said that she ran inside the house to tell her husband. He came running out to see the apparition. However, when they glanced up the street nothing could be seen or heard.

When such events occur, the observer believes that such an event should coincide with the dictates of natural law, but they do not! The old couple had died and yet there was the old man seemingly alive and well! Such experiences operate outside of the boundaries of reality that we normally experience. Such *counter coincidences* appear otherworldly to the percipient, although there may be a yet-to-be recognized rational explanation for them. They truly appear to be *Supernatural Synchronisms*.

9

Flying Saucers

> *Jung came to the conclusion that UFOs were examples of the phenomena of synchronicity where external events mirror internal psychic states.*
>
> —John Fraim
> *The Symbolism of UFOs and Aliens*

JUNG AND UFOS

The reader may well wonder what the subject of *Flying Saucers* [UFOs] has to do with the phenomenon of synchronicity in my life. It is a legitimate question and the reading of this chapter will provide the answer. However, prior to doing so, I believe that some introductory data are in order regarding UFOs and Synchronicity.

It might come as a surprise that Carl Jung was what one would call a dedicated UFOlogist today. Indeed, he even came to believe that the element of synchronicity was a common element of the UFO phenomenon. In the event that this fact is unknown to some, I have extracted the following from Jung's book entitled: *Flying Saucers.* [1] It portrays his initial reaction to the appearance of unidentified flying objects. This in turn led to his detailed studies and the book in question.

As early as 1946 Jung had begun to collect data on unidentified flying objects—newspaper clippings, reports issued by groups dedicated to their study, statements from the scientific, military and governmental establishments, letters from people all over and he read virtually every book on the subject. His published letters give us a vivid notion of his preoccupation with the phenomena. [2] Typically, in February 1951 he wrote to an American friend:

> I'm puzzled to death about these phenomena, because I haven't been able yet to make out with sufficient certainty whether the whole thing is a rumor with

concomitant singular and mass hallucination, or a downright fact. Either case would be highly interesting. If it's a rumor, then the apparition of discs must be a symbol produced by the unconscious. We know what such a thing would mean seen from the psychological standpoint. If on the other hand it is a hard concrete fact, we are surely confronted with something thoroughly out of the way. [3]

After a decade of study, Jung came to a conclusion about the so-called flying saucer phenomenon. He writes that:

This obviously complicated phenomenon had an extremely important psychic component as well as a possible physical basis. This is not surprising, in that we are dealing with an ostensibly physical phenomenon distinguished on the one hand by its frequent appearances, and on the other by its strange, unknown, and indeed contradictory nature...One often did not know and could not discover whether a primary perception was followed by a phantasm or whether, conversely, a primary fantasy originating in the unconscious invaded the conscious mind with illusions and vision. [4]

Simply put, Jung was stating that whether the object seen in the sky was real or not it coincided with psychological effects upon the observer. In either case, he theorized that unidentified phenomena seen in the sky produced psychic manifestations. These, in turn, emanated from the collective unconscious of humankind in response to *precarious conditions* in the world. However, the question remains: how do UFOs enter into Jung's definition of synchronicity? Jung continues in the statement quoted above that:

To these two causal relationships we must add a third possibility, namely, that of a "synchronistic," i.e. acausal, meaningful coincidence. [5]

Concerning this "third possibility," psychologist John Fraim comments that:

Jung came to the conclusion that UFOs were examples of the phenomenon of synchronicity where external events mirror internal psychic states. As usual, he saw the UFO situation in a broader perspective than most. For Jung the UFO images had much to do with the ending of an era in history and the beginning of a new one...Jung felt that modern man projected his inner state into the heavens. In this sense, the UFOs became modern symbols for the ancient gods, which came to man's assistance in time of need. The need perhaps was for wholeness again out of the increasing fragmentation of the modern world. In the early 50s and the beginning of the Cold War, when UFOs began to infiltrate popular culture, there was a great fragmentation in the world. Jung writes: "At a time when the world is divided by an *iron curtain*, we might expect all sorts of funny things, since when such a thing happens in an individual it means a complete dissociation, which is instantly compensated by symbols of wholeness and unity."

The UFO events of the 50s that Jung turned his focus on have certainly not gone away. In fact they seem to increasingly dominate contemporary American popular culture. In the almost half century along the way they have gone a long way towards creating and boosting the literary/film/television genre of science fiction, as well as creating a huge marketing empire and a division in culture between the believers (contactees) and non-believers. In the process, UFOs and aliens have moved out of cults and into the mainstream of popular culture, their symbolism continually evolving. [6]

Jung, however, was hesitant about supposing that psychic projections could manifest themselves on radar screens. His primary interest was how a UFO sighting [physical or imagined] affected the percipient in a synchronistic sense. Thus, his main interest was studying the psychological effects upon a person who sighted a UFO. Indeed, he states that:

> As a psychologist, I am not qualified to contribute anything useful to the question of the physical reality of UFOs. I can concern myself only with their undoubted psychic aspect. [7]

Psychologist, John Fraim writes that:

> "It was very relevant to Jung that the shape of the *flying saucers* was round, the shape of the ancient *Mandala,* symbol of wholeness throughout history. [8]

Jung came up with this concept of *wholeness* after seeing the round *Mandalas* used for meditation in the Far East, especially those of Tibetan Buddhism. The belief was that the *Mandala* would appear in dreams and visions during times of mental disruption. Such an appearance would be compensatory. They suggested that a resolution of the disruption was at hand. Aniela Jaffe, an experienced analyst, Jung's confidential private secretary and biographer writes that:

> The symbol of the circle has played a curious part in a very different phenomenon of the life of our day, and occasionally still does. In the last years of the Second World War, there arose the "visionary rumor" of round flying bodies that became known as "Flying Saucers" or UFOs [unidentified flying objects]. Jung has explained the UFOs as a projection of a psychic content (of whole-

ness) that has at all times been symbolized by the circle. In other words, this "visionary rumor," as can also be seen in many dreams of our time, is an attempt by the unconscious collective psyche [i.e., the collective unconscious] to heal the split in our apocalyptic age by means of the symbol of the circle.[9]

This ends our brief discussion of Jung's thoughts about UFO's and synchronicity. Again, Jung was primarily interested in the psychological rather than the physical aspect of UFOs. Now, the question at hand is—what is my connection with UFOs and *Synchronicity*? Again, some introductory data are in order before this question will be answered.

AUTHOR AND UFOS

Jung's fascination with the UFO mystery coincides with mine. I saw a flying disc in broad daylight in July of 1947. I too began collecting news clips, magazine articles and books on the subject. In 1963, I began investigating this phenomenon. Over a period of years, I became internationally known as a respected UFO investigator. Astronomer, Dr. J, Allen Hynek, chief scientific consultant to three USAF UFO projects, wrote the foreword to my first book on UFOs. The following is a brief extraction from his foreword. I present it here only to establish my credentials to those who are not familiar with my work in UFOlogy.

> This foreword is primarily a tribute to an outstanding UFO investigator and fact-finder. I know of none who is more dedicated, trustworthy or persevering than Ray Fowler.[10]

Over the years, I have written ten books on the subject of UFOs. My reports have been published in magazines, military and scientific literature and congressional hearings. I have been a guest on hundreds of radio and TV shows in the U.S.A. since 1963. Examples include the *Today Show, Dick Cavett Show, Mike Douglas Show, Good Morning America, Unsolved Mysteries, Encounters* and *Sightings*. On a number of occasions, I have been a consultant to a number of TV UFO Documentaries and *Time-Life* Books.

Childhood Experiences

My experiences began in childhood in Danvers, Massachusetts. I can remember waking up to a bright light beam shining through a window onto my bed. It was so bright that I could see dust particles moving around in it. Each time that I saw it, I would crawl out of my bedcovers and allow it to shine on me. When I entered the light, I would feel what could only be described as pure love. I called it the *love light*. I wish that I could remember more about what happened after entering the light, but that is where my memory of these events terminates.

My next memory of such a beam of light involved both a UFO and an entity. I was sleeping on a couch in what we called the *Big Hall*. My use of it as a bedroom was short. It is remembered because of two traumatic events that took place during my stay there.

The first incident was being awakened at night by the telephone downstairs. I heard my father yell upstairs to my mother that her mother had died. Death frightened me. I lay quietly listening to the commotion and pretended to be asleep. I also pretended ignorance in the morning. When my sister Dorothy told me, I tried to show no emotion as I did not want to feel sad. I can remember Dot being very upset about that. Even at this young age I feared death and wanted to deny it.

The above traumatic event was natural. The second was supernatural. Strangely, it elicited excitement and curiosity rather than fear and denial. My grandmother died on August 1, 1942. I was born in 1933, so I was eight years old at the time.

I awoke to find the *Big Hall* lit up by light shining through the window beside my bed. I sat up to see a robed lady encased in brilliant light. I felt no fear. Instead, I felt an overwhelming sense of love that vibrated through my body. It was the same feeling that I experienced with the aforementioned *love light*.

The rest of my memory is sketchy. I wanted to show her my children's Bible Storybook and Dot's Book of Knowledge. She asked me to get them off the bureau. I cannot remember what we looked at in the Bible Storybook. However, I can still visualize myself sitting with her looking at the Astronomy section of Dot's *Book of Knowledge*. It contained my favorite pictures. One was a black and white photograph of Saturn. The other was of airplanes flying to the planets. My memory goes blank after that.

Next, I remember being engulfed in light and floating through the closed window beside the couch. I felt weightless and was kicking my legs in the air. It was terrifying to look down at the illuminated flower garden far below. I thought that I was going to fall. The light stretched upward to lights in the sky. I think that the lady made me close my eyes because of my fear. I do not know what happened next. However, I can visualize coming back down to the house in the light and opening my eyes. What I saw when my eyes opened is still etched in my mind. I saw the small crescent-shaped attic window as we descended by it. The front side of the house was bathed with light. Then I remember standing before the glowing lady in the middle of the *Big Hall*. She told me that I was going to do something important for mankind.

When I awoke in the morning, I remembered everything. I was terribly excited and ran downstairs to tell my mother. She was already up and dressed. She was standing in slippers dry mopping the linoleum covering the floor in the living room. I could hardly get the words out to describe what had happened because of my excitement. Much to my surprise, she would not listen to me. She said it was a dream and ordered me upstairs to dress.

I was frantic and protested, but when she got angry, I started back up the stairs. I can still remember the utter frustration as I started up the stairs as if it were yesterday. As I plodded up the stairs, the memory of what happened began slipping away. As it did, I started crying and ran back downstairs. I insisted that Mom listen to me. My persistence and tearful face finally made her take notice.

Mom's face broke into a kind smile. She leaned against the mop and patiently listened. She gently repeated that it was just a dream. I was again told to get upstairs and dress. I reluctantly obeyed. However, before I dressed, I began looking for the *Lady*. Even today, I can see myself looking under the eaves of the attic stairs. I even climbed the attic stairs to see if she were hiding in the attic. I can remember trying to lift the heavy trap door into the attic.

In the meantime, the memory of what happened continued to slip away. However I distinctly remember a name associated with the visitation. It was *Amelia Earhart*. I wondered if this were the lady's name. When I went back downstairs, I asked my mother who she was. She told me that she was a pilot and to ask Dad about her when he came home from work.

I vividly remember waiting at the front door to greet my father. I can still see him in my mind's eye opening the door. He was wearing a blue overcoat. Upon opening the door, Dad was taken aback when I greeted him with—"Who is Amelia Earhart?" Dad told me that she was an aviator who had disappeared while flying an airplane. He thought that she probably crashed and was dead. One would think that both of my parents would have paid more attention to Amelia's connection with what they considered a dream, but they did not.

The strange thing is that over the years, I have encountered some remarkable synchronisms involving the name of *Amelia Earhart*. I wish that I had recorded them all. Some examples follow in *SynchroFile*. I might add that such synchronisms appear shortly after I am thinking of *Amelia Earhart*.

The Earhart Synchronisms

March 8, 1996: I came in from shoveling snow and decided to take a brief nap as I had been up late the previous evening. As I dozed off, I wondered about the glowing entity that I had encountered during my *Big Hall* experience that I seemed to equate with **Amelia Earhart**. I wondered if I had seen what others have described as a guardian angel. When I awoke, my wife brought in the mail. I received a letter from a woman UFO abductee who mentioned that as a child she had an encounter with an angelic-like being that she had called **"Air-hart"**!

The next entry also seems to have the earmarks of a premonitory power working in my life.

February 19, 1997: I inadvertently glanced at clocks twice today, at 2:22 and 3:33. In the evening during my UFO class, I experienced another interesting synchronism. I told the class about a connection between my childhood *Big Hall* experience with the glowing lady of light and **Amelia Earhart**. After class, I turned on the TV. During the program, **Amelia Earhart** was mentioned in a discussion relating to conspiracy theories and the assassinations of Martin Luther King and the Kennedy's.

February 22, 1997: Another synchronism regarding **Amelia Earhart**! I flipped on the TV while I ate a late dinner after teaching a kid's astronomy class. Just before turning the set off, I inadvertently flipped to Channel 11 just as someone mentioned the name **Amelia Earhart** in connection with mysteries!

August 11, 1998: In the evening as I was watching the news, I flipped to another channel just as the name **Amelia Earhart** was spoken. This happened before on February 19 and 22, 1997.

October 19, 1998: I woke at 3:33 when my wife (I think) poked me in her sleep. Later I awoke at 5:55. This evening I sat down to watch a movie on TV and no sooner was it underway than **Amelia Earhart** was mentioned. This is the 4th time this has happened, i.e. on 2/19 and 2/22/97, 8/11/98 and today.

November 8, 1998: I sat down to watch TV with Margaret and **Amelia Earhart** was mentioned.

December 3, 1998: I awoke to see the clock switch to 4:44. I sat down with Margaret to watch the TV news in the evening. **Amelia Earhart's** name appeared on the screen! This has happened several times in the recent past. Later in the evening, I glanced at the clock at 5:55.

March 13, 1999: At 12:34, I flicked to Channel 44 after watching the Channel 7 news. Within a minute, **Amelia Earhart's** name was mentioned during a discussion on Feminism.

May 29, 1999: I turned on the TV and again heard **Amelia Earhart** mentioned.

August 3, 1999: I came up from the garden to hear the rest of the morning [TV] news. I entered the room as an announcement was being made about making a statue of **Amelia Earhart**! This is beginning to be a habit!

Then a week later [Can you believe it?] a *surrogate* **Amelia Earhart** visited my neighborhood!

August 11, 1999: Here we go again. I picked up the local paper and was looking through local entertainment. My eyes fell upon a one-woman show being presented at Burnham Hall. It is located behind the library parking lot about 1500 feet from the house! The show will be on **Amelia Earhart**!

August 18, 1999: Margaret and I attended the show on **Amelia Earhart**. It was very well done.

June 26, 2000: I waved goodbye to my wife and turned on the TV show entitled *Chronicle*. I sat down to watch. A group was listening to a talk on memory retention. The speaker handed a ball to someone in the audience. She said **Amelia Earhart**! Here we go again!

December 17, 2002: Yesterday I was glancing through diary entries about **Amelia Earhart** for my book on synchronicity. This morning I turned on the TV. **Amelia Earhart** was being mentioned in connection with the 99th anniversary of the airplane.

I guess that is enough about Amelia Earhart. Let us return to the *Big Hall* experience. Curiously, memories of this experience would be forgotten for long periods of time. They would only return as temporary flashbacks. These were triggered by a variety of synchronistic associations.

Synchronistic Flashbacks

Shortly after the *Big Hall* experience, I looked again at the black and white picture of Saturn in Dot's book. I felt that I had seen Saturn in color. It did not look like it was depicted in the book. The experience with the lady in the light disappeared from memory until prompted by certain catalysts. After a period of regressive hypnosis as an adult, I am now able to recall when and why these memory flashbacks occurred. It was instigated by a scene from the *Wizard of Oz* movie. When I saw the good witch descend to Dorothy in a ball of light, it brought back the incident full force. However, later, it again faded from memory.

The next remembered incident is interesting. It evoked an exceptionally strong sense of guilt. Paul had just moved into the house next door on Dodge Court, in Danvers, Massachusetts. While playing in front of my house, I happened to glance up at the attic and *Big Hall* windows. The sight of these windows provoked memories of my childhood experiences to flood my mind. [Yes, there were other childhood experiences involving a *Little Hall* in our house.]

I looked at Paul and pointed to the *Big Hall* window. I told him about floating out the window with the lady. Earlier experiences flooded my mind. These involved being taken somewhere by someone that looked like a China man. However, no sooner had I begun to relate these things, I suddenly was overcome with guilt. I felt that I was betraying a trust and was not supposed to be telling others about these things. Paul just gave me a funny look. I changed the subject and we continued playing.

Other flashbacks erupted when a wingless aircraft called an auto gyro swooped over Dodge Court. It was kept at nearby Beverly Airport. I became terrified each time that I saw it. I would run and sit on the top attic stair, look out the window at it and shout, "They're coming for me!" My mother got upset at me when I did this and shouted, "Don't be silly, Buster!" [My nick name.]

The next two flashbacks occurred in adulthood. One occurred when I saw the first close up color photos of Saturn released by NASA. The other happened during my investigation of UFO abductee Betty Andreasson. She also had similar childhood UFO experiences with small entities with large black slanting eyes. I called them China men. They would come concurrent with a tingling sensation in my body. I would awake and see one of these small beings approach my bed. When it did, I became completely paralyzed and could not yell for help. In the morning, I would tell my parents about these visitations. They dismissed them as nightmares. On several occasions I would wake up and find myself walking with the China man. I would lose consciousness again when he looked into my eyes.

Other childhood experiences include a small glowing ball of light that came into the room while I was sitting up in bed. It hovered inches from my face. I screamed for my mother to come upstairs to help me. When she did, it whisked away as she started upstairs.

Another experience occurred in my teens. It happened while walking in the woods one early afternoon. One moment I was walking beside a pond in bright sunlight. The next moment I awoke lying on the ground a few hours later. It was almost dark. The sun was setting behind the trees. Terrified, I ran wildly through the woods and back home. By the time I reached home, it was pitch dark. My parents were about to call the police. I could not account for the missing time.

I do have occasional visual flashbacks concerning this experience. I see myself descending from above to my curled up body lying on the ground. I also have dreamed of seeing a bright object darting back and forth in the sky on that day.

The next experience did not involve a light from the sky. I only mention it here because of its similarity to the *love light* and *Big Hall* experiences. It involved an unseen woman and that same vibrating feeling of love experienced in these two incidents.

Channeling?

I remember the next experience as if it took place a short time ago. I have no explanation for it. I am ashamed in a way to record it. Nevertheless, I feel that I must. It is just one of many paranormal events experienced by myself and family members.

As an older teen, I became acquainted with a girl several years older than myself. She told of many sexual encounters and of mothering a child which she gave up for adoption. I was a virgin. Even as a teen, I was still innocent about the facts of life. She took it upon herself to be my practical teacher. When we were about to have intercourse, I felt a cloak of unconditional love engulf me with a vibrating tingling feeling.

The next thing I knew, someone else took control of my mental facilities. I had no control of my voice at all. My mouth moved. I spoke, but it wasn't me. I sensed that *a woman* began speaking to both of us through me. She told us that what we were planning was not right. I cannot remember her exact words. She went on for several minutes gently chastising us. Both of us seemed to be frozen in time as we listened. When she stopped, we went no further with our plans. In fact, my young lady friend was terrified. I had occasion to meet her decades later. She still remembered the experience and how it had scared her.

That Light

Not long after, I again experienced that wonderful vibrating feeling of unconditional love. This time it coincided with a brilliant anomalous beam of light that illuminated the area all around the house.

At the time, I was the oldest kid in our neighborhood. I was leader of what was known as the High Street Gang. It is hard to believe, but we had regular rock and apple throwing fights with the Lawrence Street Gang. It is amazing that no one got seriously hurt during these encounters. The fights centered on obtaining control of Day's Hill near my house. I took pride in being the gang's leader. However, I was taken aback when Dave, a boy of my age, moved into the neighborhood. I did not want any competition. Dave was from a broken home and was a temporary foster child. His foster parents were the local Baptist Minister's family who lived around the corner. Dave and I became great friends. He told me that unless he found another foster family, he was going to be sent to an orphanage. I persuaded my parents to take David in and agreed that he could share my room.

It was then that I discovered that Dave was very religious. He read his Bible and prayed before going to bed. He attended Church, Sunday school and a Church Youth Group. I felt out of place with these things. I had quit going to Church years ago. However, after getting to know David and his friends in the church youth group, I decided that I wanted to be like them. So, on the evening of May 19, 1950, I silently prayed what Dave had earlier taught me to pray.

Dave had no idea what I was doing. He was in bed on the other side of the room looking out the window. No sooner had I begun to pray when it happened again. I was suddenly filled with that same unique overpowering feeling of unconditional love and total acceptance. It vibrated with the same tingling sensation experienced in the past. It was the same unique feeling that I encountered with the lady in the light. It was the identical feeling I experienced when someone took over my voice.

It is significant that these feelings also began at the *same moment* Dave shouted that there was a bright light illuminating the whole area outside the window. However, I was so entranced by my experience that I did not answer him. I think he thought that I was asleep, as I do not remember him saying anything else. I must have fallen asleep right away although I do not remember doing so.

I did not tell Dave about my prayer until the next morning. I do not remember telling him the strange feelings that I had experienced. I showed no interest in his excitement about the light. Decades later, I equated this experience with the other of my paranormal and UFO experiences. This realization would be the catalyst for another amazing psychic-like event. It would reunite me with not only Dave but also with the house that held memories of my bizarre childhood experiences.

Telepathic Synchronism

For years, I persistently wondered about that light that Dave saw from our bedroom window. I wondered if this light was from a UFO and if something else happened to us that night. This was because I now recognized the light and tingling experience as harbingers of UFO and other strange experiences! On a sudden impulse, I felt constrained to look up Dave and ask him more about *that light*.

I had lost track of him over the years. Once, he showed up for a brief visit over two decades ago. At that time, he excitingly reminisced about *that light*. However, I changed the subject and we concentrated on catching up on our mutual activities. At that time, UFO and associated beams of light were not in my UFO-logical vocabulary. In retrospect, it is significant that one of the first subjects David had brought up was *that light*. Knowing what I know now, I can now see why it has had such a lasting impression on him.

I began to search in earnest for David. It became an obsession to find and ask him more details about *that light*. I went through a number of telephone books checking for his name. I phoned other persons with his last name hoping to find a relative who might point the way to him. I obtained a CD-ROM that listed the telephone numbers and addresses of all persons in the U.S. I checked persons listed with his name in and around Eastern Massachusetts but still could not locate him. I had reached an impasse. Then, on a whimsical impulse, I decided to try something that I had never tried before. I attempted to reach Dave by *mental telepathy*!

On or about September 26th or 27th 1998, I began to visualize Dave's face. I mentally asked him to contact me. At night, after retiring to bed, I would reminisce about the many activities that we shared together as teens. I would literally call up mental pictures in my mind. I relived going fishing and hunting together, playing sandlot softball and shooting off homemade rockets and bombs.

My attempts at trying to reach Dave in this unorthodox way went on for several days without any result and I eventually gave it up. I thought myself rather silly for even attempting such a thing. So, you can imagine my shock when David telephoned me a few days later on the evening of September 29! The following *converging coincidence* indicates that contact with David was telepathic in nature.

It appears to have been in direct response to my concentrated thoughts about him.

> **September 29, 1998:** I had searched for years for a dear friend named David Harris. He was a foster child that shared my room in 1950. He visited me in 1980, but I had lost track of him. **A few days ago, he was very much on my mind** and I began to make mental images and concentrate on them, thinking that perhaps it would influence him to contact me. Amazingly, this evening I received a telephone call from him. He was having a personal problem and said **that he began thinking of me a few days ago**!

Dave said that not only had he been thinking of me, but he also had been thinking about *that light*! He too wondered if *that light* had some connection to the UFO subject. I had not found him in telephone directories because he had no telephone listed in his name. He used the landlord's phone.

After excitedly talking with each other for awhile, I asked him if he could remember details about *that light*. He said that it lit up the whole area around the house. It was there as long as he looked, but he does not remember what happened next. He thought that he must have fallen asleep. We made plans for him to visit me. I wanted to tell him about my UFO experiences but was a bit reticent to do so. I thought he might think I had mental problems.

Dave soon visited and again emphasized the brilliance of *that light*. As it turned out, I need not have worried about Dave thinking that I had mental problems. When I described my experiences, he was empathetic and confessed bizarre things in his life. Two incidents involved *contact with the dead!*

When Dave's young daughter was killed in an automobile accident, she contacted him audibly. She assured him that she was all right and in a better place. Shortly after his mother died, he received the same type of audible communication. It was always preceded by a buzzing sound in his ears. His mother told him that her jewelry was in a hidden section of her sewing basket. She said that her housemaid had inadvertently taken it to her home. Dave visited the woman and examined the sewing basket. Sure enough, the jewelry, unknown to the housemaid, was under a false bottom of the basket!

Dave has become part of the family once more. Our children and grandchildren call him Uncle Dave. During his visits, he often mentions *that light*. He remembered feeling a keen sense of well-being as he gazed at it. It may be significant that David does not remember how that light disappeared. Both of us had thought that we just fell asleep. Did we fall asleep or did something else happen?

Adult Experiences

I have summarized my childhood anomalous experiences as a prelude to a number of adult experiences. These involved UFO sightings and dreams of being abducted by the same type of alien entities experienced in my childhood. The sightings themselves are synchronistic. They link a physical event [sighting a UFO] with a psychic condition in the observer that Jung calls numinosity. Numinosity is the powerful psychological effect that the UFO invokes in the witness. More will be said about this term later in the book.

Jung, during psychoanalysis of patients, found that numinous experiences, whether encountered inwardly by a UFO dream or outwardly by seeing a UFO, were meaningful. Meaning, according to Jung, was often symbolically indicated through dreams that coincided with the event.

Since childhood, I have consciously observed UFOs on several occasions. On July 4, 1947, while working on a farm, I observed a disc-shaped object approach and then descend with a falling leaf motion behind distant trees. Later, the headlines of the local newspaper reported UFO sightings on the same date and location. Shortly after that, my mother, sister, brothers and I observed a white cylindrical object engulfed in a cloudy haze hovering high in the clear blue sky above our house. We watched it on and off for over a half-hour before going in the house for lunch. When we came out later, it was gone. In retrospect, I wonder if this object were observing the world war two Navy fighter-bombers practicing bombing runs at nearby Beverly Airport.

In 1966, I observed a red oval object with no conventional running lights. I gave chase and was able to get ahead of it. I got out of the car. As it passed overhead, it emitted a slight humming sound. Then it suddenly performed a quick descent in an arc behind trees. Later, I learned that just a mile up the road from where I had seen it, others at nearby Gordon College had seen a glowing UFO pass over and perform a right angle turn over the college grounds. During the same time frame, in nearby Beverly, over a dozen witnesses watched a UFO hover over the Beverly High school. At one point it dived at two witnesses and hovered low over their heads. I investigated this sighting with a USAF-contracted team of scientists. They wrote in their report that if the statements by witnesses were accurate, the object must have been *alien* in nature.

My next sighting was more mysterious. It occurred on July 21, 1969, during a family visit to Margaret's parents in England. It was a beautiful sunny day with not a cloud in the sky. Margaret's father had rented a large car so that all of us could go to Hornsea Beach together. We started out early so that the children would have plenty of time to wade and use a playground. As we drove along, suddenly, up ahead of us, a disc-shaped object dropped out of the sky in an arc so fast that I thought it would crash behind trees ahead of us. I yelled to my father-in-law and the others if they had seen it and waited for signs of an explosion, but none came. No one had seen it although I suspected that Margaret's father had because he seemed nervous.

When we arrived at the beach, my father-in-law looked at his watch and was amazed *how long it had taken to get there*. He was upset and promised us that we would come back again, as there was little time for the children to play. We did return two days later with no missing time. Back then I had not dealt with UFO sightings involving missing time and abductions. I did not make a connection between the two. However, I have had weird flashbacks. In these, I see my father-in-law frozen at the wheel as if time stood still. My daughter, Sharon, is seen in the same state. I also have a flashback of a disc-shaped object slowly and wobbling back in forth in front of a car that I was in or was driving. I do not know whether the latter took place then, at another time or is just a product of my imagination.

During our flight home from the family trip to England, I may have shared a UFO sighting. My daughters and other passengers witnessed two silver objects from windows on the other side of the plane. The pilot ordered everyone to be seated and seat-belted. He said that there might be turbulence. I was upset that I could not leave my seat to look out the window on the other side of the plane. Several minutes later, I did see two shiny objects in the distance behind the plane through my window and took a photograph.

My last conscious sighting of a UFO was a *concurrent coincidence* that strained my credulity. It jarred my emotions to the very core of my being. Afterwards, I just sat limply wondering how such things could happen. Again, I was in an aircraft with my wife, flying back from a visit to her mother in England.

> **September 28, 2000:** While flying home from England, we passed off the shore of Newfoundland. Half in fun, I glanced out the **window to see if I could see a UFO**. Shocked, I **saw a light brownish disc-shaped object** pass northeasterly under the plane smoothly. It moved as if it were a hockey puck gliding over the ice. It was around 4:35 p.m. EDT.

The disc-shaped object passed through a break between the clouds thousands of feet below. At first I thought I was watching a reflection from the plane, but it had sharply defined edges. The lighting would have made it impossible for it to have been a reflection from the plane. The way it flew stirred my emotions. It moved as if it were attached to a perfectly straight track. It is hard to describe.

FAMILY EXPERIENCES

Members of my family have also had UFO experiences. Indeed, as we shall see, one of the most intriguing benchmarks of the UFO abduction experiences is that an overwhelming number of reports indicate that it is a **family phenomenon**. Investigations reveal that the grandparents, parents, brothers and sisters of an abductee have experienced UFO sightings and benchmarks of UFO abduction experiences.

Stranger still is that an abductee may unknowingly marry into another family of abductees and discover this truth later in life. One wonders if such marriages are directed by the powers behind the UFO phenomenon. This may be true regarding my mother and father. As mentioned, my Dad's first known UFO experience occurred after being hit by lightning in a Naval Radio operating station. The station was located on Mount Desert Island, Maine. His experience included three robed entities. They descended into and ascended out of the radio station in a beam of light. The light was beamed down from a glowing object in the sky. What I did not mention was the synchronicity involved in his meeting my mother who lived on the island in Bar Harbor.

Dad met Mom just a few years after she also had a close encounter with a UFO. It happened as she and her girlfriends were returning home from a youth group at Bar Harbor's Episcopal Church. While taking a shortcut through a golf course, a large silent object with flashing colored lights descended out of the sky. It stopped and hovered directly over them. They were terrified and ran home as fast as they could. One girl became hysterical. Their parents told them not to mention it. Mom did not remember if they experienced any missing time.

It is significant that Mom and Dad's UFO experiences took place in the early 1900s. This was decades away from modern UFO sightings. In addition to UFO sightings, Mom, Dad, and other family members have also experienced many benchmarks of a UFO abduction experience.

Mom's next UFO sighting was of a disc-shaped object in 1945 while riding a bicycle. She watched in astonishment as it descended from and then re-entered a cloud. Mom and a friend watched two UFOs fly into a bay near her home in Surrey, Maine in 1966. Later she had two sightings in 1976. One involved sighting a disc-shaped object hovering over Pease Air Force Base in Portsmouth, New Hampshire. The other was from her home at South Berwick, Maine. During the early morning hours, she was awakened by bright light shining through a window. When she looked out, she saw a glowing object moving along the railroad tracks behind the house.

After Dad's Near Death/UFO experience, he had follow-on OBEs with robed entities. He had further UFO sightings and the *typical abductee scoop mark* on his ankle. These are tiny round plugs of flesh removed from the abductee that look like punch biopsies.

My three brothers have had UFO sightings. A brother and his son have these same *scoop-marks*. My brother's scoop-mark occurred after a realistic abduction dream. It involved small entities that abducted him from a motel. Prior to that, he had a close-encounter with a large oval object. It hovered over him as he crossed a parking lot on the way to work on a night shift.

I have already mentioned that two of my brothers have had startling precognitive dreams. One of them and his family have also experienced apparitions and the physical actions of a poltergeist.

Another brother's wife has the typical scoop-mark. One night, she awoke to see small *gray* entities approaching the house just outside a large picture window. She screamed without effect for my brother to wake up and then fell asleep. Her mother also had experienced poltergeist phenomena. One night, her mother screamed for help. When my sister-in-law rushed to help, her mother exclaimed that she had found herself being levitated out of bed! Her brother also has experienced the same phenomenon.

One of my sons sighted a domed-disc hovering over a lake during one of our vacations. As mentioned, my daughters and other passengers sighted two UFOs from an aircraft over the Atlantic Ocean

Two of my mother's sisters and her aunt observed an oval object with flashing colored lights right outside of their window in April of 1966. Perhaps significant is the fact that my wife's mother [now deceased] once made two intriguing remarks to me. She had no knowledge of my abduction experiences at anytime in her life, although familiar with my book, *The Andreasson Affair*. One day while sitting with company sipping tea, she blurted out "Do the little men come and take you too?" Everybody fell silent wondering what she was talking about. Embarrassed, I changed the subject and the former conversations continued. Another time while retiring for bed, Margaret's mother pulled the drapes over her windows and said, "I do this so the little men can't get in." When I got the chance to be alone with her, I asked if she would tell me more about these statements. She asked why I wanted to know. I said that if she was willing to share her experiences with me that I in turn would to the same for her. She refused.

It is not my intent to go over the history of my family's UFO experiences in detail. [For those interested in exploring them further, I would refer you to my book, *The Andreasson Legacy*.] Suffice it to say there is abundant evidence to indicate UFO experiences have been alive and well in my family as far back as 1916!

The synchronistic effects of UFO sightings and [as we shall see] UFO dreams have caused a good part of my life to be devoted to near fanatical UFO research. I believe [to put it in Jungian terms] that it has been due to the inner psychic response of my unconscious to the external events of personal, familial and societal UFO experiences. Let us now turn to *dreams about UFOs* and what they may represent.

10

Stigmatic Synchronicity

After dealing with several UFO 'abduction' cases in private therapy, I'm struck—in all instances—by the sincerity and humility of the folk involved, and by the genuinely traumatic nature of what they've experienced...I'm also struck by its blatantly archetypal nature—people receiving the equivalent of **stigmata**. *(Jung relates an intriguing instance in his* **Flying Saucers** *book of a guy who received on his arm a centered circle mark, or basic mandala, after an alien encounter).*

—Maureen B. Roberts, Ph.D.
The New Mythology

UFO dreams are synchronistic in and of themselves. Persons who experience them report details within the dreams that coincide with others that report the exact details in their dreams. These details, in turn, coincide with details reported by people who have had a *conscious* UFO abduction experience. These synchronistic details are called *benchmarks* of a UFO abduction experience. Many of them fall into the *counter coincidence* category as their catalyst appears to originate outside our concept of reality. They [according to Jung] would be acausal in nature. A detailed list of them follows:

BENCHMARKS OF A UFO ABDUCTION EXPERIENCE

Awake paralyzed in bed.	Dreams of floating through windows.
Awake with a panic attack.	Dreams of floating in a beam of light.
Awake in other position/place.	Dreams of aliens, doctors, operations.

Awake suddenly with a start.
Awake and find clothes affected.
Awake with sore genitals/navel.
Awake with blood on bedding.
Awake with scars, bruises.
Childhood visitations by entities.
Compulsion to study UFOs.
Compulsion to become vegetarian.
Compulsion to improve ecology.
Compulsion to study Astronomy.
Compulsion to study Quantum Physics.
Compulsion to study the Paranormal.
Compulsion to go to a certain place.
Compulsion not to reveal experience.
Compulsion to sleep against a wall.
Compulsion to resolve experiences.
Compulsion to perform a mission.
Dreams of flying, weightlessness.
Dreams of owls or deer in/out of house.
Dreams about UFOs, Entities.
Dreams of large black staring eyes.
Experience nose bleeds, implants.
Experience missing fetus.
Experience Paranormal Phenomena.
Experience Missing Time.
Experience synchronistic happenings.
Experience being out of body [OBE].
Experience affecting electric devices.
Experience hearing anomalous sounds.
Experience electric-like tingling sensation.
Experience Flashbacks [strange craft, conference, corridors, glowing-misty oval room with table, alien exam, instruments, babies, hybrid children, UFO sightings, etc.]
Have fear/wariness of a certain place
History of family UFO experiences.
See same numbers on clock lined up.
See anomalous fog or haze.
See apparitions.
See anomalous balls of light.
See hooded figure, strangers dressed in black.

If you recall, sometimes my nighttime experiences with *clock coincidences* coincided with physical effects on my body. Clock coincidences and a variety of physical effects are among the benchmarks of a UFO abduction experience that are listed above. This chapter will detail the synchronistic benchmarks that I personally have experienced.

BLOOD ON THE BED

Sometimes I awake with **blood on my bed** without a known causal connection. The following are examples from *SynchroFile*:

April 14, 1991: I woke up briefly in the middle of the night. I felt very apprehensive and up-tight, as if something was about to happen again, but then went right back to sleep. I woke up to find blood on my pillow again.

April 15, 1991: The inside of my right nostril felt tender/sore to the touch when I placed my finger inside. There was no sign of any cuts or other sources for the blood. As before, the blood was localized on just one section of the pillow. This time, instead of one smudged streak, there were two smudged streaks. Each of them was between one to two inches long and one-half to three quarters of an inch in width. There were blotted out streaks in between them.

November 13, 1991: I woke up with the same type of blood clot in my nose noticed other times. This time it was in my left, rather than my right, nostril. A round spot of blood about ½ inch in diameter stained my pillow.

February 2, 1993: This morning there were two spots on my pillow, approximating the distance between my nostrils. One spot was blood, the other a lighter grayish substance. Neither would scrape off and both were soaked into the pillow. Each is about three sixteenths of an inch in diameter with pinpoints of blood around the large spot.

October 6 & 7, 1994: While visiting my son in Florida, I woke to find spots of blood on my pillow twice. They appear to have come from my nose, but my nose was not bloody or sore.

October 14, 1994: Returned home from Florida on 10/13. I woke up in the morning on 10/14 to find blood on my pillow. [Note: According to diary entries throughout October, my right nostril was very sore.]

April 25, 1996: I awoke and found a spot of blood on my pillow where my nose would have been against the pillow.

June 15, 1996: Awoke with an elated feeling saying to myself, "I can hardly wait for my soul to come home." Three drops of blood on my pillow.

October 1, 1996: There was blood on my pillowcase where my nose would have been pressed against the pillow when I woke up in the morning. The blood had soaked right through the pillow slip and stained the pillowcase as well. I do not remember anything strange happening during the night.

March 30, 1997: The town fire whistle went off and woke us at 2:22. [Still later, I was awake at 4:44 but cannot remember what woke me up.] I found two tiny spots of blood on the pillow that look as if they came from my nose.

However, there are times when there is no doubt as to why bloodstains are found on the bedding. Their origin is painfully obvious. They coincide with my **awaking with scars and bruises** on my body. However, there is no natural cause for the scars and bruises

SCARS AND BRUISES

March 11, 1990: I woke up and there was one round spot of blood on the pillow. It was about three sixteenths of an inch in diameter. There was a three eighths of an inch trail of three dots of blood coming from its right side. I examined my head area and found a small pinpoint of dried blood behind the fold of my right ear.

May 16, 1991: This morning I again found blood on my pillow. When I looked in the mirror later, my left cheek had a bloody scab on it next to a pockmark that has been there since my teens. Sometimes, when I have noticed this pockmark while shaving, I get the mental impression of a needle pricking me at that spot and being maneuvered with a circular motion. I also get the impression that my skin is being sucked up into the needle.

This impression has surfaced off and on over the years. I have not mentioned it before as I had assumed that it was just my imagination. I attributed the mark to perhaps being left by chicken pox or a pimple, etc. It used to be much larger and deeper and is a smaller version of the scoop mark on my leg.

However, today, when I examined the bloody spot (now a scab), this thought surfaced very strongly. Perhaps there is nothing to this. The blood could have been caused by an insect bite, but there seemed to be more blood than an insect bite would cause and the scab is quite large. I thought I had better record this "for the record."

Later in the morning, while answering correspondence that has been piling up over the past several months, I came across a letter and some photographs. The writer, who has reportedly had UFO/paranormal experiences, suspects that two types of marks on his body may have been connected with them. Coincidentally, one photograph of small puncture-like wounds on his back that appeared overnight sometime in November of 1989, is identical to some that appeared on my back in the same area on October 30, 1988. Even the pattern is somewhat similar, except his are more closely spaced. His dermatologist told him that they were fleabites. He believed that this was not possible under the circumstances.

October 21, 1991: I have thought about recording the following on several occasions. It may be nothing, but it is strange enough to be put on the record. From time to time, I have felt something at the base of the back of my head like an insect bite. When I touch it with my finger, there is a scab of dried up blood. This by itself would not be a cause of suspicion, except it always occurs in the same place!

It just happened again. In fact, there always seems to be some tiny wound there that never heals. It scabs over, but the scab never goes away. Occasionally, the scab is covered with dried blood. This may be because I scratch at it or because something else may have happened. I am recording this now because yesterday morning it again had a small wad of dried blood over the scab.

In looking at a schematic of the brain and spinal chord, this wound seems to be just above the cervical region. This is where the brain and spinal chord join and where the nerves from the spinal chord emerge as two roots [the posterior and the anterior roots]. I feel funny even mentioning this, but the fact of its location and that it does not ever heal may possibly have something to do with what has been happening to me over the years. This scab has been there on and off for several years.

Again, and there is no way for me to verify this, the night before it scabbed up again with fresh dried blood, I had gotten up to go to the bathroom. I thought that I noted the time as 01:05 when I left the bedroom. However, when I returned, it was 01:26! At the time, I thought I must have misread the time. Nevertheless, since this coincided with the fresh blood on the wound, I thought it was worth recording. I wish that if something were happening, there would be no question whether it did or did not. However, I shall continue to record things as time goes on. Perhaps they will contain a clue to what may be going on with others and me.

November 4, 1991: This is an update on the last message noted above. This time I examined the area daily. I found that the sore/scab did heal. I could feel it no more after several days. However, I continued to check out the area and on November 2, there were two new wounds in the same area. One is more prominent than the other. They are diagonal—one below the other. I am wondering if something is biting me, but if so, why in the same area. That's it "for the record." I'll continue to monitor this area. [Note: As I am writing this in *SynchroFile's* manuscript in April 2000, this scab continues to appear, heal and disappear periodically in the same location!]

December 15, 1991: While watching TV, I happened to reach up to where the scab/sore above the cervical area has appeared from time to time. The last time I had checked, it had healed completely. However, I now have a new scab in this area.

January 30, 1993: I woke with a pain above my left breast and found a round wound of raw flesh and blood. It looks circular, but a magnifying glass reveals the interior to be deeper. It is roughly keyhole shaped.

July 18, 1993: I woke up and went to the bathroom. The clock in my classroom read 2:22. I went back to bed. In the morning, I had deep scratches and puncture marks on my right buttock. It looked very similar to what happened to me back on January 14, 1993 and January 13, 1992. Bloodstains on my underwear matched the scars. These marks were not there before going to bed and I had done nothing during the day that would account for their presence. My underwear from the previous day had no blood on it. There were bloodstains on the right side of the toilet seat. They matched where I sat at 2:22. I do not remember feeling pain then. When I walk or sit, it causes a dull pain. I did not feel this yesterday nor prior to going to bed.

January 14, 1994: I noticed a sharp pain in my right buttock. There was a circle, two to three inches in diameter comprised of many small individual fresh dried scabs of blood. My wife examined this with a magnifying glass. She said it looked like I had been slashed. I have had similar marks in this location before. These are deep punctures and very painful.

March 29, 1994: I felt the familiar [new] scab of dried blood on the back of my head. I wonder if it has to do with possible *missing time* a few days ago.

November 4, 1994: When washing, I happened to notice a triangular pattern of red spots of dried blood below my upper right shoulder. This pattern was similar to one that had appeared on my body in the past. I decided to examine my body for other scars. I found what look like claw marks on my back, just behind the shoulder blades. They look fresh, but there is no pain. Similar marks have appeared in the same place in the past and were recorded in this diary on January 14, 1994.

January 1, 1995: I woke up with a start, got out of bed to go to the bathroom, and noticed that the clock read 1:11. Later I woke up again and opened my eyes that were facing the clock. It read 5:55. Still later, when taking a shower and soaping the inside of my right thigh, I felt a roughness. After showering, I pushed my skin around to see what it was. There is a straight-line scab that measured are one inch long and about one sixteenth of an inch wide. I could not see it without a mirror or pushing my skin around. I never would have noticed it unless I just happened to rub my hand against it while soaping my leg. The hardened blood has the same appearance and texture as the cut that appeared on the hairline of my forehead on the night of 12/26/94. It is perfectly straight. It looks like a razor cut that bled.

February 7, 1995: For some reason, I reached up and touched the back of my upper neck. There is a new scab of dried blood in the same area that similar scabs of dried blood have appeared many times before. Right nostril still sore.

September 21, 1998: Awoke sometime after 3:00 a.m. to a sound similar to my wife's alarm clock. Currently, she has the clock while visiting in England. Later I heard a female voice say "Dad" very distinctly. By the time I stirred and turned around to look at the clock it read 5:56, but I bet it had read 5:55 when I first heard the voice! Later, I noticed three tiny pricks that had left tiny hardened blood scabs behind in the shape of a triangle on my left forearm. The sides of the triangle measure exactly one and one half by one and one half by two inches.

December 24, 1998: Awoke at 2:22. Inadvertently glanced at clock at 10:10 and 4:44. [Note: I keep forgetting to mention that the scab behind my neck that I have mentioned in the past still periodically appears. I remembered to note it this time as the scab has reappeared with lots of matted blood around it.]

January 18, 1999: A few days ago, I noticed what I had thought [a few months ago] to be a slow-to-heal tick bite. It has left a fading scab over what appears to be a round mark on the left side of my left shin. It is amazing that I had forgotten all about this and had not thought further about it. At the time, it appeared it was a bloody puncture and it left a scab that did not go away. Why I did not think more about it is strange. I just forgot about it. It is in such a location that I cannot see it unless I twist my ankle. It is in such a location that I cannot take a photo of it. It is also in the exact position of an anomalous scoop mark on my right shin. I measured both as being four inches from the same bone in my ankle. Both also are on the left side of my tibia. Is this a remarkable coincidence or another "operation"?

August 15, 1999: Awoke at 1:11 and 3:33. I have not been keeping track of the clock phenomenon. I am mentioning it this time because when I awoke in the morning I found a large ¼ inch bloody stain. It surrounds a fresh scab of what looks like a tiny puncture. It is located a little over an inch from my scoop mark. Like the scoop mark, it is located in the flesh above a bony section of my right tibia. I noticed it first thing this morning. I did not notice it last night, so this may mean it appeared overnight. I am trying to remember if I did anything to cause it yesterday. Thus far, I do not remember anything. I took a picture just in case it may be anomalous.

>Shortly after discovering this, I took a shower. When I soaped my legs, I felt pain just above my left tibia. This was caused by a series of tiny abrasions located in exactly the same area as the marks on my right tibia. They were fresh and felt sore to the touch especially when touched by soap and water. I took a photo of these marks as well. I might add that I do not remember anything out of the ordinary that happened last night—no noises, tingling sensation, etc.

Such physical marks also coincide with *bizarre dreams*. The dreams are about deer, wolves and strange entities entering my room. Sometimes I dream of being operated on in a laboratory by strange entities. Again, these *stigmatic* synchronisms are typical benchmarks of a UFO abduction experience. They mirror what UFO abductees have *consciously* experienced in waking life—abduction by entities from a UFO.

Three theories are offered as explanations for such dreams:

1. They are dreams instigated by UFO books and television shows.

2. They are flashbacks of real but forgotten abduction experiences of the past.

3. They are actual abductions remembered as realistic dreams.

UFO abduction dreams are synchronistic because:

1. The dream's content *coincides* with dreams of other abductees.

2. The dream's content *coincides* with UFO abduction experiences.

3. The stigmatic effects *mirror* the effects of dreamt physical operations upon the very areas of the body that the stigmata appear.

4. The synchronistic stigmata fall in the category of *counter coincidences*.

If we accept accounts of UFO abductions at face value, the abductees are made to forget their traumatic experience. This appears to be done by a type of mind control akin to hypnosis. Usually, all the abductee is left with consciously is a realistic nightmare or unaccounted for *missing time* and anomalous physical effects upon the body.

However, the traumatic experience, buried within the unconscious, sometimes bursts through to the conscious mind. This may be caused by word or picture association. Sometimes it is caused by passing by the location of the abduction. Any one of these catalysts can be the synchronistic connection between the two. However, many times memories surface in an *abduction dream*. In this case, a person is actually taken from bed at night to a UFO and given a physical examination.

An abduction dream is not a normal dream. Abductees may be having a normal run-of-the-mill dream. They awake suddenly with a start when their body is moved or touched. When they open their eyes, they find themselves in what they believe to be another dream. This dream feels more real than the dream that they have just left. In this dream, they find themselves lying on a table in a bright room with strange entities.

The room contains consoles and instruments that remind them of a doctor's office. The entities, in most cases, are small *gray* entities. They have oversized heads shaped like inverted pears. Their large eyes are pitch black and their stare effects mental control over the abductee. Many times, a taller entity appears familiar to the abductee. This entity seems to be in control of the operations that are being performed on the abductee. Sometimes entities that appear human provide assistance to the alien entities.

During the abduction, certain physical procedures are performed by alien entities. Afterwards, the person is then placed back in bed and awakes with a memory of a realistic nightmare. Later, the person finds bruises, cuts or burns that correspond to procedures dreamt about in the nightmare. Pajamas may be unbuttoned or put on backwards. Earrings may be missing or put on the wrong way. Anomalous traces of dirt and grass may be found on the floor beside the bed. In some cases, the person awakes in another bed. Sometimes shocked parents have awakened to find their child missing from their crib. They are doubly shocked when the child is found playing outside their locked house.

The synchronistic numinosity elicited by UFO sightings and abductions can produce deep, psychological life-changing effects in those who experience them. These experiences do not correspond to everyday reality. Religious, philosophical and scientific belief systems may be shattered or changed depending upon personalities and worldviews.

Some theorize that the *clock coincidences* associated with abduction dreams may be associated with the *times* that past bedtime abductions have taken place. The abduction causes a disruption of the abductee's sleep patterns. Such a stress response might cause the abductee to wake up at a certain time each night. The times would coincide with the times the past abductions had occurred. They would be *wake-up-and-protect-yourself alarms* sounding from the unconscious. Others believe that clocks may be used for post-hypnotic suggestions, that is:

"When you wake up and see the clock hands lined up at such-and-such a time, you will forget what happened to you."

The experiences examined thus far certainly reflect just the synchronistic *benchmarks* of a UFO abduction dream. They do not contain memories of an *actual encounter with alien entities*. This type of dream is the subject of the next chapter.

11

UFO Abduction Dreams and Synchronicity

> *Not only are UFOs seen, they are of course also dreamed about. This is particularly interesting to the psychologist, because dreams tell us in what sense they are understood by the unconscious.*
>
> —Carl G. Jung
> *Flying Saucers*

As I write this particular chapter, two significant events have occurred in the past few weeks that are pertinent to the UFO abduction phenomenon.

> (1) Steven Spielberg's epic 20-episode miniseries *Taken* is being televised twice weekly and is the biggest miniseries ever seen on television. According to Barry Diller, chairman and CEO of USA Networks, Spielberg's treatment starts from the premise that "there are abductions, that they're real and not made up." It weaves together the lives of three families over four generations and their crucial roles in the history of alien abduction and government conspiracy.
>
> (2) Coincidentally, my latest book *UFO Testament—Anatomy of an Abductee* [1] was published at the same time as Spielberg's *Taken* was about to be launched on television. Although it is fiction, Spielberg extracted data for *Taken* from accounts of those who believe that they have been abducted by entities from UFOs. It has been estimated that about 30% of reported abductees remember all or part of the abduction consciously.

UFO abduction reports demonstrate that a person or persons can be captured and examined by aliens under many conditions and situations. Such abductions are not limited to bedtime visitations! Many reports are of abductees taken from automobiles. Some are taken while on a stroll in the countryside. One of the reports that I thoroughly investigated involved four campers being drawn up from a canoe into a UFO by a beam of light.

However, most reports involve the abductee being captured from and returned to bed. The majority of persons taken in this manner never suspect that anything so bizarre could have happened to them. They believe that they just have experienced a vivid life-like nightmare.

I decided to begin keeping a record of my abduction dreams in 1990. The following account is my first abduction dream entry into *SynchroFile*. I also am including an entry describing my panic attack when I shared the experience with a friend.

> **November 8, 1990:** I remember portions of a strange dream of being in some kind of a laboratory. The man who ran the laboratory was a friend, but I cannot remember who he was. It was no one I know in real life. He jokingly told me that he would sign a document indicating that I had been abducted by alien beings if I wanted. He indicated that he would only do it because I was his friend. He laughed as he signed it and passed it to me as if to say that he did not really believe that I had been abducted. I felt angry and asked him if he would really like to see an alien. He said yes. I began to stare at his eyes. It was at this point that I instantaneously felt the inception of the typical tingling sensation felt in the past during bedroom visitation experiences.
>
> The dream abruptly ended at this point. Instantly, I felt pressure enveloping my whole body. I felt myself rising vertically and then moving horizontally along somewhere. I could not open my eyes. I felt exhilarating tingling sensation—a feeling of release—weightlessness—I felt as if I was just floating horizontally. The feeling was similar to what I felt during the Dodge Court *Big Hall* experience when I went up the beam with the glowing entity.
>
> I do not know how high I was. I felt as if I were just floating along horizontally. I then said to myself, "I'm going with them. I want to go with them, but I want to come back." I stopped and hovered weightlessly. I still could not open my eyes, but I now could see a small, concentrated, bright patch of light through my closed eyelids. It was just a small, blurred, shapeless mass, somewhat like what a distant light bulb would look like through closed eyes in a dark room. Then I felt someone touch me and hold me. I felt *love* coursing through my body and I asked, "Is that you mummy?" [Note: I thought that I was dead and was being touched by my deceased mother.]
>
> I began to move horizontally again. Then, I stopped and felt myself descending. I stopped and at this point began to feel weight and bodily sensations. I began to feel the presence of my arms and legs, but they were still paralyzed. I felt a tingling sensation all through my body. I knew that I was now lying back in bed and tried my utmost to come back to full consciousness. I did not believe that I was dreaming because I knew that I was lying in bed. I

knew that I could not move. I knew that I was trying to get out of that strange state of semi-consciousness.

Then, slowly it dawned on me that it was my mind saying that I could not move. I felt that if I exerted mental pressure, I would be able to open my eyes and move my limbs. I strained to do so and finally was able to open my eyes. I realized then that I was lying on my back in a very strange position. My legs were tightly crossed at my ankles and my arms were crossed over my chest. [I never sleep in such a position.] Now that I could feel my limbs, I strained mentally to move them and slowly was finally able to move them in a dream-like way. As I raised them up slowly, my limbs felt almost weightless. It was as if they were floating up and off my chest. They still felt as if they were just barely a part of me.

I suddenly wondered if I had just had an abduction experience or if I had nearly died. Then, for some reason, I slowly placed my legs and arms back into the folded positions and closed my eyes. Remnants of the tingling sensation were still with me. I mentally said, "I want to go with you again. I want to see you. I want to come back, though." I felt part of me trying to rise vertically again. I felt totally relaxed. It was a feeling of near-freedom, but I could not let go.

Slowly, I opened my eyes again and tried to move my limbs. I lay there for awhile again, either not able to or not willing to move. I was enjoying and trying to retain the tingling feeling. Then, slowly but surely, I found myself raising my hands off my chest. again. It was as if time had slowed down and I was moving in slow motion. I did the same with my feet as the prickling sensation slowly dissipated.

I told myself that I must remember this extraordinary experience. I reached for a Kleenex box at the head of the bed and placed it on my bureau to remind me of what I had experienced. I noted that the clock read 2:23 a.m. [Note: 2:22 is a component of the *clock phenomena*. This was one minute later.] I slowly got out of bed and walked in a dream-like state to use the bathroom. On the way, I stopped and looked at the sky through my study picture window and wondered if I had had an abduction experience. I glanced at the study clock. It read about 2:26 a.m. I used the bathroom and went back to bed. The clock read 2:28 a.m.

When I returned to the bedroom, I wondered if I should try to re-enter the strange state of consciousness again. I lay on my back and re-folded my arms and legs as before, but I thought of death and the possibility of not coming back if I succeeded. Something told me to roll over into my normal sleeping position and go to sleep. I did this. When I awoke in the morning, I had a clear memory of what had happened. I got a pad of paper and wrote down everything that I could remember "for the record" in the event that it might be significant for future study.

The following entry was made twelve days late. It was about the above-mentioned experience It is significant because of my reaction when I shared it with a friend over the telephone.

> **November 20, 1990:** I talked with David Webb about the Allagash report and mentioned the November 8 experience. I said that I thought that it represented much more than I could remember. I told him that I thought the familiar man in the lab could have been something other than what my mind conjured up. After hanging up, I thought about my statement. I wondered if the man could have been an alien. I began feeling fearful and literally began shuddering all over uncontrollably [Panic Attack].

Persons awaking from an abduction dream feel confused about the realness that such dreams engender. They are bewildered to find coinciding anomalous physical effects on their bodies. The nightmares contain the **mixed nonsense** of normal dreams along with fleeting dream-like memories of an actual abduction. The following are examples from *SynchroFile*:

> **May 22, 1991:** I had a strange dream that may be of significance I remembered it vividly when I woke up in the morning. I dreamt that Margaret showed me an opening into a small place. She told me that if I went through it, it would be much larger inside. I tried to get in but did not follow directions the first time. The second time I succeeded. As I entered this place, I found it to be a round area, and white, with translucent dimly-glowing walls.
>
> There was mist throughout the room about knee-high from the floor. I immediately experienced the euphoric tingling feeling felt during some of my other experiences. I found myself alone and went toward an opening in the wall. Here I came face-to-face with a non-human being mopping the floor. It came right at me waving the mop. I said to myself, "This time I am not going to be afraid." I stood my ground and stared at it. It then became non-aggressive and led me to other entities.
>
> We sat down at a table and talked about something before I was told that I had to go back. I do not think that I wanted to go back, but I did. I cannot remember what happened after this. I only mention this dream because of several elements in it. (1) Entering what seemed to be a very small place but that was huge, comparatively speaking, inside; (2) Experiencing the typical euphoric feeling upon arrival; (3) The round, white area; (4) The mist; (5) The non-human entity. [It had a round head and big eyes and was thin. I do not remember how it was dressed.] and (6) A conference. These are all typical benchmarks of a UFO abduction experience. I wondered if surfacing past memories caused the dream or if it was a screen memory of what may have

occurred during the night. Of course, it could be neither, but I felt that it would be worth mentioning.

November 18, 1991: I woke up in the middle of the night experiencing the usual tingling feeling but not as strongly as other times. I tossed and turned trying to get to sleep and finally mentally asked—"If you are coming for me, come now and get it over. But if you do, let me see you and not be afraid." I crossed my arms at the wrists and crossed my legs at my ankles and mentally said, "Okay, I'll go." I finally fell asleep and had a crazy dream that I cannot remember except, I was going to see a **doctor**.

June 9, 1992: Last night I awoke and glanced at the digital clock that had all numbers lined up to 3:33 a.m. I decided to get up and go to the bathroom. On the way back, I went to the picture window in my classroom. I gazed at the sky and thought about abductions. I glanced at another clock. It read 3:34. I continued on the way back to my bed. Mid-way, I felt the tingling feeling that I have had before having an experience

I glanced at the clock after I got in bed. It read 3:38. I then got into my normal sleeping position on my side and closed my eyes. Then, as if no time had passed, I opened my eyes as my wife got out of bed to go to the bathroom. The clock read 4:57. I was lying on my back in that same strange position that I have been in before during an experience. My legs were tightly crossed at the ankles, my arms were upwards on my chest with my wrists crossed and tightly pressed together.

On this occasion, I was not paralyzed. I was just in this very strange position. If it were not for this, I would have thought nothing about what had happened. However, this event seemed strange enough to record, especially in light of the dream that I had experienced.

I was in a doctor's office or hospital. I was sitting in a chair. Two persons were behind me. I was being tested with a strange instrument. It was a small black capsule attached to a black cord like an electric extension cord. The capsule was placed behind the left earflap against the side of my head. The capsule was about a quarter of an inch in diameter and about one and one-half inches long.

After the exam was over, I was asked if I worked fast when I awoke. I said—"Yes" even though I didn't know what he meant. Then I awoke or opened my eyes. Another strange thing is that I kept on forgetting to record this. I did not even remember the dream until I was typing this. It suddenly came back to me, at least, what I could remember about it.

November 22, 1992: I retired to bed and drifted off to sleep around 11:15 feeling completely normal. I awoke with a start, turned over and stared at the clock—it read 4:44. I felt startled, but I think that I drifted back to sleep. I then had the following dream:

I was sitting at the kitchen table at my childhood home at 4 Dodge Court, Danvers, MA. With me were my mother and father and a doctor whom I knew in my dream but cannot identify now. We were talking about my scoop mark. I told the doctor that my doctor had examined it but could not explain it. I also told him that a dermatologist had found it strange. I told him about my weird dream during which I levitated from bed with my eyes closed and was brought to a place where a bright light shined on my face. I could see it faintly through closed eyes. After I told him these things, the doctor told me that it sounded like a UFO abduction experience.

The reason we were gathered at the table was because another scoop mark had appeared beside the other one. My mother and father were concerned because it was very swollen around the area. After examining it, the doctor took out what looked one of those X-Acto knives that have a tubular handle. He cut into the area and removed a round plug of flesh. [This did not make sense as it would have made a third scoop mark and there were still only two.]

I don't know if this dream was a partial flashback to another scoop mark that I remembered as a child at 4 Dodge Court or not. When I returned from the woods after my missing time experience, I first confronted my parents in the kitchen. They were concerned and about to call the police. I do remember such a mark appearing and bleeding. At the time, I attributed it to the snaps on my boots for some reason. This would have been impossible because they were located on the outside of the boot and not pressing against my shin.

I wonder if this is when I got that other scoop mark, i.e., a dream about a doctor that I know in the dream but cannot remember when I wake up. The silver, pencil-shaped instruments may be a flashback to the time when I received one or the other scoop mark. Perhaps all of this was mixed up since I cannot remember the entire dream. It began to depart from my memory as soon as I woke up. Interestingly enough, the area below my current scoop mark was itching when I woke up in the morning. It is still itching. However, there are no new marks in this area. I cannot find remnants of the childhood scoop mark.

October 20, 1992: I dreamt that I was in a room with a group of nude human children who appeared to be two to three years of age. One whom I noticed differed from the others had long, unkempt, shoulder-length hair.

March 16, 1993: I had an abduction dream but cannot remember details. I remember trying to move a cylinder attached to something that was putting pressure on my chest. I could not budge it. I was in pain and moaning.

March 29, 1993: I went to the bathroom at 1:41 and went right back to bed. As soon as my head hit the pillow, a strange dream began. I can only remember the first part of it. It began with being confronted by a familiar figure. For some reason, I equated him with an alien entity that took my brother somewhere in the past. I thought that he would do the same again. I felt that I must warn my brother. I do not remember which brother. The tall figure looked at me with its eyes. That is all I could remember until shortly before 2:41. I say shortly before 2:41 because the next thing I knew, I was lying in bed totally paralyzed.

It felt as if only my consciousness existed. My body felt like a cement block. I felt as if I had been somewhere and returned but now was just consciousness locked in stone. I did not panic but calmly wondered how I would get out of this strange state. Then, after what seemed a long few minutes, I suddenly felt my body again. My eyes opened. I glanced at the clock. It was exactly an hour since I returned from the bathroom, but it seemed as if no time had lapsed. I felt that I had just put my head down on the pillow, closed my eyes, saw the entity and then found myself in this strange state of paralysis. I also felt as if I had been somewhere and had been returned. I wonder if I was taken somewhere in an OBE state.

December 15, 1994: I awoke out of a deep sleep and thought to myself—"They floated me back to bed." I then got up to go to the bathroom. When I started out the door, something told me to look at the clock on the bureau. It read 3:33! I went back to sleep but awoke again at 4:44. Later, I awoke and watched the clock flick from 5:54 to 5:55!

December 21, 1994: I went to the bathroom and returned at 4:42. I felt that I must stay awake until the numbers changed to 4:44. I had a dream earlier of sticking a pencil in my ear. It was realistic. I could feel it probing inside my ear. [Was something really being stuck in my ear?]

May 8, 1995: I had a dream of two personages [could not see faces] advancing down a corridor toward me. Each pushed a rectangular machine on a cart that measured about two feet by two feet by three feet. Each machine had two extended lenses, like projector lenses, on their upper front surfaces. I was only wearing a white johnny and was retreating from them. I ducked into a room. They followed and forced me to lie down on a bed. I was embarrassed, as I was nearly naked. I thought they wanted to take my picture. I woke with a start at 4:44.

November 6, 1995: I awoke remembering a very detailed dream. The contents were slipping away as I tried to recall the details. I remember suddenly finding myself floating just above the ground. There were typical *gray* entities on each side of me holding me under my arms. I was not frightened. I felt that it was just another experience among many that I was now used to. We seemed to be waiting for something. It was a warm summer night. The mosquitoes were vicious. I asked them to go up higher above the ground so I would not be bitten. They accommodated my request. We rose higher and waited. Suddenly we were in a bright room!

There were more *gray entities* and a human woman in the room. I think she had blond hair and wore coveralls. The woman stayed near me as the *grays* proceeded to examine and prod me with instruments from a console in the wall. I did not put up any resistance and merely let them do anything they wanted to me. I can't remember what they did, except I think they drew blood from my finger. The woman told the *grays* that she wanted some time with me. They seemed reluctant to let her do this but allowed her to bring me to a table.

We sat and talked. I asked all kinds of pertinent questions and got answers. However, I cannot remember my questions or her answers. I only remember begging them all to let me remember everything this time. The next thing I can remember is waking up in the morning. Strange. I wonder if this was related to an abduction or was just a dream.

February 23, 1996: I got to bed around 11:30. I had a realistic dream during the night. I could only remember the first part. I was standing in a room filled with mist or fog. I was facing a door with diffuse light shining from it through the fog. Then four or five figures came through the door. I could only make out silhouettes but immediately recognized the typical *gray* UFO entities. They were short with spindly arms and legs and large heads. That's all I can remember of the dream.

Just dreams? Skeptics [especially in my case] would readily dismiss these as nightmares. They would suggest that my association with the UFO abduction phenomenon instigated them. I am certain that some dreams might fall into that category. However, what if the abduction dream contains a number of abduction benchmarks? What if these other benchmarks occur during a wakeful state before and after the so-called abduction dream? What if physical effects on the body correspond to alien operations on those same locations on the body in these supposed dreams? The following are examples of abduction dreams which I have experienced that have left **physical [and other] benchmarks** behind in their wake:

SYNCHRONISTIC SCOOPS!

The aftermath of the next dream was a typical benchmark of a UFO abduction—the overnight appearance of a scoop of flesh removed from my ankle. I should add that the UFO abduction phenomenon is often a family affair. Many family members have had UFO sightings and experiences. The same type of scoop marks are located just above the ankles of my father, my brother John and me. We all have experienced abduction dreams. My dream and the circumstances surrounding it are as follows:

On Monday, August 14, 1988, a day after returning from vacationing, I received a phone call from Betty (Andreasson) Luca. Her voice sounded very nervous. She told me that three scoop marks in the form of a triangle had suddenly appeared on her arm. She told me that they were similar to one on her leg that she had written me about some time ago. To be truthful, I had forgotten all about that letter. I immediately went and found it in my file. It was dated June 1, 1987. I had not paid much attention to it. At that time, I did not realize that it was typical of scars that appeared on other abductees. I asked her to send photographs of the scars and waited to see what they looked like.

On the following evening [Tuesday], I gave a presentation on Astronomy to some children at the Manchester Beach and Tennis Club. I returned home and retired to bed. Shortly after lying down, I suddenly began feeling very strange. I felt pressure engulf my body and a tingling sensation. I could not get to sleep at first. I tossed, turned, and wondered why I was feeling this way.

I remembered feeling this way in the past. I had been puzzled about it then. During the night, I had a frightening nightmare. I felt myself being taken from bed and moved somewhere. I tried to wake up as I thought it I was dreaming, but I could not wake up. When I did wake up later, I almost blurted out loud that—"They were operating on my leg!"

I found the scoop mark on the following day while taking a shower. It was about a quarter of an inch in diameter and appeared as if a tiny round scoop of flesh had been removed. Betty's photographs showed similar scoop marks. Shocked, I made an appointment with my personal physician to examine it. He was alarmed and referred me to a dermatologist.

The dermatologist insisted that I must have had a recent punch biopsy. He became frustrated when I insisted that I had had no such thing. His examination showed that it was healing but that it did not seem to be dangerous. As he walked out of the examining room, he turned before closing the door and said that: "It looks like a punch biopsy!" **(Photo 1)**

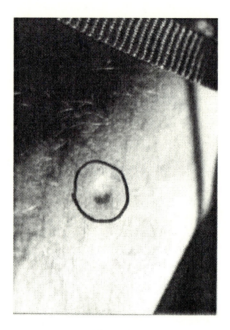

Photo 1

Again [and I feel that I must stress this] such physical synchronistic effects are found upon awaking from such a dream. They appear overnight with no apparent explanation except in their relation to the content of the dream. Thus, abduction dreams are revelatory. They provide an explanation for anomalous physical effects upon the body that appear simultaneously with such dreams. They provide strong circumstantial evidence that the dreams are the way an abductee remembers an abduction. These physical [and other non-physical] benchmarks of a UFO abduction experience have appeared repeatedly in my life.

The following are examples of synchronistic abduction dreams that left other kinds of physical [and other] benchmarks behind in their wake:

OTHER PHYSICAL BENCHMARKS

December 26, 1994: I dreamt of learning and teaching a repetitious code of raised white dots and other things that I cannot remember. Then I dreamed that I was in the ocean floating. As I slowly awakened, I said to myself: "I've been with those people again. I must not forget this." Everything faded away except the latter statement. The clock read 5:52. I fell asleep and woke again at 5:55! In the morning, there was a scab of fresh blood on my forehead at the hairline. I removed it to find a deep abrasion shaped like fat V tilted 90 degrees to the left. The area is about 1/8 of an inch. I found two spots of what looks like blood on the pillow. I think that a similar wound has appeared in this same area in the past but was ignored.

As mentioned, my life and those of other abductees have been plagued with various kinds of synchronistic events. I am mentioning the following such event because of its uncanny connection with the above abduction dream entry:

November 23, 1990: In one of those amazing synchronisms, I received a letter today from an abductee [dated 11/14/90. It is postmarked 11/20/90.] I had referred her to a MUFON investigator. In the letter, she described some recent events. She had experienced them on October 8, 20, 21, 23, 27, 28, November 4, and 8. These experiences included being paralyzed in bed at night, floated out of her body to a craft with her eyes closed. She too was somehow blindfolded so that she could not see her abductors! She too wanted to see them, but this was not allowed. In addition, she experienced a nosebleed.

This last fact suddenly made me realize the possible significance of what I had first thought was just a small pimple inside my right nostril. It had appeared exactly during the week of the strange nighttime happenings to me. When it didn't go away, I took a mirror and looked at it. It was not a pimple but a large clot of dried blood! Each day I would gently scrape the dried blood away to make my nose more comfortable. None the less, each day, the scab would be back just as big as ever. Today, it is still there but is finally much smaller and appears to be healing. I have doused it with antiseptic several times. It stings when I do, but it seems to have helped the healing process.

Again, am I being paranoid thinking that this could be connected to my experiences? How did it get there? I thought it might be from shaving, but it is just inside my nose. In addition, when I do cut myself shaving, I feel it and it bleeds noticeably. It's just another interesting thing to record.

February 19, 1996: I woke up in the early hours of the morning and used the bathroom. I went back to bed but awoke with the familiar uptight tingling sensation that I believe precedes an *event*. I was very restless but fell asleep to awake later from a terrifying dream. I saw a familiar man. I could not see facial features except his two round, pupil-less non-blinking, pitch black eyes that were staring at me. As soon as I saw him, I knew that he was going to accost me, so I walked quickly away from him. I could feel him coming up behind me, so I swung around and hit him in the stomach with all my might. I immediately awoke to find that I had flipped around in bed and had punched my pillow.

The tingling sensation was strong. My legs had become crossed tightly at my ankles. This position has occurred in the past during this kind of an event.

I tossed, turned, and slept restlessly the rest of the night. In the morning, I noticed a new five eighths of an inch hairline cut above the bone of my left shoulder. There were also two tiny puncture marks of dried blood just below the left shoulder on my arm. I found no blood on the sheets or pillow.

February 7, 1998: On the way to bed, I happened to glance behind me. I saw what appeared to be a human, perhaps female, figure at the top of the stairs. As my eyes made contact with it, it dissipated into thin air. I cannot remember if anything happened during the night. However, my wife called my attention to more drops of fresh blood on my pillowcase that appeared overnight.

June 18, 1999: Awoke at 2:22 after having a dream of being in a tunnel looking at the very close glowing face of a lady with large black eyes.

As mentioned, the tingling sensation, anomalous scars, the staring black eyes [typical alien eyes] and strange entities are also benchmarks of a UFO abduction experience.

According to UFO researchers, some abduction dreams incorporate *screen memories*. The entities are remembered as animals with big eyes such as deer, wolves and owls. They also are remembered as ordinary doctors and human beings. The UFO itself might take on the appearance of a conventional craft. Examples of both of these types of *screen memories* are as follows:

SCREEN MEMORIES

May 1, 1993: I awoke and glanced at the clock, which read 3:33. I went back to sleep and dreamed about deer visiting the house. I saw a group of deer coming out of the woods. One of them came towards the house and stuck its big head through the window. It stared at us with its big eyes as we lay in bed. I woke up my son to look at this unusual sight. The adult deer then came through the window and went by us into the house.

Then a baby deer appeared at the window and hopped into bed with us. I petted it. It was very friendly and I did not want it to leave. It wandered around the bed and explored the room. I woke up feeling very tired after the dream. I glanced at the clock, which read 5:56. If I had looked at it when I first awoke, it would have read 5:55. I mention the dream about deer as others have had screen memories of aliens as deer with big eyes.

July 30, 1996: I had a dream in which I was chosen to go on a shuttle spacecraft. I remember seeing a pitch-black sky and stars out a window. I remembered that I had been on this shuttle before. This time there was an elderly man and woman on board with me. I distinctly remember saying to them excitedly—"Just wait until you see the mother ship!" In addition, I remember seeing long corridors but have forgotten the rest of the dream. I think that I also remember armed guards around the shuttle take-off area. The next morning there were two round dots of blood and a blood smudge on my pillowcase.

May 28, 1998: I awoke to hear a *clicking sound*. I thought it was just the house settling or furniture creaking due to the temperature change. I tried to go back to sleep. I felt nothing. However, the clicks would occur periodically and would keep me awake. Suddenly, there was a barrage of clicks one after another. Instantly, the familiar tingling coursed through my body. I felt like my body was locked in a vise that was pressing in on all sides. I think it stopped and I went to sleep.

I then dreamed that I was back in my childhood neighborhood. I was looking over what used to be woods bordering Dodge Court. However, all the trees were gone and there was just bare dirt. Suddenly, I was confronted by a deer. It walked right up to me and looked me in the eyes. I tried to scare it away. It backed off but then came right after me again. There was a woman present and I asked her why the deer was so tame. She told me that it was always tame with her. I can't remember anything else.

These *clicking sounds* that preceded my strange experiences had started in 1997. They had brought back memories of a probable abductee named John. John was compelled to leave his sleeping daughter and drive to a remote area of Maine called the Airline. His car engine failed and he heard a clicking sound out his right window. When he glanced out, he saw that the sound came from a hovering UFO that aimed a beam of light at him that caused him to slip into an unconscious state. Such sounds had become all too familiar to me. They will be mentioned from time to time in my diary entries.

December 17, 1998: I awoke to use the bathroom. I believe that I noticed the clock read 12:20 as I passed by it. However, when I returned from the bathroom, it read 1:00! As soon as I got into bed, I heard a few clicking sounds and the tingling sensation began. I think I fell asleep but woke up with a start at 4:44. Sometime, either before or after I got up to use the bathroom, I dreamt that I was walking by an apple tree in the woods. There were several deer eating apples off the tree. They stopped and looked at me but did not run. I thought that was strange. Stranger still was when the larger deer walked over to me. It looked at me face-to-face and began nuzzling me.

I do not remember any more of the dream. I wish that I could be sure of the clock and apparent missing time, but it is hard to remember. I had entirely forgotten about the dream of the deer until something brought it to mind after breakfast.

Sometimes Margaret would experience possible *screen memories* in a dream. I mention her following dream because it coincided with my experiencing benchmarks of an abduction experience during the same night. This indicates that both of us may have been abducted. Note that *clock coincidences* continue to occur during these events.

> **November 17/18, 1992:** Shortly after retiring to bed, I got a feeling that something was going to happen—a feeling of apprehension. I dozed, woke up and looked around the room to see if anyone was there. I could see nothing. I dropped off to sleep. Later, I woke up with a start and glanced at the LCD numbers on the clock. They read 3:33. I was experiencing the tingling feeling all through my body. It continued through the morning hours and I found it hard to sleep. It finally dissipated shortly after I got up. Another curious thing was that when we woke up, my wife told me about a scary dream. It involved two scary-looking wolves looking through a window at us. I got up and brought them in. I told her that I could tame them and not to be afraid, but she was terrified.

The following diary entry records another occasion when Margaret's UFO dreams coincided with my abduction benchmarks:

> **November 12, 1990:** I awoke during the early morning hours several times with a feeling of great apprehension. It was the same feeling that I had the night that I received the scoop-mark on my leg. I do not remember anything unusual. I did not mention this to Margaret. Thus, it may be significant that she told me in the morning that she **had dreamt about UFOs during the night**. She could not remember her dream. I should add at this juncture that Margaret and I have also awakened from the same night with anomalous physical benchmarks on our bodies.

I should mention in passing that Margaret also has experienced UFO dreams and similar benchmarks.

> **December 19, 1991:** While returning from a visit to my son, Ray, in our car, Margaret suddenly remembered something that she had meant to tell me but for some reason had forgotten to do so. Several days ago, she woke up with a sharp pain on the inside of her right thigh. Upon examining the area, she saw a badly bruised area.
>
> When she went to bed that evening, there was no pain and no bruise. Since it is on the inside of her thigh, she could not understand how she could have received it in bed. She could not remember the date, but it seems to have been during the *same time period* that a scab/sore reappeared on me. She told me

that it hurt so badly when she first got up [before me] that she was limping for awhile. I examined it this evening. There were two localized irregular fading bruise marks about an inch apart that were red and yellowish in color and a about an inch and one half in length and about one inch in width. I could not really examine them more closely as she would have suspected my intentions and their equation with the UFO phenomenon. That would have caused new problems.

The next entry is particularly interesting as it concerns both Margaret and I finding identical anomalous punctures on our bodies.

November 10, 1995: I have had a small puncture on my thigh for a few weeks. It is probably just some kind of an insect bite. It itches and bleeds easily if disturbed. I mentioned it to my wife this evening. She told me that she had the same thing on her thigh. It had itched for a few weeks and had filled with pus. I would not have mentioned it in this diary except for the fact that both of us experienced the same thing. Biting insects such as mosquitoes, black flies, etc. have long disappeared.

As mentioned earlier in the book, many times I would experience strange phenomena at the onset and conclusion of my abduction dreams. I would sometimes hear a voice call my name, "Ray," or hear a strange sound. The following are some examples of my abduction dreams that were accompanied by **other strange phenomena**. They were also accompanied by other typical benchmarks of an abduction experience.

OTHER STRANGE PHENOMENA

April 17, 1996: I woke up abruptly when I heard a voice [female?] say "Ray!" and something about "the *other side*." I sat up in bed. The room was lit up with a dim soft light. However, there were no lights on. It was a strange light because everything in the room seemed to be lit-up equally. It should have been pitch-dark. My body had the familiar electric-like tingling feeling. I had a feeling that someone other than my wife [sleeping] and I were in the room. I remember saying in my mind—"Will you show yourselves this time please?" and that "I am ready to see you" but no one appeared. Then, I think I just laid back and went to sleep. I can't remember what time it was. I do remember that it was in the early morning hours.

January 26, 1997: I watched the post-Super Bowl interviews. I dressed for bed in my study, as Margaret was already asleep. I entered our bedroom and glanced at clock. It read 11:11. I lay wondering when the next strange incident would happen. I started to doze off but awoke when I heard my name, "Ray," softly called once. Again, it was a female voice. I tried to get back to sleep but began to feel familiar "tingling" sensation. I must have gone right to sleep because I awoke later hearing a "bell" sound.

My dream involved a human-looking man changing into an alien. He chased me down a large corridor. It also involved me looking at a bulletin board with a series of still photographs taken from the air. First, it appeared that they were taken from way above the earth. Then they appeared as if they were taken from up close. The pictures were of a complex of whitish buildings. They were located in the middle of a valley surrounded by mountains.

Upon awaking, I thought that the alien's face looked similar to the face of a creature shown during an advertisement for *X-Files* that I had seen earlier in the evening. I thought that this was a catalyst for my dream until I saw my pillowcase. It had a two to three inch circle of blood on it that was soaked into the pillow. I examined my head area thoroughly, including the inside of my nose, but could not find any blood anywhere.

Anomalous phenomena have also awakened me when a possible abduction dream is not remembered. A few examples follow. Note the fact that I awake with *a sore right nostril*. During a later discussion, you will recognize its significance.

January 27, 1995: I awoke twice to a brief electronic beeping sound. The second time I thought it was my watch alarm sounding and actually reached to shut it off just before the beeping stopped. My right nostril is still sore.

January 28, 1995: I woke again to a brief electronic beeping sound and again reached for my watch alarm, but it was not the watch. My right nostril is still sore.

As mentioned, an abductee awakes from a dream to find himself in another dream that in actuality is the abduction experience. The next entry may be a case of this kind.

February 11, 1998: Sometime during the night I awoke to a clicking sound and the onset of the tingling sensation. It got stronger as more clicks ensued. When I tried to resist, I fell asleep. Later, I dreamt that I woke up. I somehow knew that I was not supposed to open my eyes and look at the clock. I lay in what seemed to be a semi-awakened state or in a dream dreaming that I was awake. It seemed as if my body was in a cast. I could not open my eyes. I was paralyzed. Then, later, I opened my eyes and glanced at the clock as it flicked to 4:44. I went back to sleep and woke to see the clock flick to 5:55.

Again, dreams of being abducted may not be of an on-going abduction. It may be a memory of a past abduction. It suddenly surfaces in a dream like a flashback does in a waking state. The following may be representative of this type:

> **September 19, 1998:** I awoke with a start from an abduction dream. In spite of all the unusual things that happen, I rarely remember actual abduction dreams. In any event, I was driving in my car when an object dropped down in front of the car. I felt myself pulled up. Suddenly, I was in a bright room with shadowy figures moving around. I woke up, used the bathroom, and went back to bed. Later, I awoke with a strong feeling to turn over and look at the clock. I did. It read 5:55. In the evening, I glanced at the clock again. It read 11:11.

The next entry concerns my experiencing another benchmark: Dreams of **aliens, doctors, and operations** among several others.

ALIENS, DOCTORS AND OPERATIONS

> **November 16, 1998:** I had a dream about being abducted—probably because abductions are always on my mind. However, I feel that I should record every dream that involves abduction. Much of the dream has slipped back into the unconscious. However, there are portions of it that I am able to retain. Basically, I am with a doctor. He looks human but I know that he is an alien entity although I cannot remember what his face looked like. He is dressed in a white smock. He had conducted some kind of test on me with a needle. He seems to be injecting what he took from me into a device made up of several thin glass tubes filled with a colored liquid. The tubes are connected to each other in a vertical position.
>
> The doctor asks me to print out my home address. I do, on a scrap of paper. I am then told that it is time for me to be returned home. I look around. I am puzzled that all of the writing I see in the room is in English. I ask why this is so because they are alien. I am then shown some kind of identification plaque on a device. It is golden in color and has what appears to be hieroglyphics engraved on it. The doctor tells me that I would forget what had happened. I tell him that I want to remember and that I will remember.
>
> Then I am taken from the doctor's office into a large room. It looks like a typical commercial warehouse one would find on earth. This confuses me. I am led to a ramp that leads to what looks like a typical parking lot for cars. As I glance behind me, I am amazed to see the human-like person who had accompanied me fade into a non-human shape. I quickly go down the ramp and yell, "I still remember" and try to get away. The entity comes after me. He is still wearing human clothes, but his face is half-alien and half-human. He

grabs me and forces eye contact with me. He tells me that I must not remember. I wrestle with him and call out for what looked like two humans watching to help me. That is all I can remember.

February 11, 2000: A few hours after I got out of bed this morning I received a flashback to a realistic dream. In the dream, I was in a small rectangular room lying down on something. To my right was a rectangular window or transparent opening connected to another similar room. I sat up and glanced through the window. I was shocked to see a perfectly *nude* woman lying on a table set up parallel to the window or opening. Her head was to the left. The woman was being examined or operated on by some humanoid figures dressed in white smocks. I cannot remember what their faces looked like. That is all I can remember.

February 23, 2000: About a week ago, I had a very realistic dream about going through two shiny metal doors. They seemed to disappear or open so fast that I could not see them just before entering them. I remembered seeing some kind of panel with spark-like numbers flashing on it. The strange thing is that each of the several times I remembered the dream, I planned to enter it in the diary. I forgot it until today.

One of the most embarrassing benchmarks is awaking with **anomalous effects in the area of the genitals**. Females experience similar pain around the naval and genital areas. This is significant because the aliens' primary interest is in the abductees' reproductive organs.

SORENESS AROUND GENITALS

Female abductees report needles being inserted through their navel and eggs being removed. Male abductees report semen being taken from them during alien examinations and operations. These experiences are usually forgotten except for occasional memory flashbacks. It requires hypnosis to break through the mental block that has mercifully kept such memories from surfacing to the conscious mind of abductee. Nevertheless, such operations leave telltale clues behind. These are in the form of synchronistic soreness and physical marks on and around the navel and genitals.

I had experienced such soreness before but never equated it with other bizarre experiences. Looking back, I don't know why I did not, unless I was somehow mentally programmed to dismiss it. The remainder of this chapter will deal with this disturbing benchmark. I first decided to begin recording it in my diary in late 1994.

November 19, 1994: I awoke to a pain in the crotch like something had scraped the area under and behind my testicles. I could see no scrapes, although the sore area is concentrated in one place. It has a different skin texture that feels like a scab. I have experienced this before. According to my diary entries, the pain persisted for several days before gradually disappearing after a period of itching. It felt like a healing process was taking place.

Over the next several days, the pain became less. It was replaced by itching that, in turn, faded away. A few months later, the same anomalous ailment appeared. It coincided with a number of [perhaps connected] happenings that heralded the beginning of the New Year. The following are diary entries recorded a few weeks before the next painful period involving the area behind my testicles. They are also recorded in the chapter entitled *Clock Coincidences*. They are *repeated* because of their proximity in time to others like them. The wounds in the genital area also coincided with fleeting remnants of an abduction dream. As usual, *clock coincidences* were in high gear!

January 1, 1995: I woke up with a start. I got out of bed to go to the bathroom and noticed that the clock read 1:11. Later, I woke up again. I opened my eyes facing the clock, which read 5:55. Later, when taking a shower and soaping the inside of my right thigh, I felt a roughness. After showering, I pushed my skin around to see what it was. There is **a straight-line scab** that measured one inch long and about one sixteenth of an inch wide. I could not see it without a mirror or pushing my skin around. I never would have noticed it unless I just happened to rub my hand against it while soaping my leg.

The hardened blood has the same appearance and texture as the cut that appeared on the hairline of my forehead the night of 12/26/94. It is perfectly straight. It looks like a razor cut that bled and scabbed up. The area around it seems slightly bruised. Oddly enough, it does not hurt, although one would think a cut of this size would hurt. The one on my forehead does not hurt either. Straight hairline cuts are one of the benchmarks of a UFO abduction experience.

January 2, 1995: I woke up with a start at 1:11, 3:33. 4:44 and 5:52. I then felt as if I had to keep glancing at the clock until it read 5:55. I had a dream. It left me with a strong innate impression that people could be taken and experimented upon by entities without their knowledge. I cannot remember the actual contents of the dream. It faded away. [Note: Three days later on January 5, 1995, I woke up at 2:22 a.m. On January 7, 1995, I woke up at 5:52 but felt I must watch the clock until 5:55 a.m. On January 8, 1995, I got out of bed to use the bathroom and noted that the clock read 4:44 a.m.]

Then, the pain in the area of my genitals coincided with an apparent period of *missing time*.

> **January 18, 1995:** I woke up and went to the bathroom. It was 1:30. I returned to bed and glanced at the clock, which read 1:31. I covered up and glanced at the clock again. [I did not put my head down on the pillow.] It now read 2:31, exactly one hour later. Did I fall asleep for an hour and wake up? It didn't seem so. I felt wide-awake. Then, after falling to sleep, I awoke again to watch the clock change from 5:54 to 5:55. During the next day, I noticed the familiar pain in the area under and behind my testicles in the same place that this has occurred before. Again, the sore area is concentrated in one place. No blood was noticed on my underwear.

On the following day, my curiosity got the better of me. I decided to closely examine the painful area for a cut or puncture.

> **January 19, 1995:** The soreness under my testicles persists. It is very painful when pressure is placed upon the area. This is especially so when I sit in certain positions. As in the past, I could not get into a position where I could use a magnifying glass to examine this area. However, this time, I remembered that we have a magnifying mirror and I used it to examine the sore area. There seems to be a small one eighth to one quarter of an inch slit of exposed hardened flesh with no signs of bleeding around it. It is located directly under the testicles and intersects the cord-like structure that runs between them.

Again, the pain in the slit area persisted for a few days before scabbing, itching and finally ceasing.

> **January 20, 1995:** I woke up, turned over and glanced at the clock, which read 4:44. The pain described in the last entry is subsiding a bit unless I sit in certain ways. It is starting to itch a little. This seems to be a repeat performance of what I previously described in my 11/19/94 entry!

> **January 23, 1995:** The slit now has a white flaky scab over it. The pain and itching has stopped.

The repetition of this painful benchmark was bothersome. I did mention it in vague terms to Margaret a few times, as I did not want to worry her. I felt embarrassed to talk about it with anyone else. I wondered if I should consult a medical doctor who was involved in UFO research. It was at this juncture that I seem to have received a synchronistic answer to what might be going on. It was by another one of those incredible *corresponding coincidences of the TV kind*!

February 23, 1995: I awoke at 2:22 and 4:44. Then, around 6:30 (?), I again awoke to a sound like my wife's alarm clock, but it was not. Later in the morning, as I was preparing to teach an evening course on UFOs, I experienced a strange synchronism. For some reason, my mind was very much on the *small painful cut* that I found just behind my testicles on January 19. It concerned me so much that I was planning to call Walt Andrus, the director of MUFON, to get the name of a M.D. to see if the location of the cut was significant. However, the following synchronistic events gave me the answer that I was seeking!

Mid-morning, I went downstairs to have a cup of coffee. I decided to sit down in the living room while I drank it and switched on the TV. The *Phil Donahue Show* was on. His guests had special stories to tell about fertility problems. One woman told how she had been inseminated by her dead husband's sperm. It had been removed before his death from cancer.

Another involved a couple who had the wife's eggs fertilized outside of the womb and then frozen for future use. However, marital problems resulted in a divorce. The wife wished to use the fertilized eggs to conceive a child. The ex-husband wanted the fertilized eggs used for scientific research and then destroyed. A judge ruled that the wife could use the eggs. At this point, I was just about to shut off the TV when I suddenly received a *strong mental suggestion* to stay tuned. I felt if I did so that the answer to my question about the cut's location would be resolved. I laughed to myself and sat back to see what would happen next.

The next guest was a man who had been paralyzed from the waist up due to a motorcycle accident. He was unable to ejaculate and therefore was unable to father a baby with his wife. This was overcome by the use of an electric prod to stimulate the nerves that produced ejaculation. Sperm was obtained and the couple was able to have a baby. At this point, I thought that my premonition was imaginary. I almost shut off the TV. However, when Donahue interviewed the doctor who used the electric prod, I felt compelled to stay tuned. Again, I got a *strong mental impression* to be patient and stick around to see what was coming next.

The doctor then went on to talk about a *new procedure* being used to obtain sperm from men who were unable to ejaculate. He explained that sperm was removed directly from the male's *epididymis*. Now very curious, I went to my study, and looked up *epididymis* in a textbook entitled *Concepts of Human Anatomy and Physiology*.[2] [Interestingly, this also was part of the meaningful coincidence. I had recently borrowed it from my daughter-in-law. I was going to use it to see if the location of a certain scar had any anatomical or biological significance.]

The text stated that the tail of the *epididymis* and the *ductus deferens* store the sperm that is to be discharged during ejaculation. I then looked up the function of the *ductus deferens*. Concerning its function, the book stated that: "Sympathetic nerves from the pelvic plexus serve the *ductus deferens*. Stimulation of these nerves causes peristaltic contractions of the muscular layer. This forcefully ejects the stored sperm toward the ejaculatory duct."

Next, I read about the location of the *ductus deferens*. The textbook stated that: "Much of the *ductus deferens* is located within a structure known as the *spermatic cord*. I located the *spermatic cord* on a diagram of the male sex organ. It showed the exterior cord where the exact location of my cut was located. This exterior cord is called the *external spermatic fascia*.

Perhaps the location of the cut is strictly coincidental. Perhaps I am getting more paranoid because of the strange things that happen to me. However, it would seem that the position of the cut was significant. It would be an excellent place to insert a probe to extract sperm from that segment of the *spermatic cord*. The cut is located just above where it divides and supplies sperm to each side of the testis. This method was exactly what the doctor on the *Phil Donahue Show* was describing!

I must admit of having chills go up and down my spine when I examined the diagrams in the anatomy book. I knew that one of the primary interests shown by the UFO entities is the reproductive systems of humans. Male abductees consistently report semen extraction during their alien physical examination. At this thought, a wave of depression swept over me, bringing me to the point of near tears.

Unfortunately, incidents of this nature did not stop. They continued periodically. I continued to record this painful synchronistic phenomenon in *SynchroFile*.

August 16, 1995: Awoke at 4:43 and 5:53. Both times, I felt that I must look at the clock until it changed to 4:44 and 5:55 but think I fell asleep. My pillow had bloodstains on it in the morning. They are apparently from the nose area. However, I felt no soreness or had no visible cuts on my face. However, my right inside thigh had a cluster of three small bruises.

Again, I noticed a pain in the area under and behind my testicles on the *external spermatic fascia*. This time there was no visible cut, just a tiny sore place with flaky skin. It was not as painful as before, when it hurt to even sit down. As mentioned earlier, this would be an excellent place to insert a probe to extract sperm from that segment of the spermatic cord. It is located just above where it divides and supplies sperm to each side of the *teste*. I also have three puncture marks on my right shoulder.

August 17-23, 1995: The pain from the location described in the last entry has subsided a bit each day until all that remains now is the tiny flaky spot.

September 7, 1995: [While visiting my wife's mother in England], I was awakened from a sound sleep by a voice that said, "Hey, Ray!" We had no visible clock in the bedroom, but I believe it was during the early morning hours. Later, I noticed the usual bloody scab on the back of my neck. I can also see and feel a tiny scab in the flaky area of my *external spermatic fascia*.

The next synchronistic occurrence took place on the *same date* that I had a *similar experience* a year earlier on January 18, 1995! It, like others, was preceded and accompanied by other benchmarks of an abduction experience.

January 18, 1996: A number of strange things that may be connected have happened over the past few days that I kept forgetting to record. On the night of January 16/17, I woke with a start. I felt like I had been dropped into the bed. Since I was under the blankets, it must have been a dream unless it was an OBE. The next day, January 17, I felt soreness under my testicles. It was not as intense as it has been in the past. I fully intended to check this area in a mirror. For some reason, I forgot about it until the next day when I felt the area with my finger and rubbed off a scab. A check with a mirror revealed no visible cut under the scab as has been noted on other occasions.

Today, January 18, after taking a shower, I noticed two identical, fresh straight-line scars. There was one behind each shoulder. Each is about ½ inch long. Also located beside the scar on my left shoulder were two shallow round indentations. These resembled two small circles touching each other. One cannot see them clearly unless the light is right. However, I can feel the indentations by running a finger over them. I have no natural explanation for these things. In the past, I have found anomalous scars just behind my shoulders.

The unnerving, painful abduction benchmark in the area of the *spermatic cord* did not abate during 1996 nor did the other benchmarks that accompanied it. As usual, I would keep forgetting to examine it and record it my diary. It was as if *something within* was telling me that it was not important and to forget it. However, each day I would be reminded because of the soreness. This was so strange!

September 23, 1996: Several days ago, I felt soreness under my testicles but not as sore as on other occasions. Back on January 18, I fully intended to check this area in a mirror but for some reason forgot about it until today when I rubbed a scab off a small painful slit. One would have thought that I would have recorded this immediately. However, for some reason I kept forgetting about it. I forget even after feeling pain and noting that I must examine the area and record it.

Coincidentally, just as in the January 18th incident, I have scabbed-over gouges on my right buttock. This evening when I went to bed and turned out the light, I glanced at the clock, which read 11:11. This continues to happen in the daytime and this evening I received Email from yet another UFO investigator who also is experiencing *clock coincidences.*

October 29, 1996: I awoke at 4:44. I feel a little soreness under my testicles in the same area as other times. There is no slit or scab, just crusty skin.

Seven months later, this phenomenon struck again. It again was preceded by other benchmarks of an abduction experience throughout the month. In the meantime, something new was added to the abduction bumps-in-the-night. It had picked up in intensity in 1997. I was now being awakened by sharp snapping, clicking sounds in addition to voices, bells and tones. Sometimes this happened on a nightly basis! I found that I could not get a good night's sleep and felt overtired. My 1997 diary is filled with entries about these nerve-wracking phenomena. Several of these events occurred just before my next round with this now familiar painful experience. A few examples of these kinds of wake-up calls follow:

BELLS, CLICKS AND TONES

March 11, 1997: I woke up with a start. I heard the now familiar snap sounds in the same corner of the room. I felt a chilling sensation move slowly from my feet to my head. It felt like having a cool tingling blanket being pulled over you. I then went to sleep.

March 29, 1997: I awoke [with a start] hearing a high-pitched tone in my right ear. I lay awake listening to it for about a minute before it faded away. I then got up to use the bathroom. When I returned and got into bed, I watched the clock turn from 2:21 to 2:22. Later, I awoke again as the clock turned from 4:44 to 4:45. Still later, I awoke and tossed and turned. I finally sat up in bed looking at the clock, which read 5:55.

March 30, 1997: I awoke [with a start] at 12:02 to what sounded like my wife's alarm clock going off. However, it was not in the room nor was it set for this time. Later, the town fire whistle went off and woke us at 2:22. [This has happened before.] Still later, I was awake at 4:44 but cannot remember what woke me up. I found two tiny spots of blood on the pillow that look as if they came from my nose.

Several days later, I again awoke with a sharp pain and a scabbed cut in the same area of my genitals.

> **April 2, 1997:** I was awakened with a start by a bell-like sound at 12:09. I awoke again staring at the clock, which read 5:55. Pain under my testicles. Same as before.

The nightly bouts with anomalous sounds that brought on the tingling sensations continued on to the next occurrences of this painful benchmark. Some examples follow:

> **April 10, 1997:** I woke with a start at 2:22. Got up, went to bathroom and lay down in bed. I heard the familiar snapping sounds to the front and left of bed. I felt a cold creepy feeling covering my body and felt a presence in room. Then, I felt like I began to spin round and round. It was like being on a Ferris wheel that sped up and was out of control. I fell asleep and awoke as the clock changed from 5:55 to 5:56. This was similar to experiences recorded on February 7, March 5 and 11.

> **April 16, 1997:** I awoke and went to the bathroom. The clock read 2:22 as I got back into bed. I decided to stay awake to see if the snapping sound would come from the same area as it has before. It did. Again, I felt a presence in the room and a creepy feeling came over my body. This time I was determined not to go back to sleep although I felt like I should. I resisted sleeping. However, the feeling to do so grew stronger, stronger. It then developed into the familiar tingling feeling that I have felt before. Within several seconds my body felt like every part of it was vibrating.
>
> I have felt this before prior to what I think might be OBE experiences. The next thing I knew, I woke up to see the clock turn to 4:44. When I woke up later in the morning, my wife had left early for swimming. I stared at the corner of the room where the snapping sound had come from and heard two more snaps. Nothing happened afterwards. I still wonder if the snaps are just the house settling. Perhaps the seeming connection is only coincidental. I will continue to record these events.

At times, I would try to fight the tingling effects brought on by the snapping, clicking sounds by sheer mental exertion. Whatever was causing the click-like snaps would counter every mental countermeasure that I took. I finally would give in and drift off into oblivion. The situation reminded me of aliens called the *Borg* featured in the TV *Star Trek* series. They told their victims that "resistance is futile" when assimilating them into their hive-like society.

The next entry describes how I tried my utmost to resist the powers behind these events to no avail. I again awoke with a sore wound behind my testicles and blood on my bed sheet. The latter seemed impossible because *there were no bloodstains on my pajamas*!

> **December 31, 1997:** I had a bad night. I awoke hearing a click and feeling the usual tingling effect. I fell asleep but then awoke screaming and hitting my wife from a dream about being chased by a wild pig at exactly 3:33. Afterwards, I found it hard to sleep and the clicks started again. When I resisted the tingling feeling, it would start to subside but then another click would increase it again. This was like a tug-of-war and at one point when the tingling was the strongest, I felt part of me *rising out of my body*. I fell asleep but awoke later feeling anxious. I could not sleep well for the rest of the morning. I seemed to rest in a half-awake state.
>
> When I got up in the morning, I noticed four drops of blood on the sheet where my body had lain. I wore heavy pajamas and underwear. These would have prevented blood from getting on the sheet from my body! I again felt a sore place under my testicles. There was a tiny, rough, scab-like point in the same place as before. Unlike other times, I am not experiencing any *acute* soreness and pain. Also, the blood drops were in a similar pattern to those found on my pillow described in the December 1st entry.

Although not as painful as in the past, soreness did persist for almost two weeks according to the following diary entry:

> **January 10, 1998:** The area under my testicles is still sore. Last night, [I am note sure when.] I awoke to two loud clicks and the tingling sensation. I attempted to make it stop by sheer mental concentration. It started to subside, but I don't know what happened next. In the morning, I found the familiar dried scab of blood on the back of my head on the hairline.

The click phenomenon continued unabated through 1998. The resultant effects were similar to a sleep disorder. My wife insisted that she did not hear any clicks. She wondered what I was talking about when I casually mentioned them to her. They now seemed to be the common catalyst for the onset of the tingling sensation. It became so common that I would find myself mentally talking to it or someone. It was as if, deep within my unconscious, I knew what or who was behind the phenomenon.

Going through the 1998 diary, for example, I find myself spontaneously telling it or someone that I would not fight it. I would go, but would like to know what was going on. Or, "Why are you doing this now? I'll be getting up in an hour or so!" Or, "I'm tired and need a good night's sleep. Please leave me alone tonight!" Or, "I don't mind going, but I do want to see you." Or, once, after losing a mental battle trying to overcome the tingling effects instigated by the clicks, I said, "How did you do that?"

As in the past, the tingling sensation would be accompanied by other anomalous synchronistic occurrences that reflected many of the benchmarks of a UFO abduction experience. However, it would be over a year before I again suffered pain in my testicles.

> **April 11, 1999:** I have pain under my testicles in the same area as in the past. I cannot see any puncture or scar. It is interesting that its appearance coincides with the recent reoccurence of the tingling episodes.

The next occurrence of this particular benchmark did not occur until almost three years later.

> **March 16, 2002:** I had a flashback to an experience that took place on the previous night. It involved the tingling sensation that I have experienced in the past. It started with a clicking sound just as it has in the past. However, in this new house in Maine we often get clicking sounds when the baseboard heaters heat up. It is hard to say whether it was this or something else. However, it came on suddenly and extremely strong. And suddenly I felt as if I were vibrating all over. Then I felt as if I melted into nothingness.
>
> In the morning, I had the same pain under my testicles that I have experienced before. As in the past, there was a raised lump-like scab directly on the exterior segment of the *spermatic cord* called the *external spermatic fascia*. That same night I also had a dream of being out of bed on the floor. I was struggling with something that I could not see. I was **out of my body** looking at myself on the floor in the dream.

> **April 24, 2003:** I was having a dream about being in bed asleep. All of a sudden, a bright light shined in my face and I felt as if I were wrapped up in something dark and lifted right out of bed. When I awoke afterwards to use the bathroom, my body was vibrating with the typical tingling sensation that I have felt during past strange experiences. The last time that this occurred was on March 16, 2002.

Although this book is primarily addressed to readers interested in synchronicity, I trust that suspect abductees and UFO researchers will also find my recorded experiences helpful. Perhaps readers will be less critical and more empathetic towards those who claim abduction experiences. Those who suspect that they may have been abducted will find the benchmarks discussed valuable. They may attest to the reality of their own experiences and bring them to some kind of closure. I trust also that UFO researchers who read this book will find my recorded experiences valuable for study and evaluation. But, now it is time to discuss one more benchmark. It is distinguished from all others. It is a *physical object* left behind from an alien abduction. Researchers call it a **Nasal Implant!**

NASAL IMPLANT

The reader will have noticed that many times the blood spots found on my pillow matched where my nose had lain. From time to time, I would poke my finger up my nostrils to see if anything was there. Once, I felt something round but believed that it was just hardened blood. After awhile it disappeared and I thought nothing more about it. This in itself was unusual. One would have thought that I would have had more interest in what might have been happening to my nose. Later, I began remembering abduction dreams of aliens operating on my nose. Then I began seriously wondering if that was really the cause of these repetitious drops of blood on my pillow. The first such abduction dream that involved my nose was recorded a little over a year into my **decade of diaries** study.

> **March 29, 1991:** Last night in the early hours of the morning [I cannot remember the time], I had a very realistic dream. I suddenly found myself lying in a bright room with three entities. One looked human. He was bending over me. The other two were the typical *grays*. One was shorter than the other. I can't remember what the human entity was wearing or what he looked like. I can't remember what he did or said. The two *grays* were dressed in form-fitting white coveralls.
>
> The smaller one was reassuring me that I would be okay. He seemed nice. The taller one just stared. I had the feeling that I knew all three of them and that I did not like the tall one. What woke me up [in the dream] was the feeling that something was touching the *right nostril of my nose*. I remember opening my eyes and seeing one of them holding a needle-like device. It had a small, right-angle-like hook on its end. Before opening my eyes, I could only feel, not see. I could not move and was lying down. I felt something being pushed into my nostril and prying it open.
>
> It was painful at first but then became numb. I could still feel my nostril being expanded. Then I felt blood begin to flow profusely out of my right nostril. I felt completely helpless and thought that it might be all over for me. I resigned myself to the worst. Then, whatever it was was removed from my

nose. I found that I could now at least move my right hand. I immediately reached up, cupped it over my nostrils, and felt blood still coming out.

The next thing that I remember was being alone with the small gray, who again reassured me. I felt that he was caring and friendly. I lay there and could move again. However, for some reason I was not frightened and did not try to get away. The small gray asked me if I wanted to see something. [Telepathically?] I think it was a book or diagram that depicted what had just been done to me. I reached for it. However, no sooner had I started to look at it than the taller gray came in from my right. He saw me with whatever it was. He demanded to know who gave it to me and was angry at the small gray. I could hear and recognize his voice *in my head* from somewhere. His voice was different from the smaller ones. It was stern, uncaring and businesslike.

I then saw what looked like a paper or plastic cup of water. It was on a table-like piece of furniture pulled alongside where I had been reclining. I was now sitting up. I asked if I could have a drink of water, as I felt extremely dry. The taller one just gazed at me and said "no" very sternly. The next thing I knew was that I woke up in my bed from what seemed to be a very realistic nightmare. I felt that I must remember it so I reached behind me and put a Kleenex box up on my bureau. I hoped that it would remind me of the dream in the morning.

I got up in the morning still remembering the dream. I got dressed. When I reached to place my pajamas under the pillow, I was shocked. There were some spots of blood on the pillow! I then took a pad of paper and outlined everything that I could remember about the dream. I also examined my nose. I found no sign of bleeding and my nose did not feel abnormal in any way. Unfortunately, when I awoke some parts of the dream were drifting away from my conscious mind. I'm sure there is more to it, but I just can't remember.

Again, the remnants of blood on the pillow were located where my nose would have been. This synchronistically coincided with my experiencing a nosebleed in the dream. As I mentioned before, I would somehow forget such incidents until I reviewed my diary. Stranger still was the fact that I rarely felt any fear or distress after a day or so passed. Even as I review them now, it is as if I am writing about somebody else's experiences. What bothers me is that their content should bother me. I did feel fear and out-of-control emotions when reliving childhood experiences under hypnosis. I have not experienced such raw fear except on four occasions. As mentioned, the first occurred when I experienced a panic attack after describing an abduction dream to UFO researcher, David Webb. The same thing occurred when I started, but could not finish, describing a UFO abduction dream to my literary agent. The same thing happened twice when I met with my former pastor for counseling about my experiences.

The Pastor and I went out to lunch and were chatting away. I felt completely at ease. However, when I started to relate the above abduction dream to him, *I experienced a panic attack*. No sooner had I started to relate the dream than I found myself gasping for breath. I could hardly breathe and, although I tried my utmost, I could not continue to tell him about the dream.

Needless to say, he was shocked and sympathetic. He told me not to continue the account any further. Strangely, we talked about several other experiences without any effect upon me. It was even stranger when I met with him again a decade later. The exact same thing happened when I tried to relate this same particular dream to him. This time I recorded it in my diary. Before proceeding, it would be worthwhile to record this particular entry at this juncture in the book.

> **February 1, 2000:** I kept hearing clicks from the window. I believed that they were caused by the wind. When I got up and closed the window, the noises stopped. However, I was experiencing a mild tingling feeling when I fell asleep. While asleep I had a *flying dream* that took place in the back and front yards of my childhood home at Danvers, Massachusetts. I came to three steps that led to a path that ran along the side of the house. I jumped from the top step and began to float. I kicked my legs, rose higher into the air, and floated up the pathway to the front of the house. I do not remember anything after that.
>
> Today, I met with my former pastor for lunch. My daughter, Sharon, had gone to him and told him about my experiences. She was very upset and wanted him to talk to me about them (experiences). I told him that because of family pressures, I was going to leave the field of UFO research after I had completed my last book on UFOs. He did not condemn me for being involved and felt that the subject should be explored.
>
> The last time I met with him, I tried to tell him about one of my experiences and found that I became so overwhelmed with emotion that I could hardly breathe or talk. I thought that this time I would have no problem. So, I began to tell him about the same experience. It involved a realistic dream of waking up on a table and having something thrust up my nose. Two *grays* [one short, one tall] and a familiar human-looking entity were standing in front of the table looking at me.
>
> I was amazed to find that no sooner had I started to relate this than I almost went into convulsions. A tremendous well of emotions swept over me so fast that I found it difficult to breathe. I tried to talk but could not. I almost cried. It took a few minutes to calm down and I did not try to tell him again. I believe that these reactions spring from complete memories of the incident trying to surface from my unconscious mind. What is strange is the fact that I can describe what happened to me to my peers and to other abductees without experiencing this reaction.

I do not believe that a nightmare could be the catalyst for such dreadful panic attacks. Such panic attacks, in and of themselves, provide further strong psychological evidence for the physical reality of the UFO abduction experience! In any event, the actual climax of the nasal mystery began with another dream. It too left blood behind on my pillow that matched where my nose had lain. This time, however, I could feel *a round object* in my nose!

> **January 1, 1998**: The nighttime clock phenomenon returned, synchronized with the click phenomenon. I awoke abruptly at 2:22 and heard a click followed immediately by tingling. I decided not to resist. I turned over and closed my eyes. At this point, I saw a few rippling parallel lines of light through my closed eyelids. I opened my eyes but saw nothing. I then fell right asleep only to be awakened again at 4:44 and 5:55. When I got up, there were two drops of blood on the pillow where my nose had lain. During the day, I kept putting my finger on the upper right side of my nose next to my eye. I could feel a small, round, hard area. At first, I thought it must be just a bone, except the other side of my nose is smooth in that area. I wonder if I have discovered a bb-like implant.

Throughout each day, I would place my finger on my nose. I would press to see if the object was still there. This time my mind was in turmoil and unlike my usual unemotional responses in the past. According to my diary, the click sounds and tingling sensations continued unabated almost on a nightly basis.

I decided to share the appearance of the nasal object with some of my UFO course students and a UFO researcher who also has experienced benchmarks of a UFO abduction experience. They urged me to have my nose X-rayed. This posed a problem. How would Margaret react if I told her that I might have an alien implant in my nose! From past experiences, I knew she would go ballistic with fear and apprehension. This had been her reaction when my scoop mark appeared. After thinking the matter over, I concocted the following game plan.

One of my daughter-in-laws is a nurse. I told her that I might have a growth in my nose and asked her to feel it. She became anxious and told me that I should have my doctor examine it. I then went to Margaret and told her what she had said. Margaret too became concerned and urged me to have it checked out. I decided to wait until my annual physical to have this done.

> **April 16, 1998:** I had my annual physical today and had Dr. Price feel the object in my nose. He was not sure what it was, other than perhaps an "exostosis" [a bone extension] but felt that an X-ray should be taken in case it was a tumor.

Dr. Price ordered an X-ray for that same afternoon. After the technician took the X-ray, I asked her if I could stay behind and see it after it was developed. She complied and we chatted awhile before going into another room where it hung drying. I can still remember the look on her face and the tone of her voice when she picked the X-rays up. She held them to the light and exclaimed, "What are those things!" I looked at the X-ray, which showed a profile of each side of my nose. There, graphically outlined on the right side of my nose, was a bright, round object **(Photos 2 & 3)**. A similar but fainter object showed up on the left side of my nose. [Later it was determined that the left-handed object might be just a bleed through image of the right-handed object.] I answered that I did not know and asked her what she thought it was.

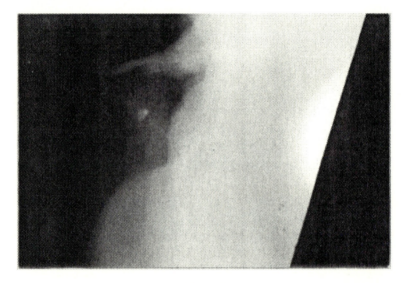

Photo 2

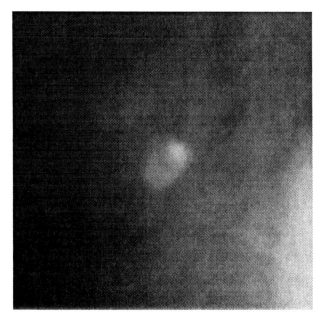

Photo 3

She looked silently at the X-ray for a moment and told me that she was not allowed to comment on what it might be. She insisted that a doctor at the hospital was the only person who could do this. I thanked her and went on my way. I felt uptight and excited about what I had seen. I could hardly wait for the doctor's analysis to come back. When it did, I was very puzzled. He did not mention the round object at all in his report!

> **April 27, 1998:** My doctor's secretary called to say that they did not have the X-rays and that I would have to obtain them from Cable Memorial Emergency Center where they had been taken. She said that she would send me a report on the results of the X-rays if I wanted it. Later, I phoned and asked her to send the report to me. The X-ray technician told me that her section had talked about my *strange* X-ray. She said that they were sent to Medical Records at Beverly Hospital. She assured me that she would request them and have copies sent to me.
>
> **April 29, 1998:** I received a report from my doctor that stated that the X-rays were "normal" but no mention was made of the round-feeling object. The clock phenomenon continues at home and on the car clock.

May 6, 1998: I phoned Beverly Radiology Associates and talked to Dr. James H. Chafey, M.D. who performed the evaluation of my X-rays. I explained to him that I wanted to know what he thought the bright object in my nose might be if it was not *exostosis*, as delineated in his report.

Later, Dr. Chafey called back to tell me that he had taken a more careful look at the X-rays. He had taken particular notice of the object. He told me that it was probably just a calcium deposit. I decided not to tell him of its *recent and sudden appearance*. However, I did ask him what, other than calcium, would show up so brightly on the X-ray. He told me that metal would but that the object would *have* to be calcium. I thanked him and hung up. It was clear that I would have to find someone sympathetic with the abduction phenomenon to evaluate the X-rays further.

May 9, 1998: I awoke at 2:22, 3:33 and later awoke to see the clock turn to 5:55. Later in the morning, I took photos of the X-rays of my nose. When I looked through the extreme close-up lens and focused on the bright round spot, I was amazed to see a perfectly round, dull, silver ball located in what seemed to be a cutout niche in my bone.

May 11, 1998: I awoke with a start at 3:33 and 5:55. I brought the film of the object in the X-ray to Short-stop Photo and picked it up later. The close-up photo shows a distinct bright sphere nestled in what appears to be a small dug-out section in the nasal bone!

July 29, 1998: I have been looking for a UFOlogist/Radiologist to examine the X-ray of my nose. When talking to another UFO researcher, I decided to tell him about the suspected implant. He said that he is a good friend of someone who knew the head of a Radiology Department at a major university who is interested in suspected implants! I'm so glad that I mentioned it to him.

Later, my researcher friend called back and said that he had explained the situation to the radiologist and that he would evaluate the X-ray, keep it confidential and charge me nothing. I will send out a copy tomorrow.

August 5, 1998: My UFO researcher friend phoned today and said that his radiologist friend is quite excited about the artifact in my nose, as it does not seem to correspond with what he has known in the past as calcium deposits. He asked for the frontal nasal X-ray exposure. He is currently analyzing the side view using a sophisticated computerized digital process that should determine whether it is calcium. I sent him the frontal exposure this morning. In the meantime, Margaret answered Peter's call. She is very upset that I am proceeding further with this.

September 8, 1998: I glanced at clock. It read 4:44. I think I feel something new in the right side of my nose. It is located lower than the other object. It could be a bite that has swollen inside, but I see no external marks. I'll monitor it to see if it remains in place or disappears. Strange. I don't feel any irritation there but again found myself inadvertently placing my finger on it before I realized it was there.

These recent, perhaps overnight, appearances of round things in my nose shattered my mind's defensive mechanisms. Perhaps my usual non-emotional response to my experiences was because I only half-believed, or denied, their reality. As long as I could alternately interpret them as nightmares and perhaps somehow self-inflicted wounds, I could contain my Mr. Spock-like composure. But, when physical objects suddenly appear in one's nose, it changes the whole picture. This situation tends to verify the reality of the other experiences. I felt the same when my scoop mark appeared in the aftermath of an abduction dream.

A month passed and still no word came from the radiologist. In the meantime, something totally unexpected happened. I experienced another realistic abduction dream during which one of the two objects was *removed* from my nose!

October 7, 1998: I had a very realistic dream about being in a doctor's office with a doctor. He was examining my nose with an instrument that looked like a slim silver wand. It had a white-lighted bulb-shaped [like a miniature pointed Christmas tree bulb] end. The wand's diameter was about one sixteenth of an inch and it had a bend in it. When he inserted it up into my nose, it acted like an X-ray and illuminated the oval object in my nose. However, I do not know how I could see this, unless I was looking in a mirror or having an OBE. Then he inserted what looked like another slim silver wand with a wire jaw that could open and close to grasp things. He pushed it up my nose, grasped the object, and pulled it out.

At first, it looked just like a rounded white ball. However, when I looked again it had changed into a tiny square object with what looked like two copper wires protruding from it. When I woke up, I checked to see if I could still feel the X-rayed round object in my nose. It was still there but the new object was not. The funny part is that I had completely forgotten about this dream until late afternoon. When I was looking in the bathroom mirror to shave, it suddenly came back to me.

I would have had to have seen my reflection in order to describe what was happening to me. What is fascinating was the fact that I received a flashback when I glanced in a mirror to shave! Seeing myself in the mirror triggered the memory. When I woke up, I felt a round object in my nose, but only the upper one. The new one that I had forgotten about was *no longer there*. I am not sure when it disappeared, unless this dream was more than a dream. Perhaps it was an actual abduction and the new object was removed that very night!

October 11, 1998: I awoke with a start at 5:55. Later, I glanced at the VCR clock. It read 3:33. My friend notified me that the nasal object mystified the radiology department at the University after using a super-computer to digitize the X-ray image. It was not tissue or bone. It was perfectly smooth and rounded, which eliminated a calcium deposit.

There was also the possibility that the object was connected to the olfactory nerve. However, the image was not clear enough to determine whether this was so. The radiologist told me only that the ovoid object had a close relationship to the olfactory nerve as it exits through the cribriform plate. He said that it could not be determined from the images whether the object was directly related to any nerve structure. However, it is interesting that recent research indicates that the olfactory nerve might be connected to the holographic abilities in the brain.

Several weeks later, I had another abduction dream. Its contents faded from my mind, but I do remember saying something to the entities at its outset.

October 31, 1998: I got up to use bathroom. I returned to bed, but before I could fall asleep the familiar clicks began. I decided to resist the usual onslaught of the tingling sensation. I thought that this succeeded when they subsided. However, they then became louder and I surrendered to the feeling. I fell asleep but awoke again to hear clicks. I again experienced the tingling sensation. I remember during one of these episodes saying that, "I don't mind going, but I do want to see you."

In the meantime, the radiologist who was working with my X-rays offered to have the object removed at his facility at the University to analyze. Margaret was really upset and insisted that I not do so. She said that it was probably just a calcium deposit as the local radiologist had stated. Again, I did not want to upset her further, so I complied with her wishes.

The object, whatever it is, remains intact in my nose. Is it an alien implant? I will probably never know. The most one can say for sure is that it, along with many of other things occurring in my life, are common synchronistic benchmarks of what has become known as a UFO abduction experience.

12

Metaphysical Musings

Of the numerous influences operating at every moment, e.g., air, electricity, we sense almost nothing: there could well be forces that, although we never sense them, continually influence us...Ultimately; we understand the conscious ego itself as a tool in the service of a higher, comprehensive intellect.

—Frederich Nietzsche (quoted in)
A History of Philosophy
Frederick C. Copleston

Those readers of my books on unidentified flying objects and near death experiences know that I always have based definitive statements on these subjects on a **what if** premise. I will continue to follow this policy as I now begin to speculate about the variety of synchronistic events experienced by myself, members of my family and others.

The following are just the musings of a layperson and are speculative to the nth degree. However, since this is a book about my experiences, I believe that the reader would be interested in knowing my *impressions* gained from them, as well as from others of a similar nature.

The experiences recorded in *SynchroFile* are varied. There are the inscrutable *concurrent, corresponding* and *converging coincidences*. Then, there are the apparently supernatural *counter coincidences* that include apparent outside intervention, out-of-the-body experiences, precognition, telepathy, time warps into the past and future, and benchmarks of UFO abduction experiences.

Some of the above imply that an *underlying intelligence* intervenes in the affairs of human kind. In my father's case, the intelligence manifested itself in the *visible* form of three robed entities from a lighted object hovering over a naval radio station. They intervened to save my father's life. Thus, is it possible that an *invisible* intelligence also intervenes to cause some synchronistic events? Such intelligence might be invisible to us physically but might interface with another part of us of which we are not normally aware—our spirit, soul or *essence*. A *casual* interacting intelligence would go a long way in taking the inexplicability out of some so-called acausal synchronisms. Where would such intelligence dwell? How would this intelligence obtain intimate knowledge about human beings and circumstances?

I believe that the answers to these questions may be found within the reports of **Near Death Experiences (NDEs), UFO Experiences** and **Contact with the Dead**. If so, it behooves us to examine the distinguishing features of such experiences. This would be a prelude to theorizing how intelligence may be one kind of a catalyst for synchronistic experiences. Let us first examine NDEs and UFO experiences. Others [and I] have found remarkable similarities between them. They appear to be the same phenomenon experienced under different circumstances.

THE NDE/UFO CONNECTION

There are what are called UFO/OBE abduction reports when people are abducted by UFO entities in an out-of-body state of being. If you recall, some of my own experiences appear to be connected to OBEs. What is it that leaves a person's body? Some call it a spirit or a soul but I will refer to it as a person's *essence*.

Conversely, there are persons who undergo an NDE but describe an experience similar to an UFO/OBE abduction. After describing such an experience, Dr. Kenneth Ring, a pioneer in NDE research, states the following:

> Is this an NDE or some kind of UFO encounter? Clearly, it has elements of both, and just as clearly, it threatens to confound our neat dichotomy between these two types of experience. In fact, it is what I have come to recognize as a "mixed motif" case, and as that phrase implies, it is not the only instance in my files. Among my respondents, I have found others who in describing what purports to be an NDE begin to talk about UFOs and aliens in the same context...Could it be that the world of the NDE and that of the UFO abduction, for all their differences, are not, after all, universes apart, but a part of the *same* universe. And, second, could it be that NDErs and UFO experiences have more in common with one another that we have heretofore suspected? Finally, what, if anything, might our two categories of experiencers have in common? [1]

Let us now examine what these two experiences do have in common as we attempt to open and peer through the crack in the mystical door that perhaps leads to the reality behind some forms of synchronicity. First, both involve OBEs.

Out-of-the-Body-Experiences

Again, an OBE involves a situation where someone finds their *essence* moving out of the body into a non-physical realm where they are not visible to those in the physical realm. Although the OBErs are able to see their physical body, other people and objects in the physical realm, they can no longer interact with it. Their body merely passes through physical objects as if they did not exist. NDEs begin with an OBE. The following are NDErs' descriptions of this initial step into another reality:

> "I saw my body in the water" [2] "I drifted up…floating right below the ceiling." [3]
>
> "I was sort of floating…above the street." [4]
>
> "I could see myself in the bed below." [5]

Compare the above experiences with those that UFO abductee Betty [Andreasson] Luca has experienced over the years.

> 1950: "And I'm standing there and I'm coming out of myself. There's two of me there."
>
> 1978: "I see myself coming out of myself."
>
> 1986: "I see myself lying on the couch. I reach down to touch myself. My hand goes right through me."
>
> 1989: "Oh-h-h, and I see myself just sitting there on the side of the bed, and yet I'm here! I'm going inside myself."

NDErs also report approaching a bright light in the OBE state. Sometimes they approach the light through a tunnel or dark place.

Light

> "I saw light going through this tunnel." [7]

> "I was floating and everything around me was dark...And then there it was, a tunnel...with a very bright light at the end." [8]

> "I moved...out through the top of my head...I noticed a bright light up ahead...with a brightness so brilliant it was beyond light." [9]

When alien entities abducted Betty as a teen in 1950, and later as an adult in 1967, she was brought before a huge glass or clear crystal-like door. She was told that she was going *home* to meet someone or something called *The One*.

> 1950: "I went in the door and it's very bright...I'm where there is light."

> 1967: "It [The Great Door] is the entrance to the other world. The world where light is.... Is this beautiful...I'm just engulfed in light."

When NDErs enter the light, they are confronted by a presence (seen or sensed) that radiates and engulfs them with pure unconditional love that is indescribable.

Love

> "I noticed...a bright light ahead...I was absorbed by it as if engulfed by a force field. I cannot describe how it felt, except to say it was inside bliss." [10]

> "I floated...into this pure crystal clear light...I didn't actually see a person in this light, and yet it has a special identity. It is a light of perfect understanding and love." [11]

Betty also found the feeling of unconditional love within the light impossible to articulate with words. When she was brought to see *The One* later in 1989, her face literally glowed with joy.

> 1989: "Oh the Light is all over. It is wonderful. I cannot explain the wonder and beauty and love and peace. It is so joyous!"

In addition to feeling unconditional love, NDErs immersed in the light receive a sense of knowing and understanding reality in its ultimate nature. Everything is part of a whole and fits at together or is *One*.

Oneness

"I could see how everything...fits together." [12]

Betty experienced the exact same understanding when engulfed by the brilliant light that the entities called *The One*.

1950: "I understand that everything is *One*. Everything fits together."

NDErs also meet with tall white-robed entities in the light that appear to be human-like in appearance. Some think that they are angels or a religious figure.

Robed Entities

"The light came closer and closer at a high rate of speed. It then took on the shape of a man in a white robe." [13]

"It was all bright then...He was tall...He had a white robe on." [14]

"He was about seven feet tall and wore a long white gown." [15]

Betty also encountered tall human-like entities. They wore white robes and led her to the great door that was the entrance to the world of light and The One. The following two excerpts are Betty's descriptions of these entities during a UFO abduction as a teen in 1950 and later as an adult in 1978. Note the child's description of the white robe.

1950: "There is a tall white-haired man standing there, and he's got a long nightgown."

1978: "looks like men in white robes."

1989: "I see someone coming now. There's someone—there's a tall person coming dressed in white."

Sometimes NDErs report that these otherworldly entities dressed in white become beings of light!

Beings of Light

"A being was at my side, a being of light." [16]

"Like two people that were coming toward me...just outlines of light."[17]

During one of her adult OBE/abductions, Betty also reported seeing glowing entities. They appeared to be shaped like humans but were composed of light.

1978: And there are other forms that look like people, but they're light...They're just like human forms, but they're light! There's no features."

TURNING INTO LIGHT

After NDErs enter the light, they find that like the light beings that they encounter, they become light beings themselves.

"Suddenly, I was suspended in total light...I was dressed in a flowing glowing light." [18]

"I left my body...I took on the same form as the light." [19]

Betty experienced the identical phenomenon during her adult OBE/UFO abduction experiences in 1978 and 1989. Note that she calls the white robed beings *Elders*.

1978: "My whole body looks like it's becoming light."

1989: "The *Elder* is changing to a white light being and...the *gray* is changing into a light blue one as we're running closer to the light and...I'm starting to change into a golden-colored light! This is beautiful."

NDErs report that communication with the light and the light beings is not audible but is by transfer of thought.

TELEPATHY

"I hear a voice...but like a hearing beyond the physical sense." [20]

"Without talking with our voices...it just registered in my brain." [21]

Betty also reported that communication between herself and her abductors was by mental telepathy.

1989: "The two of them think exactly alike, you know? When the one is talking to me, it is like they're both talking to me, because they have the same thoughts...It's like he's talking somehow to him through the mind."

NDErs describe the place where they have been brought as being a timeless environment.

TIMELESSNESS

"I learned there are no limits, no time...No past. No future. Only right now, this instant." [22]

"I realized that time as we see it on the clock isn't how time really is." [23]

Indeed, NDE researcher Phyllis Atwater writes that:

Almost every single person returns knowing *time does not exist*. They come back knowing time is a matter of consciousness: past and future are really qualities of perception. [24]

UFO abductees Betty and her husband, Bob Luca, both encountered the timelessness of the place where they were taken to by UFO entities.

Betty: "Time to them is not like our time, but they know about our time."

Alien to Betty: "Time with us is not your time. The place with you is localized. It is not with us."

Bob: "There's no time up here. There is no time! And nothing changes. They said: "beyond my understanding."

Both NDErs and Betty were told that the world of light is their real *Home*.

NDEr: [Suddenly he regained consciousness before again dying. He also said] "I shall go to my home. Angels have come to take me away." [25]

NDEr: "I could see my mother...just saying, 'Come on home, come on home.'" [26]

Betty: "They [UFO entities] said, "We're going to take you home...Home is where The One is."

Once at the light-filled door to the world of light called home, neither NDEr nor UFO abductee Betty [Andreasson] Luca wanted to return to their bodies and to earth.

WISHING TO REMAIN IN THE LIGHT

NDEr: "I didn't want to go back. That was the last thing I wanted to do...So, I threw a tantrum...'Why can't I stay?' I yelled." [27]

Betty: "I don't want to go. I don't want to go back. I want to stay!"

The consistent message given to NDErs to bring back to earth with them is that love is the most important thing in the universe. Betty was told the same thing.

LOVE

NDEr: "Love...is the main reason for our existence as human beings in our physical bodies...We cannot fully experience love unless we also know compassion...the ability to know pain and loss—not just our own pain and loss, but the ability to feel the pain and loss of others." [28]

Betty: "He says...love is the greatest of all...because of great love, they cannot let man continue in the footsteps that he is going."

Some components of the NDE are not experienced by UFO abductees. They do not [as many NDErs do] recognize the entities dressed in white robes as deceased relatives or friends. Although Betty was shown a *past* event that occurred in her life, she did not experience a *life review*.

LIFE REVIEW

During this process, the NDEr *instantly* experiences his or her complete past life experiences in a dynamic three-dimensional format. Some feel as if they are actually reliving their lives. They also report that when they are communicating with other people during the review, they also experience their feelings and reactions. Sometimes this is very unpleasant when they involve conflicts with other persons. They feel the other person's hurt and anger as if it were their own.

NDErs are not judged by the otherworldly light or entity. They judge themselves and learn from the experience. What happens after the life review is not known because the NDEr is sent back to earth. NDE Researcher Kenneth Ring provides the following six summarized examples of a typical life review by NDErs for comparison:

1. "The Life Review was absolutely, positively, everything for the first thirty-three years of my life...from the first breath of life right through the accident."

2. "It proceeded to show me every single event in my twenty-two years of life, in a kind of instant three-dimensional panoramic review...The brightness showed me every second of all those years, in exquisite detail, in what seemed only an instant of time."

3. "My whole life was there, every instant of it...Everyone and everything I had ever seen and every thing that had ever happened was there."

4. "Then I was seeing my whole life from beginning to end, even all those little things you forget along the way."

5. "I had a total, complete clear knowledge of everything that had ever happened in my life—even little minute things that I had forgotten."

6. "My life passed before me...even things I had forgotten all about. Every single emotion, all the happy times, the sad times, the angry times, the love, the reconciliation—everything was there. Nothing was left out." [29]

The point to be made here is that the entities that NDErs meet at the doorway to a world of light reportedly are aware of every facet of our past life to the present. They *also know our future*. They know when we are supposed to die!

FUTURE KNOWN

Those who greet NDErs typically give them this same basic message. They are commanded to go back to their body because *it is not their time*. The reason given for sending them is intriguing and relevant to our discussion.

> "It is not time yet…You have work to do." [30]

> "Go back. Your work on earth has not been completed. Go back now." [31]

> "And a voice, a clear voice, said, 'You can't go yet. You have unfinished business.'" [32]

Although UFO abductee Betty [Andreasson] Luca did not experience a life review, the entities that she encountered appeared to have known her life intimately. They physically interfaced with it from time with her abductions since childhood. The entities told her that all things were planned, and predicted things that would happen in her life. They told her about the imminent upcoming death of her two sons, which they could not prevent. Betty was horrified and visited me in a distraught condition just two days before her sons were killed in an automobile accident. I tried to dismiss her anxiety as pure imagination until I received word of their death a few days later.

Another component of the NDE that UFO/OBE abductees do not experience is sensing the potential of attaining *absolute knowledge*.

ABSOLUTE KNOWLEDGE

Dr. Robert Aziz writes the following about the unconscious's potential connection with absolute knowledge and how the NDE is one of the prime synchronistic catalysts for making such a connection:

> For Jung the individual is, through the unconscious, coextensive with the totality. Thus we find in the deepest levels of the psyche the presence of an "absolute knowledge," which moving into consciousness, provides the astute observer with insights into the event of outer reality, past, present, and future. [34] That the individual is conjoined with the totality through the unconscious is indeed *one of the fundamental concepts of the synchronicity theory* [italics mine]. [35]
>
> Some of the most dramatic examples of synchronistic experiences of *absolute knowledge* occur in connection with the power constellation of the arche-

type of the self. And indeed, one very critical situation in which we often find the self powerfully constellated is with experiences of *near-death* [italics mine].[36]

Aziz continues by describing one of Jung's patients near death experience:

> Below she could see herself lying on the bed, "deadly pale, with closed eyes," yet she knew she would not die, and thus was not alarmed by her situation. She knew that there was behind her a world of indescribable beauty and peacefulness. She knew also, however, that as much as she was supported by this knowledge, she could not turn to view this world directly, for if she did, and attempted to enter it, she would certainly die.[37]

Aziz quotes Jung, who states that his patient was able to prove that she was able to observe the physical environment around her when she left her body:

> Only, [Jung relates], when she described in full detail what had happened during the coma was the nurse obliged to admit that the patient had perceived the events exactly as they happened in reality.[38]

Jung states the following about this NDE:

> [This is] an example of an inner synchronistic vision...An experience of the *absolute knowledge* of the unconscious.[39]

It might surprise some not acquainted with Jung's works that he had a near death experience himself during which he too was privy to this sense of *absolute knowledge*. Jung wrote in his autobiography that during his NDE he approached a temple. He felt that if he entered the temple, he would know the full meaning of his existence

> There I would at last understand what had been before me, why I had come into being, and where my life was flowing.[40]

I ascertained from Jung's comments about his experience that had he entered the temple, he would not have returned to the land of the living. Indeed, his experience parallels that of Steve [a church friend of mine], who suffered a major heart attack. He was clinically dead for a short time. During my interview with Steve, he described how his *essence* left his body. He said that he found himself in front of a gate with a bell hovering in mid-air on each side of it. He told me that somehow he knew if the bell rang, he would enter that gate and have absolute knowledge. Steve commented that he also knew that if he entered through the gate that there would be no return.

Another unworldly *intelligence* that reportedly interfaces with human beings is called a *ghost*. Such an event has been dubbed an **After Death Communication** [ADC] by researchers into this phenomenon.

If ADCs correspond to reality, they too could be behind some forms of synchronistic events in our lives. Many books have been written on such events. Witnesses have experienced auditory, visual, olfactory, sleep state, tactile, telephone, symbolic and OBE ADC's. An excellent and well-researched book on this subject is entitled *Hello from Heaven* authored by William and Judith Guggenheim. [33]

Two common types of ADCs are interventions by the deceased *to provide comfort* and *to provide protection*. I have come across a number of these two types myself. Rather than quote from accounts by other researchers, I will restrict the following to those that I have recorded from family and others. If such incidents reflect reality, they indicate that our lives are being watched by those who have passed on.

AFTER DEATH COMMUNICATION

To Provide Comfort

The following incidents involve family members. They appear to have happened to assure us that those who have passed on are all right and are looking after us. If you recall, one of these experiences involved my mother while she was recovering from a heart attack in the critical care unit at the York, Maine hospital. Her mother appeared by her bedside, gave her a reassuring smile and then faded away.

My mother's two sisters, Pricilla and Lois, also had similar experiences. Pricilla had taken care of her mother [my grandmother] in her aging years. She was devastated when she died. She claims that she appeared and comforted her as she had for my mother years later. Lois, on the other hand, had taken care of her Uncle Charles in his aging years and missed him terribly. She claims that he suddenly appeared sitting in his rocking chair, gave her a comforting smile and then faded away.

My Brother John's wife, Kathy, was away on vacation when her grandmother died and felt sad and guilty that she could not have been with her to say goodbye.

John and Kathy have a bell on the door which, when rung, is connected to an intercom so that callers can identify themselves. Shortly after returning from vacation, the doorbell rang and the voice of Kathy's grandmother called her twice. John told me that Kathy turned white as a sheet and hurried down to open the door. When she opened it, there was no one there, but hearing her grandmother's voice gave her much comfort.

I hear about such incidents often from friends and students. Indeed, you will recall earlier in this book that my best friend, Dave Harris, was temporarily comforted by his daughter's voice after she was killed in an automobile accident.

To Provide Protection

Recall also that Dave Harris's deceased mother contacted him to retrieve and protect her jewelry. She told him that it was in a hidden section of her sewing basket that her housekeeper had in her possession. Dave investigated and retrieved the jewelry from the basket. Thus, intervention by the deceased is not only to protect from danger. Sometimes [such as in the next incident] intervention occurs to assure that promises are kept.

My mother was living with us when her youngest sister Pricilla died. My brother and I traveled to Bar Harbor, Maine to represent the family at her funeral. She had left property to my cousin and he promised to pay for the funeral. A few days after I returned, my mother awoke from sleep and burst into the kitchen with a frightened look on her face. Apparently, her sister had appeared and told her that my cousin was not going to keep his promise and that she wanted the undertaker to be paid. However frightening her experience, it must have given my mother assurance that her sister was all right. She told my father to make out a check to the undertaker immediately and send it to him. Nothing was ever said to my cousin about the incident.

My mother passed away on March 8, 1988. Several times since, I have heard or imagined hearing her voice call to me by my nickname, "Buster," and awaking me from sleep. Recently, I had a different kind of experience with my late mother. I have a mild case of *apnea*, which is a temporary cessation of breathing while sleeping. I always wake up suddenly with a snort and have had no serious problems with this condition until one night in September of 2002. The following is recorded from *SynchroFile*:

> **September 22, 2002:** A strange dream? I woke up in the early morning hours after a very realistic double dream. I was dreaming about being in my senior high school class when suddenly I felt someone pulling my left arm. I awoke

out of that dream to see my mother's face and part of her body glowing and hovering over the left side of my bed saying, "Buster, you just stopped breathing!" I believe that there was a brief conversation, which I cannot remember, before she faded away. Then I suddenly found myself back in my first dream.

I was in the classroom again. I walked up to my teacher, Mr. Nolan, and excitedly told him that I had just talked to my mother, who had died some years ago. I felt elated. He did not seem impressed, so I walked back to my desk. The dream continued for awhile. Later, I woke up and used the bathroom wondering if I had really seen my mother or whether it was a dream.

The above experience did not seem like a dream. I distinctly remember waking up abruptly when I felt my left arm yanked. When I heard and saw my mother, I half sat up on one elbow looking up at her for a short time. I think that we conversed for a short time. When she faded away, I sank back onto the pillow and fell asleep. The dream continued, but now it contained what I had just experienced. I wonder if I really had stopped breathing for a dangerous amount of time and that my mother intervened to wake me up

The next examples again involved my cousin Betty and her father, my uncle Charlie. On this occasion, Charlie took drastic measures to warn Betty of the impending death of one of her sons. My sister Dorothy was with Betty at the time and was privy to some very weird events.

It was January 14, 1972, and Dorothy and Betty's two brothers were visiting Betty at her house in Beverly, Massachusetts. It may be significant to mention that one of Betty's brothers lost one of his sons named Peter in an automobile accident in the summer of 1971. Betty also had a son named Peter and another named Paul.

Betty's brothers left for home in the evening. Dorothy remained, as she was to spend the night and the next day with Betty. Later, Betty began showing off some expensive china that she collected as a hobby. One piece was a china plate, hung on the wall by a clasp attached over a screw in the wall. Betty told Dorothy that she took this precaution to assure that it was securely fastened, as it was her favorite piece.

On a table, parallel to the wall and about one and one-half feet from the wall, was another piece of china—two *boy figurines*. Sometime between 11:00 p.m. and midnight, my sister caught a glimpse of the plate suddenly falling outward from the wall and smashing the figurines sitting on the table. They could not understand how the clasp on the plate could move up and over the three eighths of an inch screw head and fall one and one-half feet outward to hit the figurines.

Betty equated the two-boy figurine with her own boys, Peter and Paul. She wondered if this was a sign that they were in danger.

Later, midnight passed into January 15. Dorothy and Betty were sitting in the living room talking when all of a sudden a loud sound of clinking glass erupted from the kitchen. They rushed in and saw glassware shaking on a shelf. Dorothy, startled, asked Betty what was going on. Betty calmly replied that when members of the family get together, her deceased father Charlie made himself known! Nothing else occurred and they went to bed. The next day, around 4:15 p.m., the telephone rang. It was Betty's son, Peter, calling from a payphone in a restaurant. My sister listened to a strange conversation and, after Betty hung up, asked her, "What in the world was all that about?"

Betty told her that Peter's first excited words to her were—"What did Grandpa look like?" When Betty asked why, Peter told her that he and a friend were seated together eating when an old man entered the restaurant and walked right up to him. The man called Peter by his first name and began calling him his "golden boy" and his "Peter Rabbit." Peter was taken aback when the man told him that Peter would soon be coming to live with him!

Peter became annoyed and told the man that he did not know him. He jokingly asked him where he lived if, indeed, he was going to "live with him." When the man replied that he lived with Jesus, that was quite enough for Peter. He told the man to go away and stop bothering them.

The man complied and headed for the door of the restaurant. As he went, Peter yelled out, "Who are you anyway?" The man stopped, turned around and replied, "My name is Charlie and you're coming to live with me in six months!" With that, the man opened the door and walked out.

Peter was shaken. He asked the waiter if he had ever seen the man before, but he had not. As soon as he finished his meal, Peter telephoned his mother, Betty, and asked her what his deceased Grandfather Charles looked like. The man fit Charlie's verbal, and later, photographic description! Not only that, but Betty told Peter that "golden boy" and "Peter Rabbit" were his grandfather's pet names for him as a small child.

Dorothy told me that Betty was upset. She said that Betty did her best to pick up the pieces of the *two-boy figurine* and glue them back together as best as she was able. In doing so, she thought it would save Peter's life. Six months later, Peter was still alive and well, but two years later her son, Paul, died at a young age.

I should mention that my cousin Betty had once died while giving birth to one of her children. She had been pronounced dead from the effects of post-surgical complications. After being pronounced dead, she found herself floating above her body in the operating room prior to the typical tunnel and light experience. Then, she went to and through the light. There, she was escorted by an entity to a beautiful place with buildings. The entity told her that she would have to return to her body. But she was so enthralled with the feeling of absolute love that she did not want to return. The entity reminded her of her husband and baby. This changed her mind and she returned to her body in the hospital room.

Uncle Charlie's physical appearance indicates the ability of the deceased to take on solidity to perform certain tasks. Another example of this type of ADC became known to me during my two-decade investigation of Betty [Andreasson] Luca and her family. If you recall, during one of Betty's encounters with an alien entity, she was told in advance that her two sons were going to die. Their names were Jim and Todd. Betty, however, has another son named Scott. Scott had never gotten over the tragic deaths of his two brothers. They were never far from his mind. However, something that took place several years after their death will be imprinted on his mind for life. The reader will find it incredible, but Scott swears that it actually happened. Here is his story.

Scott travels all over the country installing skylight windows for high-rise buildings. He was working in New Jersey in the fall of 1985 when the incident occurred. One evening, he stepped into a restaurant lounge and got into an argument with three men. Trying to avoid a physical confrontation, he turned his back on the men and walked out of the building. Scott declined to discuss what happened with me personally. It was so bizarre that he only felt comfortable discussing it with family members. Therefore, I had his sister Becky sit down with Scott and take notes as he related his experience to her. I also talked to Betty at length about the incident. The following are quoted excerpts from Becky's written notes and a recorded conversation with Betty about the otherworldly intervention that saved Scott's life:

> Scotty went to leave the restaurant. When he did, they followed him outdoors and into the back alley where he was walking to his hotel room. And they pulled a knife on him. They stabbed him in the lower back, threw him in a dumpster and left him there, probably thinking that he would die.
>
> Some time later, Scotty came to and found himself lying on the cold tar about twenty yards from the dumpster. Evidently, he must have climbed out, stumbled a ways and passed out. It was early in the morning, around three or four o'clock. As he lay there, he felt someone grab him around the waist and lift him up. He heard someone say, "You'll be all right, Scott." Then, as Scott turned around, he was shocked to see his brother, Jimmy, who had been dead for eight years! Jimmy said again, "You'll be all right, Scott." Scott grabbed his

brother's shoulders and said, "Take the knife out!" Jimmy did so, and Scott suddenly felt relaxed.

Scott was holding Jimmy's shoulder and Jimmy was holding him as they walked from the dark alley to a lit street. Scott said the he felt stronger as he walked with his brother to a hospital. When they arrived and walked into the hospital, Jimmy looked down at him and said, "Scott, you did well walking into the hospital." Someone then hollered, "I need a doctor!" A doctor arrived and Jimmy swung Scott to the left as the doctor pulled his eyelid up, checking his eyes. Nurses came running and put Scott on a gurney. And Jim kept on telling him that he was going to be fine and that everything was going to be all right and that Scotty was strong and that he would make it. And Scott watched Jim turn around and leave as they wheeled him away on the gurney into the emergency room. There he had three interior and four exterior stitches because of the knife wound. He never saw his brother again. He still has the scar from the knife wound.

PUT THEM TOGETHER—

And what have you got? You would not have the *Bippity-Boppity-Boo* magic of Cinderella's fairy godmother's magical interventions. Instead, you would have glimpses of a reality that would seem to be truly magical in nature.

For instance: Who or what intervened to save my wife from a falling ladder? Who or what pulled out an electrical plug to prevent our house from being set afire by a blanket on a heater? Who or what warned me about a truck backing out of a driveway as I biked down a hill? These and others recorded in *Synchrofile* certainly exclude chance and strongly imply intervention by *intelligence*. In addition, if we take the accounts of NDEs, UFO experiences and ADC's at full face-value we are faced with *entities* with powers hitherto equated with a divine being.

Such experiences also imply that these entities are controlling our affairs at times to assure that our work on earth is brought to completion. Why do they care? Perhaps it is because we are the larval forms of them. It may be that our connection to them is symbiotic in nature. Charles Fort, a pioneer researcher of anomalous phenomena, concluded that we are somebody's property. He may have been correct! Perhaps we are being *raised* for future life in the timeless realm experienced by NDErs.

It is significant to note that the robed entities and beings of light are humanlike in form. Dead relatives seen during a NDE or an ADC also appear in human form, although at times they appear as *a light being*. The so-called *grays* experienced by UFO abductees appear to be workers for these entities. Their activities are akin to ranchers carrying out medical procedures and genetic experiments upon their cattle. Betty [Andreasson] Luca was told that these workers are *mature human fetuses* taken from surrogate human mothers. They are raised in an artificial womb to maturity. They call themselves *Watchers*. Betty was told that they have been given the physical task of overseeing and *caring for the spirit* in life forms on earth. They told her that their physical operations on humans [and animals] were necessary because life on earth was becoming sterile.

NDEs, UFO experiences and ADCs also give glimpses of a reality beyond the grave that is beyond human description. How can one fathom the concept of *timelessness*? It is no wonder that those who enter such a place believe that they instantly acquire *absolute knowledge*. Time is no longer experienced in a linear fashion. Everything is *now*. They also report entering a realm where they perceive the oneness of all things. This should not seem strange as we are just one of countless interrelated manifestations that *evolved from the light* of the *Big Bang* that also created time and space. If the so-called oscillating theory of the Big Bang were true, the universe would collapse back to the beginning. Everything, including humankind, would revert back to light and to whatever the catalyst was for the beginning of the universe. Perhaps this ultimate *oneness* of all things provides a clue to one of the mechanisms behind synchronistic phenomena.

What if Time really does not exist? Betty [Andreasson] Luca's alien captors told her that our so-called future and past are the same as today to them and that time to them is not like our time. They tried to explain to her that our time is *localized*, but it was not with them.

If what they told Betty is true, perhaps all of the constituents of reality are happening all at once. We, like the needle on a groove of a completed phonograph record of grooves, may be sensing the whole of reality just one needle touch at a time. Maybe tomorrow's events are already occurring in other room-like realities separated from us by the illusion of localized time. What we sense as time may be our passing on to each room one at a time in a linear fashion. We do not sense that all of reality and what we call Time is happening simultaneously.

If the above is true, it would go a long way to account some forms of synchronistic happenings. It would certainly account for people reporting past and future events in the apparent present. It would explain why my father, brothers, others and I have experienced precognitive dreams. It would provide an explanation for how I could see my boss in his office and Margaret on the bed *in the past*.

Conversely, it would show how I could see myself *in the future* walking in my cellar or getting into my car. It would explain my seeing a woman walk by me in old-fashioned clothes and then disappear into her past reality. It would explain why Margaret's niece could experience seeing an old man, long dead, drive by her house in his automobile. It would explain why near death experiencers are able to review all of their life experiences simultaneously. It would provide a reason why NDErs believe that they temporarily acquired a sense of absolute knowledge.

The key to such experiences may lie in the out-of-the-body experience. The OBE experiences of my father and others indicate that this state of being is not restricted to near death experiences. Some people reportedly have artificially induced these experiences. Others report OBEs when they are suddenly confronted with a life-threatening event. In such an event, one's *essence* abruptly leaves the body to escape the pain such an event would engender. People who have been in comas also report their *essence* leaving and returning to the body. Some researchers believe that OBEs occur while we sleep but that we forget these experiences or remember portions of them as *flying dreams*. I like to use the analogy of rooms to visualize our illusion of Time. It is inadequate because time would flow. In this analogy, our past would be still going on in rooms behind our present room. The future would already exist in the rooms ahead.

This being the case, I wonder if the *essence* associated with OBEs at certain times [unknown to the conscious] leaves our physical body during waking hours. What if our *essence* has the capability to travel back to one of the so-called past *rooms of yesterday* where everything is still occurring as now? What if it could bring back what it *experiences* to our conscious minds so that we could experience what it is seeing and experiencing as happening *now*?

Conversely, what if our *essence* could leave our body and travel ahead to the next day's "room of future activities" and transmit what it sees and experiences to our conscious minds to re-experience? If this takes place, it raises the question of why the conscious mind is not always aware of these forays by our *essence*. The answer may be a catalyst that opens a momentary pathway between our *essence* and the conscious mind of our physical body or self. What could it be?

Catalysts could be one's death, an impending danger or other traumatic experience. Such might draw our *essence* forward in what we psychologically experience as time and then back again to the conscious mind in the form of a synchronistic premonition or vision. This could explain why my friend Alan [and many others] had a premonition of his death.

This could also occur in a backward fashion. NDErs [before their *essence* is drawn to the light] describe an ability to instantly travel anywhere they wish. Thus, it would possible for their *essence* to visit and interface with a loved one's *essence* to inform them of their passing. Indeed, many persons have either envisioned or felt the presence of a loved one at the moment of their death.

However, death [and other trauma] would be only one type of catalyst to draw our *essence* to meet and report back on future events. The so-called *essence*, as mentioned, may have the ability to access the collective unconscious. There may be a constant interplay between the two of which we are not normally aware. If the collective unconscious is a repository of the past experiences of humankind, might it also contain the future experiences of humankind? It would be the sum of all the analogized "rooms" of the future that we subjectively move through in a linear fashion. The so-called *collective unconscious* would be analogous to *The One*. It would contain absolute knowledge.

Perhaps during an NDE [and later at final death] our *essence* merges with and becomes one with the collective unconscious when it enters the world of light. Perhaps this gives the NDEr's *essence* the impression of obtaining absolute knowledge. If so, it raises the possibility that our *essence* may be able to make *momentary forays* into the collective unconscious before death *at any time*. In doing so, it could obtain and transmit future objective or symbolic information to our conscious mind or self through synchronistic happenings and dreams.

The above theoretical speculations could account for a number of synchronistic and paranormal events. However, they are based upon two-edged sword premises. The existence of absolute knowledge and the non-existence of time imply that what we experience as freewill is, like time, an illusion as well. Perhaps freewill somehow still could exist under such circumstances, but it is hard to envision. It still might be that each of us freely restructures our personal future into one of many possible futures. If not, the absence of freewill raises uncomfortable moral and philosophical questions. Unfortunately, reality may care little whether we are comfortable about what form it takes.

NDEs, UFO experiences, ADC's and, I might add, ESP experiments, all manifest another possible catalyst behind some forms of synchronistic happenings. These experiences all involve reports of communication by the *transference of thought*. NDE, UFO and ADC entities communicate by *mental telepathy*.

ESP experiments with remote viewing indicate that thoughts are a form of energy that can be transmitted over great distances. If so, perhaps our thoughts are constantly interfacing with Jung's theorized collective unconscious. If so, perhaps the thoughts of all human beings are part of the collective unconscious. This would mean that the *like-thoughts* of everyone would be embodied within the collective unconscious.

Perhaps [because of their like-ness] at times *like-thoughts* would be drawn together and meaningfully interface with the unconscious to the conscious minds of multiple persons via synchronistic events. Those experiencing such events would think they are unique to themselves. They would be unaware that their amazing coincidences were also being simultaneously experienced by others.

If indeed humans are put here for a purpose and are expected to complete a work before going to, or perhaps returning to, the light, it is conceivable that some synchronisms might be staged to induce psychological and emotional growth of character—Jung's concept of individuation. The numinosity caused by such experiences of synchronicity has a powerful effect on human personality. They cause and/or strengthen belief systems and effect deep changes in personality. Therefore, it is possible that they are part of a conditioning program conducted by overseeing intelligent entities. Such would better prepare us for our future in the world of light that lies beyond an earthly grave.

There is, perhaps, the possibility that consciousness is not restricted to what we perceive as organic living systems. There are researchers who theorize that the universe is *holographic* in nature and that consciousness pervades all matter. Remote viewing experiments have shown that people can accurately describe distant locations even when there are no human observers present at the locations. Some psychics are able to identify the contents of a sealed box randomly selected from many similar sealed boxes. Others are able to discern the history of seemingly inanimate objects. Michael Talbot, author of *The Holographic Universe*, writes that:

> If such assertions are true, and we can obtain information not only from the minds of other human beings but from the living holograph of reality itself, psychometry—the ability to obtain information about an object's history simply by touching it—would also be explained. Rather than being inanimate, such an object would be suffused with its own kind of consciousness. Instead of being a "thing" that exists separate from the universe, it would be part of the interconnectedness of all things. It would be connected to the thoughts of every person who ever came in contact with it, to the consciousness that pervades every animal and object ever associated with its existence via the implicate to its own past, and connected to the mind of the psychometrist holding it.

I reluctantly became a witness to the phenomenon of psychometry after being badgered by a woman who wanted me to write a book about her exploits in using it. As proof of her ability, she sent me a box of news clips detailing her assistance in police investigations to find lost persons by holding an object belonging to them. I finally agreed to see her perform and set up an appointment to meet my wife and I.

When she arrived, I gave her a handkerchief. I had carried it in my pocket during a recent vacation in England in July 1980. Margaret, in turn, gave her a necklace that belonged to her deceased grandmother. Neither of us expected anything unusual, so we were shocked by what she had to say.

When she held the handkerchief, she turned to me and gave an excellent description of the isolated modern building that we rented in the rolling hills of Yorkshire. At one point, she described another place that we visited. She said that she could see me standing on something out in the water looking back to land. She also sensed a terrible shipwreck. Coincidentally, I had walked out on a very long dock to view Margaret's uncle's sailboat. While examining the boat, he gave a vivid account of a shipwreck involving a ferry!

The most astonishing results came when Margaret handed her the necklace. She described her grandmother's house inside and out. The grand finale came when she said that she associated the word *Lenwood* with the house. We were shocked. *Glenwood* was the name of Margaret's grandmother's house! There was nothing written on the necklace that would have given her this information. Unfortunately for the woman, my publisher was not interested in a book on the subject.

Obviously, if everything somehow exhibits consciousness, this fact would also be a causal factor behind some synchronistic happenings. Jung felt that many synchronisms are generated by strong emotions on the part of the experiencer. If you recall, my father witnessed an automobile accident and associated weather conditions that had occurred many years ago. Perhaps the emotional trauma experienced by persons in that automobile accident of the past are embedded in the consciousness of the road that Dad traveled. For reasons unknown, he, and others before him, were in the right mental equilibrium that allowed them to telepathically experience the accident.

As I look back of over my *Metaphysical Musings*, it is still hard for me to conceive of a reality that exists without linear time and without cause and effect—especially in regards to synchronisms. Nonetheless, if there is no conscious guiding intelligence of some kind behind synchronistic happenings, then we must accept, at least for the time being, the acausal nature of synchronicity. The seemingly inexplicable nature of synchronistic events may be akin to the inexplicable randomness of nature at the sub-atomic level and will always remain a mystery. It all depends whether Einstein was right or wrong when, rebelling against such randomness, he insisted that, *"God does not play with dice!"*

13

Conclusions

If I were a reader of this book, my first question of the author would be, "How have these experiences affected your life?"

My pastor once asked me how I integrated my experiences into the everyday life of normal reality and, from his perspective, *my faith*. He knew nothing of the repeated incidents of synchronicity in my life. He was referring to my UFO research and abduction experiences. I answered then, and I answer now, that I can find no credible place for UFOs and abductions in theology nor in the reality of everyday living. There very well could be a connection between [for example] these current phenomena and recorded events in the Bible, but such a thought would be highly speculative. Thus, I find myself forced to live a schizophrenic-like double life.

On one end of the spectrum are the reality of family, friends and all the facets of normal everyday life. On the other end of the spectrum are the incredulous otherworldly anomalies that continually challenge that so-called normality. It causes everyday tension as my mind attempts to find a bridging worldview that encompasses the two. Indeed, the very *act of trying to do* this is the catalyst for radical changes in my way of thinking about reality.

Earlier, mention was made of *numinosity* and how it could grip and mold one's personality and worldview. Numinosity is the "emotional glow or fascination or power that an activated archetype inspires in the inner experiences it gathers to itself." [1]

As a child, my experiences with—the *love light*, the *China men* abducting me from bed, the *ball of light* that hovered near my face, the *lady in the light* that floated me toward lights hovering in the sky, the *missing time* experience in the Burley Woods and the *channeled message* to a young girl and myself—did not consciously effect me numinosly until adulthood. However, they most likely had an effect deep in my subconscious life.

Later in life, numinosity did erupt when I recognized their historical connection to my adult experiences. It caused a deep transforming effect upon my worldview. This *converging coincidence* between childhood and adult experiences led to serious self-investigation and even hypnosis to find the answers lying behind such experiences.

The one childhood teen experience that at that very time *consciously* and radically changed my life took place on May 19, 1950. The synchronistic effects directly associated with my teenage conversion experience caused this change. This so-called *born again* experience coincided with a brilliant beam of light from the sky, a rapturous feeling of unconditional love and the now recognized tingling sensation associated with my anomalous experiences. Whatever/Whoever it was, God, UFO entities or Other, I felt that the numinosity of this experience was not *self-caused*. I was thoroughly convinced that it was generated by a power *from outside* my self. Indeed, Jung writes that:

> In speaking of religion, I must make clear from the start what I mean by that term. Religion, as the Latin word denotes, is a careful and scrupulous observation of what Rudolf Otto aptly termed the numinosum, that is the dynamic agency or effect not caused by an arbitrary act of will. On the contrary, it seizes and controls the human subject, who is always rather its victim than its creator. The numinsoum—whatever its cause may bem—is an experience of the subject independent of his will. At all events, religious teaching as well as the consensus gentium always and everywhere explain this experience as being due to a cause *external* to the individual.[1]

That numinosity of that early experience engendered a belief system that changed my whole way of thinking. I became a fundamentalist Christian. After serving in the USAF, I attended Gordon College of Liberal Arts where I majored in Bible and New Testament Greek. I began attending what is now Gordon Conwall Seminary to study for the Christian ministry. However, I dropped out after one semester because of intellectual problems with theology.

I still attend church but am much more liberal in my theology and way of thinking. My main interest now is in the practical, rather than the theological, side of Christianity. Nevertheless, because of that childhood conversion experience I could never break away from Christianity in some form. This numinous experience was my initial conscious initiation into metaphysical or spiritual reality. It has given me [as Jesus taught] life more abundantly. It gave, and still gives, me a feeling of oneness with *what is right*. Jung writes that:

> A religious numinous experience mobilizes philosophical and religious convictions in the very people who deemed themselves miles above any such fits of weakness. Often it drives with unexampled passion and remorseless logic towards its goal and draws the subject under its spell, from which, despite the most desperate resistance, he is unable, and finally no longer even willing to break free, because the experience brings with it a depth of fullness of meaning that was unthinkable before. [2]

Jung also uses the term *individuation* to describe the psychological process that I am experiencing. It is the process by which a person integrates unconscious contents into consciousness, thereby becoming a psychologically whole individual. If such integration can be attained, we become more at one with the collective unconscious. This is exactly the kind of numinous feeling that I receive when I experience synchronicity.

Synchronistic happenings in my life leave a strong impression that I am part of a greater *one* unknown reality that controls all things. To me, these uncanny happenings are intrusions from a mega-reality into my particular reality via some kind of paraphysical osmosis. The various forms of synchronicity have led me down paths that I never would have imagined treading in younger days. In retrospect, it seems as if I am being schooled by *something other* via these acausal manifestations. But, enough about the subjective impact of these strange phenomena, I now will address how they have affected me in an objective way.

UFO investigations and experiences strengthened my childhood fascination with astronomy and cosmology. They did so to such a degree that I built a planetarium and observatory on my property and operated it for over three decades. In addition, I have taught basic UFO, astronomy and cosmology courses for community colleges for over 17 years. I continue to study astronomy and cosmology through video courses and reading in order to keep abreast of these sciences.

My study, of and experiences with, the UFO and synchronistic phenomena have been the catalyst for writing ten books on the subject. These studies, in turn, have prompted serious studies of other esoteric subjects, especially the Near Death Experience (NDE) and After Death Communication (ADC). More recently, my ongoing experiences have led me to study synchronicity in a formal way, which has resulted in my writing this very book. There was a time that I never would have even thought of reading books written by Carl Jung and others about acausal coincidences. Their bringing to light the connection [at least in an analogous sense] between Quantum Mechanics and Synchronicity has been the catalyst for introducing me to the *New Physics*. I have just finished a video-recorded course on the subject.

The events recorded in *SynchroFile* have deepened my interest in exploring synchronicity's relationship to clairvoyance, pre-cognition, religious experiences and telepathy. These events have sparked an interest to study synchronicity's analogous relationships with a number of other disciplines. [See Appendix B.]

Now, it is time to give my answer to the question posed at the beginning of this chapter. My answer is that all of the above are ways that I am integrating my acausal experiences into everyday living. Doing so is a marvelous adventure that I am enjoying sharing with the readers of this book. I actually miss the numinosity generated by my so-called abduction dreams. They seem to have ceased, at least for the time being.

However, the integration of my experiences into everyday life is bittersweet in nature. The *bitter* side is that the experiences are beyond understanding. They can only be comfortably shared through writing a book or conversing with a certain circle of empathetic friends and students. My experiences and those of probably millions of others are still at odds with the belief systems of society at large. This is particularly so with that segment of society that represents scientific materialism and fundamentalism in religion.

The conflict between *Materialism* and *Romanticism* mentioned in the Introduction to the book is alive and well. It still rages on. The former is upset and perplexed by the influence of the so-called New Age movement upon society. This has led to frontal attacks on what is considered pseudo-science. The most current portrayal [at the time of this writing] of this ongoing conflict is a recently published book approved by the National Academy of Sciences (NAS).

The book attempts to undermine one of the crown accomplishments of parapsychology: the unqualified successes of Rhine's scientific-controlled experiment with Extrasensory Phenomena (ESP). It is entitled *Quantum Leaps in the Wrong Direction*.[3] The book attacks parapsychology, out-of-body experiences, ghosts, near-death experiences, UFOs, creationism, and astrology. I am including an abbreviated review of this book by *The Journal of Parapsychology*[4] in Appendix A. It is an excellent portrayal of the current attitude of mainstream science towards acausal phenomena.

On the other hand, religious fundamentalism, (especially within the Christian context that I am most familiar with) would brand the phenomena discussed in this book as Satanic in nature. Such anomalies would be considered a threat to its very narrow and restricted view of reality. Paradoxically, Christian fundamentalists and Materialists, [usually archenemies] find themselves in the same bed regarding these phenomena because they pose a threat to their world views

Irregardless of these societal opposing forces, the *sweet* side of my integrating these phenomena into everyday living is the numinosity that synchronisms generate in my life. These powerful innate *feelings* flow like a refreshing stream through my life's activities. They are a soothing counterbalance to the tension that separates the explicable from the inexplicable.

As I bring this book to a close, synchronistic phenomena continue to occur in my life. These sudden unexpected happenings leave me with a comforting feeling that I am in the right place at the right time, doing exactly what I am supposed to be doing. They leave me with a strong impression that everything in creation is and has been connected from its beginning. They give me the assurance that I am currently playing my designated part in the wondrous Oneness of reality before passing on to yet another of its constituent locales to continue *becoming*!

APPENDIX A

Book Review: Quantum Leaps in the Wrong Direction.

(By *The Journal of Parapsychology* Volume 66, No. 3, September 2002 Pages 321-324).

There are no footnotes or endnotes, and the text rarely acknowledges any recognized authorities. I suspected that the book was aimed at a juvenile audience, but neither my local library nor the Library of Congress classifies it that way. The tone is deprecatory throughout, and 30 cartoons, many of which are full page, reinforce the ridicule and derision.

The additional reading section (six pages) lists no scientific journal articles but includes debunking books by Houdini, Henry Gordon, James Randi, Martin Gardner, Joe Nickell, and Michael Shermer...The reader of this Journal may then wonder why the book is being reviewed. Quantum Leaps is published by Joseph Henry Press, an imprint of the *National Academy Press*, the publishing arm of the *National Academy of Sciences* (NAS). The NAS is chartered by the U.S. federal government and provides advisory services to government agencies. It is one of the most elite scientific bodies in the world; only the very top scientists are elected to membership.

The NAS imprimatur carries enormous clout. Adding to the book's apparent credibility is a blurb on the back cover from Nobel laureate Leon Lederman and a glowing review in the Journal of the American Medical Association. Normally, one would expect such a volume to be written by well-qualified authors. Charles Wynn is a professor of chemistry at Eastern Connecticut State University. Arthur Wiggins is a physicist at Oakland Community College in Michigan. They apparently have no credentials or specialized expertise that would qualify them to write the book. Quite otherwise, for example, the authors assert: The Rhines used a 153 [sic] of cards designed by their colleague Carl [sic] Zener (p. 154) and that

Rhine coined the term parapsychology (p. 154). They also severely misdescribe blind-matching card tests (p. 155).

The book begins with a description of what the authors believe to be the scientific method. Their presentation is simplistic and uninformed by any scientific study of scientific processes (e.g., sociology of science). No mention is given to sociologists' demarcation problem, that is, determining the difference between science and nonscience. No anthropological, cross-cultural, or historical perspective is included. One redeeming factor is that the entire volume can be viewed online free of charge at the publisher's Web site (though the process is cumbersome). The topic of parapsychology is allotted 14 pages of text…The casual treatment subtly, but effectively, conveys the message that these topics do not merit serious examination. The publication and reception of this work say something profound about the status of parapsychology. In fact, they should serve as a wakeup call for the field.

APPENDIX B

The Other Faces of Synchronicity

Jung's early study of synchronicity was initially relegated to the domain of psychology. Later, he discovered and researched its analogous connections with other disciplines. These included astrology, Chinese philosophical concepts, ESP research and the New Physics. Jung carried on a voluminous correspondence with Physicist Wolfgang Pauli on the latter. Today, the concepts underlying synchronicity continue to infiltrate and affect Psychology, Biology, Physics, Cosmology and Creativity.

For those interested in studying the phenomenon of Synchronicity further, I am providing extracts from the following overview by Jane Piitro of Ashland University who graciously posted it on the internet in a non-copyrighted form. [1] Piitro's article will summarize and expand upon what I have written regarding Jung's theory of synchronicity and introduce the reader to *The Other Faces of Synchronicity* as an impetus for further study.

I. GLOSSARY OF TERMS

Formative causation: A hypothesis proposed by biologist Rupert Sheldrake: all biological and chemical systems at all levels of complexity are organized by morphic fields. Under standard conditions anywhere in the world, permutations in one morphic field will occur more readily over time in similar organisms through inheritance of habits.

Implicate Order: A theory by physicist David Bohm. The universe is organized from within as well as from without. The implicate order underlies and enfolds all matter.

Morphic resonance: According to Rupert Sheldrake, "Formative causation is the kind of causation responsible for form, structure, and pattern, and the causal influence on this is the morphogenetic field...from the Greek word morphi meaning form. Each kind of thing has a field, which gives its form, pattern, field or structure. This field is like the plan, the shaping influence. It has the kind of form it does because of its memory by the morphogenetic fields. An influence of similar things on subsequent similar things. Fields have a kind of inherent memory within them that is nonmaterial but physical. The gravitational field is physical, it has physical effects, and is part of nature, but it's not material in the sense it's made of matter."

Trickster: a mythological character found in many cultures, who transforms aspects of the world and who plays pranks. Often in the form of the raven, the coyote, the spider, the mink, the blue jay, or the rabbit, in North American Indian cultures; of the monkey in Asian cultures; of Hermes and Prometheus in Greek mythology; of Loki in Norse mythology

II. SYNCHRONICITY IN PSYCHOLOGY

The simultaneous occurrence of a certain psychic state with one or more external events that appear as meaningful parallels to the momentary subjective state and in certain cases, vice-versa. Synchronistic events rest on the simultaneous occurrence of two different psychic states. One is the normal, probable state (the one that is causally explainable) and the other, the critical experience, is the one that cannot be derived causally from the first. [2]

1. A woman in therapy dreamed of receiving a scarab pin. While she was describing the dream, Jung heard a buzzing rap at the window. There, simultaneous with the woman's story, was a golden beetle, similar to the Egyptian scarab beetle, which is a symbol of rebirth in Egyptian mythology. This was an example of synchronicity in which a psychic state simultaneously occurs with an external event that coincides with the content of the state.
2. A woman saw birds gathered outside the rooms in which her grandmother and mother died. Jung was treating her husband for a neurosis. The man seemed to exhibit signs of heart trouble. Jung sent him to see a doctor. The man was given a clean bill of health. On the way back home after his appointment with the doctor, with the papers in his pocket, the man collapsed of a heart attack. The woman reported that soon after her husband had gone to the doctor, she saw a flock of birds land on their house. She remembered what had happened at the deaths of her mother and grandmother, and was very fearful. Her fears were justified. Jung said this was an example of synchronicity where the woman's unconscious had already perceived the danger to her husband. The first two incidents of birds landing were coincidences that set up a correspondence in her that could only be proved when the man's dead body was brought home.
3. A man in Europe dreamed the death of a friend in America. The next morning he received a telegram that the friend had died an hour before the

dream occurred. Jung said that such experiences commonly happen almost simultaneously with the event, just before, or just after it happens. The person had unconscious knowledge of the event.

The two necessities for synchronicity to take place are (1) the presence of emotion; and (2) an unconscious image that comes to consciousness either directly or indirectly. The melding of space and time are crucial and how the energy is transmitted is not known, and perhaps unknowable. Jung said that there is no explanation for the transmission of energy in these cases. He conjectured about three different ways of understanding synchronicity, focusing on how intuition has worked in a way that is statistically significant.

> 1. One could look at the ESP experiments that provided statistical empirical evidence that such events exist. In the ESP experiments, the subjects did better when the tasks were fresh and their emotion and interest was focused. As the tasks repeated, boredom set in, and they did not do as well. This shows that emotion is indeed necessary for synchronicity to occur.
> 2. If we look at the Chinese way of holistically seeing the world, rather than the western way of seeing the world by analyzing small parts and generalizing to the whole, we can see that the concept of synchronicity is more explainable. The ancient Chinese practice I Ching, based on the concept of the Tao, where one throws stalks of yarrow (or, in the west, three coins) in order to grasp the meaning of an event or to predict the future, is based on intuitive principles. (Jung did much work with the I Ching and first used the word synchronicity at the funeral of his friend Richard Wilhelm, who had translated the I Ching). When an intuitive person who understands the 64 mutations of Yin and Yang interprets the tosses, the interpretation taps into the inner knowledge of the person, which is the same as the person's psychological state at that time. This state is synchronous with the chance falling of the coins or sticks. Thus the results are meaningful but there is no cause or explanation for the meaning.
> 3. Jung settled on another intuitive technique based on ancient science, and that was astrology. He conducted an experiment with 80 married couples and found that their signs were compatible to a degree that was statistically significant. A mathematician colleague of Jung's looked at the data and found that 25 percent of the couples had signs that were compatible. Of course, the other 75 percent did not. Jung said such astrological coincidence has little chance of being proved by mathematical law, and that astrologers would argue that probability mathematics is not subtle enough to decipher the many permutations that influence the married couple's charts and signs.

Jung reviewed historical antecedents to the idea of synchronicity, cautioning that the rationalistic view of people in the West is not the only possible explanation for events, and in fact, the rationalistic view shows short-sightedness, prejudice, and bias. He cited the western practices of astrology, alchemy, and mantic practices such as tarot and I Ching as being open to synchronicity.

Jung referred to Schopenhauer's idea of the unity of primal cause, Leibniz's idea of pre-established harmony, and Kepler's idea of a geometrical principle that underlies the physical world. Jung said there must be some girding idea or principle, which can explain these seemingly coincidental happenings. Noting that both primitive and medieval people did not doubt the existence of synchronicity as explanation for seemingly acausal events, Jung asserted that it is the role of psychology and parapsychology to take into account the fact that synchronicity might explain such events.

Jung pointed to dream analysis, and focused on his principle of the collective unconscious, which is an underlying species memory, common to Homo sapiens, that is expressed in Archetypes, overarching mythic figures that appear similar in myths and fairytales in all societies. They are primordial images that exist in the unconscious and surface in dreams, images made in art forms such as poetry, painting, and music, and in fantasy, delusions, and delirium states of people alive today. In 1961, Jung stated that the form of Archetypes is comparable to the form of a crystal, which is preformed in the liquid from which it rises, even though it does not exist materially by itself.

Jung worked with physicist Wolfgang Pauli, who postulated that synchronicity is the fourth pole in a unity of time, space, and causality. Pauli pioneered with his explication of the exclusion principle, which stated that electrons cannot share the same path of orbit in an atom. This led Pauli to assert that quantum physics did not uphold the idea of universal principles and thus began the era of "new physics." Pauli and Jung proposed an addition to classical physics, that of synchronicity.

In 1980 Arthur Koestler described synchronicity as even more enigmatic than ESP such as telepathy and precognition. Humans have been infatuated with such riddles since the beginning of mythology. These riddles contain the perhaps accidental and coincidental meeting of unrelated events, which seem to have no cause, but which also appear to be very important and significant.

Koestler felt that Jung's relating synchronicity to the idea of the collective unconscious was a mistake. Koestler applauded Jung for working in concert with the physicist Pauli as he developed his theory. While Jung used Pauli as a "quasi" tutor in theoretical physics, Koestler faulted Jung for not following up on Pauli's ideas, but rather descending into the obscure by attributing synchronicity to the collective unconscious and to Archetypes. Koestler said, "This was sadly disappointing but it helped turn synchronicity into a cult word."[3]

III. SYNCHRONICITY IN BIOLOGY

Synchronicity is expressed by the principle of morphic resonance in formative causation described by Rupert Sheldrake. According to Sheldrake in 1994, "the hypothesis of formative causation suggests that self-organizing systems at all levels of complexity including molecules, crystals, cells, tissues, organisms, and societies of organisms are organized by æmorphic fields. These fields include morphogenetic fields that have to do with the how organisms, molecules, and even crystals inherently remember what previous bodies have done."

The case of the blue tits is an example. Over time, ornithologists noticed that small blue tit birds learned to pierce the tops of milk bottles left on the doorstep in the morning in Great Britain. The phenomenon was first reported in 1921. By 1947 the behavior had been noticed throughout Europe. Blue tits do not usually travel far from their homes and live only two or three years. In the Netherlands, milk delivery had been all but stopped during World War II. When milk delivery resumed in 1947 and 1948, the blue tit behavior also resumed. Sheldrake used this as an example of how organisms remember habits established by previous generations.

Sheldrake said that space and distance do not matter to morphic resonance, for information and not energy is exchanged. That is, the universal principles of space and causality do not apply. The hypothesis of morphic resonance explained by formative causation explains the patterns and events in nature to be "In effect, this hypothesis enables the regularities of nature to be understood as regulated by inherited habits and not by universal and eternal underlying principles."

Mechanistic science after Descartes took for granted that there were universal principles that were inviolable, and that the task of science was to discover these principles. Thus memory was "stored" in cells in the brain or body; Sheldrake said this was not true; memory is part of a collective memory of the species inherited from former members of the species. In 1994 Sheldrake said that this is a concept similar to Jung's concept of the collective unconscious: "The hypothesis of morphic resonance enables the collective unconscious to be seen not just as a human phenomenon but as an aspect of a far more general process by which habits are inherited through nature."[4]

Sheldrake commented that these two hypotheses of formative causation and of morphic resonance may seem mysterious, but the mechanistic idea that there are laws of mathematics that transcend nature are more mysterious, as they also rely on a metaphysical explanation for what happens in nature.

IV. SYNCHRONICITY IN CHAOS THEORY

In 1987, Ervin Laszlo formulated a hypothesis about mathematical wave functions that assemble themselves into forms and nested patterns or psi-fields. Laszlo theorized that once patterns are made, they probably will occur again. This is an expression of creativity in the universe, or cosmos.

V. SYNCHRONICITY IN THE NEW PHYSICS

In physics, the principle of correspondence was cited by Niels Bohr to illustrate the discontinuum between the particle and the wave. Bohr later changed the term to "argument of correspondence." The idea of correspondence is related to the concept of the natural philosophers of the Middle Ages, who talked of the "sympathy of all things," and to the Greek philosophers such as Plato who postulated an underlying ideal form.

David Bohm expressed the theory of the implicate order, which is the order that underlies what is external, or the explicate order. The implicate order is part of and contains the explicate order. Bohm saw the universe as a hologram, where each part is enfolded into each other part. The synchronicity in this theory is that locality disappears. Time, space, and causality are not evident in events that happen. What may seem to be creativity may instead be the expression of synchronicity. Bohm also proposed a superimplicate order, which may contain a unifying principle. Intuition may be an expression of the superimplicate order functioning to perceive the implicate order and therefore the explicate order. The notion of the "sixth sense" is similar to the notion of synchronicity.

VI. SYNCHRONICITY AND CREATIVITY

These and other theories evolving simultaneously from many branches of knowledge converge in the root definition of creativity, which means "to make." The root of the words "create" and "creativity" comes from the Latin cre tus and cre re. This means, "to make or produce," or literally, "to grow." The word also comes from the Old French base kere, and the Latin crescere, and creber. The Roman goddess of the earth, Ceres, is an example, as is the Italian corn goddess,

Cereris. Creativity as a word has roots in the earth. Other similar words are *cereal, crescent, creature, concrete, crescendo, decrease, increase*, and *recruit.*

The Dictionary of Developmental and Educational Psychology in 1986 defined creativity as "man's capacity to produce new ideas, insights, inventions or artistic objects, which are accepted of being of social, spiritual, aesthetic, scientific, or technological value." In 1988 the Random House Dictionary of the English Language, Unabridged Edition noted that creativity was an ability, the ability to "transcend traditional ideas, rules, patterns, relationships or the like, and to create meaningful new ideas, forms, methods, interpretations, etc."

Synchronicity has thus two relationships with the concept of creativity. First is that seemingly acausal coincidences may jar a person to have new ideas, to see the old in new ways, and force a person to pay attention and perhaps change the old ways of behaving, acting, doing, making. Second is that in the new cosmology where universal principles have been shown not to exist (except perhaps in Jung's concept of the collective unconscious and in Bohm's of the superimplicate order) creativity is found in the constantly evolving and perhaps accidental forms and patterns that are being developed.

The former may be illustrated with the following: A woman wakes up. Last night she dreamt about a coyote coming out of a cave and licking her hand. At the dentist, she flips through a fashion magazine and sees there a new perfume called Coyote, in which the model is dressed in Indian fashion, petting a coyote. She goes to work and receives a letter from a man called William Coyote who wants her to give a speech at his school. At lunch, she tells her friend about these unforeseen coincidences. Her friend pulls from her purse a novel she is reading. It is called Coyote Justice. By the fourth coincidence, the woman has a strong feeling that there is something going on. She and her friend talk about the coyote as trickster in American Indian mythology. This begins a search that leads the woman to a life change as she begins to embrace the significance of the trickster figure in her life. These coincidences with no seeming cause are called "synchronicity."

An example of the latter is the following, as explained by Sheldrake. When random mutations occur, organisms must react in new ways. Organisms adapt to the genetic mutation by making a creative leap, which synthesizes into a new pattern. These patterns are instituted by morphic fields, which get more powerful and instill habits into the organism if the organism is preserved through natural selection.

Thus, the creativity that gives rise to new bodily forms and to new patterns of behavior is not explained by the random mutations alone. It involves a creative response upon the part of the organism itself and also depends on the ability of the organism to integrate this new pattern with the rest of its habits. [5]

Thus, synchronicity is basically creative whether at the level of the atom, the molecule, the cell, the organism, or the system. Enigmatic, inscrutable, mysterious, seemingly acausal, playful and funny, synchronicity makes us laugh, cry, pay attention, and shake our heads in amazement. In 1996, Combs and Holland stated it well: "Nothing is closer to the heart of the experience of synchronicity than the feeling that the world itself expresses creativity in synchronistic coincidences. Such coincidences often have more the feel of poetry than physics." [6]

APPENDIX C
A Recommended Reading List

A Anderson, Ken, *The Coincidence File*. New York: Sterling Publishing Co., Inc., 1999.

Atwater, P.M.H., *Coming Back to Life*. New York: Dodd, Mead & Co., Inc., 1988.

Aziz, Robert Aziz, *C.G. Jung's Psychology of Religion and Synchronicity*. New York: State University of New York Press, 1990.

Burrow, Barron, *PS: Pauli-Jung...by 50 yrs. [Pt A]*. http://www.shef.ac.uk/~psysc/psychoanalytic-studies/msg00154.html

Chalquist, Craig, *Glossary of Jungian Terms*. http://www.tearsofllorona.com/jungdefs.html.

Copleston, Frederick C., *A History of Philosophy*. New York: Image Books, 1993.

Bell, Craig S., *Comprehending Coincidence: Synchronicity and Personal Transformation*. West Chester, PA: Chrysalis Books, 2000.

Davis, Stephen J., *Synchronicity: Trick or Treat?* http://www.viewzone.com/synchronicity.html.

Fowler, Raymond E., *UFOs: Interplanetary Visitors*. New York: Exposition Press, 1974; New Jersey: Prentice-Hall, Inc., 1979; New York: Bantam Books, 1979.*

Fowler, Raymond E., *The Andreasson Affair*. New Jersey: Prentice-Hall, Inc., 1979; New York: Bantam Books, 1980, 1988; Tigard, OR: Wildflower Press, 1994. *

Fowler, Raymond E., *Casebook of a UFO Investigator.* New Jersey: Prentice-Hall, Inc., 1981.

Fowler, Raymond E., *The Andreasson Affair—Phase Two.* New Jersey, Prentice-Hall, Inc., 1982, Tigard, OR: Wildflower Press, 1994. *

Fowler, Raymond E., *The Watchers.* New York: Bantam Books, 1990, 1991.

Fowler, Raymond E., *The Allagash Abductions.* Tigard, OR: Wildflower Press, 1993. *

Fowler, Raymond E., *The Watchers II.* Tigard, OR: Wildflower Press, 1994. *

Fowler, Raymond E., *The Andreasson Legacy.* New York, NY: Marlowe & Company, 1997. *

Fraim, John, *The C.G. Jung Page,* "The Symbolism of UFOs and Aliens." (www.cgjungpage.org/articles/fraim3.html).

Guggenheim, William and Judith, *Hello from Heaven.* New York: Bantam Books, 1997.

Jung, C.G., *Synchronicity: An Acausal Connecting Principle.* Tr. R.F.C. Hull. Princeton, NJ: Princeton University Press, 1973.

Jung, Carl. G., *Flying Saucers: A Modern Myth of Things Seen in the Skies.* New Jersey: Princeton University Press, 1978, 1991.

Jung, C.G., Memories, *Dreams, Reflections,* Tr. R. & C. Winston. New York: Vintage Books, 1965.

Jung, Carl G., *Letters,* Vol. 2, New Jersey: Princeton University Press, 1975.

Jung, C.G., *Collected Works,* "Synchronicity: An Acausal Connecting Principle," vol. 8, par. 995, Trans. R.F.C. Hull, New Jersey: Princeton University Press, 1978.

Jung, Carl G., Ed., *Man and his Symbols, Part 4*: "Symbolism in the arts" by Aniela Jaffe. New York: Anchor Press, Doubleday, 1988.

Kent M., Von De Graaff and Stuart Ira Fox, *Concepts of Human Anatomy and Physiology.* Dubuque, IA: Wm. C. Brown Publishers, 1988.

Laszlo, Violet Staub De., Ed., *The Basic Writings of C. G. Jung.* New York: The Modern Library, 1993.

Mansfield, Victor, *Synchronicity, Science, and Soul-making.* Illinois: Open Court Publishing, 1995.

Meir, C.A., Ed., *Atom and Archetype: The Pauli/Jung Letters, 1932-1958,* Tr. Roscoe, David, New Jersey: Princeton University Press, 2001.

Moody, Raymond A., *Life after Life.* New York: Bantam Books, 1976.

Morse, M.D., Melvin with Paul Perry, *Closer to the Light.* New York: Villard Books, 1990.

Morse, M.D., Melvin with Paul Perry, *Transformed by the Light.* New York: Villard Books, 1992.

North, Carolyn, *Synchronicity: The Anatomy of Coincidence.* Oakland, CA: Regent Press, 1994.

Peck, Scott M., *The Road Less Traveled.* New Jersey: Simon and Schuster, 1997.

Piitro, Jane, *Synchronicity: An article for The Encyclopedia of Creativity, Academic Press,* 1999. http://www.ashland.edu/~jpiirto/synchronicity.htm.

Reagan, Nancy, *I Love You Ronnie.* New York: Random House, 2000.

Redfield, James, *The Celestine Prophecy.* New York: Warner Books, 1994.

Ring, Kenneth, *The Omega Project.* New York: William Morrow and Co., 1992.

Ring, Kenneth and Elsaesser Valarino, Evelyn, *Lessons from the Light.* New York and London: Insight Books, Plenum Press, 1998.

Roberts, Maureen B., *The New Mythology: Angelic, Apocalyptic and Alien Dreams.* The Jung Circle: http://www.jungcircle.com/index.html, 1997.

Sabom, Michael B., *Recollections of Death—A Medical Investigation.* New York, Harper & Row Publishers, Inc., 1982.

Russell, Peter, *How to be a Wizard.* http://www.dharma-haven.org/keys/#Synchronicity.

Talbot, Michael, *The Holographic Universe.* New York: HarperPerennial, 1991.

The Journal of Parapsychology, Volume 66, No. 3, September 2002.

Worden, Greg, "A UFO in Townshend? Something was there," *Brattleboro Reformer,* December 21, 1974, p. 1.

* Contact author at 249 Maguire Road, Kennebunk, ME 04043 for availability of autographed copies.

Notes

Introduction

1. Carl G. Jung, *Synchronicity—An Acausal Connecting Principle* (New Jersey: Princeton University Press, 1973), p. 24.

2. *Ibid.*, p.109, 110.

3. *Ibid.*, pp.102, 103.

Chapter 2

1. C. A. Meir, Ed., *Atom and Archetype: The Pauli/Jung Letters, 1932—1958*, Tr. Roscoe, David (New Jersey: Princeton University Press, 2001), p. 38.

2. Carl G. Jung, Synchronicity: *An Acausal Connecting Principle.* Tr. R.F.C. Hull (New Jersey: Princeton University Press, 1973), p.110.

3. *Idem.*

4. *Idem.*

Chapter 3

1. Craig S. Bell, *Comprehending Coincidence: Synchronicity and Personal Transformation* (West Chester, PA: Chrysalis Books, 2000), p. 3.

2. C. G. Jung, Synchronicity: *An Acausal Connecting Principle*, Tr. R.F.C. Hull. Princeton (NJ: Princeton University Press, 1973), p. 107

Chapter 4

1. Raymond E. Fowler, *The Andreasson Affair—Phase Two* (New Jersey, Prentice-Hall, Inc., 1979, 1982; Tigard, OR: Wildflower Press, 1994).

2. Ibid.

3. Raymond E. Fowler, *The Watchers* (New York: Bantam Books, 1990, 1991).

4. Nancy Reagan, *I Love You Ronnie* (New York: Random House, 2000), p. 89.

Chapter 5

1. Raymond E. Fowler, *Casebook of a UFO Investigator* (New Jersey: Prentice-Hall, Inc., 1981).

2. Greg Worden, "A UFO in Townshend? Something was there," *Brattleboro Reformer*, December 21, 1974, p. 1.

3. Raymond E. Fowler, *The Allagash Abductions* (Tigard, OR: Wildflower Press, 1993}.

4. Robert Aziz, C.G. *Jung's Psychology of Religion and Synchronicity* (New York: State University of New York Press, 1990), p. 136.

5. *Ibid.*, pp. 136-138.

6. Raymond E. Fowler, *The Watchers II* (Tigard, OR: Wildflower Press, 1994).

7. Raymond E. Fowler, *The Andreasson Legacy* (New York, NY: Marlowe & Company, 1997).

Chapter 9

1. Carl G. Jung, *Flying Saucers: A Modern Myth of Things Seen in the Skies* (New Jersey: Princeton University Press, 1978, 1991).

2. Carl G. Jung, *Letters*, Vol. 2 (Princeton University Press, 1975).

3. Carl. G. Jung, *Flying Saucers: A Modern Myth of Things Seen in the Skies* (New Jersey: Princeton University Press, 1978, 1991), vii.

4. *Ibid.* p. 7.

5. *Idem.*

6. John Fraim, *The C.G. Jung Page,* "The Symbolism of UFOs and Aliens." (www.cgjungpage.org/articles/fraim3.html).

7. Carl G. Jung, *Flying Saucers: A Modern Myth of Things Seen in the Skies* (New Jersey: Princeton University Press, 1978, 1991), p. 7.

8. John Fraim, *The C.G. Jung Page,* "The Symbolism of UFOs and Aliens." (www.cgjungpage.org/articles/fraim3.html).

9. Carl G. Jung, Editor, Man and his Symbols, Part 4: "Symbolism in the arts" by Aniela Jaffe (New York: Anchor Press, Doubleday, 1988), p. 249.

10. Raymond E. Fowler, *UFOs: Interplanetary Visitors* (New York: Exposition Press, 1974; New Jersey: Prentice-Hall, Inc., 1979; New York: Bantam Books, 1979.

Chapter 11

1. Raymond E. Fowler, *UFO Testament—Anatomy of an Abductee* (Lincoln. NE: iUniverse, Inc., 2003).

2. Kent M. Von De Graaff and Stuart Ira Fox, *Concepts of Human Anatomy and Physiology* (Dubuque, IA, 1988), p. 936.

Chapter 12

1. Kenneth Ring, *The Omega Project* (New York: William Morrow and Co., 1992), p. 110.

2. Raymond A. Moody, *Life after Life* (New York: Bantam Books, 1976), p. 85.

3. *Ibid.*, p. 85.

4. *Ibid.* p. 36.

5. *Ibid.*, p. 37.

6. *Ibid.*, p. 38.

7. *Ibid.*, p. 55.

8. Melvin Morse, M.D. with Paul Perry, *Transformed by the Light* (New York: Villard Books, 1992), p. 52.

9. P.M.H. Atwater, *Coming Back to Life* (New York: Dodd, Mead & Co., Inc., 1988), p. 43.

10. *Idem.*

11. Moody, op. cit., 1976, p. 68.

12. Melvin Morse, M.D. with Paul Perry, *Closer to the Light* (New York: Villard Books, 1990), p. 117.

13. Ring, op. cit., 1992, p. 102.

14. Michael B. Sabom, *Recollections of Death—A Medical Investigation* (New York: Harper & Row Publishers, Inc., 1982), p. 49.

15. Morse, op. cit., 1990, p. 29.

16. Morse, op. cit., 1992, p. 142.

17. Sabom, op cit., 1982, p. 44.

18. Ring op. cit., 1992, p. 96.

19. Moody, op. cit., 1996, p. 102.

20. Ibid., p. 57.

21. Sabom, op. cit., 1982, p. 47.

22. Atwater, op. cit., 1988, p. 77.

23. Morse, op. cit., 1992, p. 75.

24. Atwater, op. cit., 1988, p. 82.

25. Morse, op. cit., 1990, p. 49.

26. Sabom, op. cit., 1982, pp. 49-50.

27. Morse, op. cit., 1992, p. 53.

28. Ring, op. cit., 1992, p. 178.

29. Kenneth Ring and Evelyn Elsaesser Valarino, *Lessons from the Light* (New York and London: Insight Books, Plenum Press, 1998), pp. 148, 149.

30. Ring, op. cit., 1992, p. 101.

31. Moody, op. cit., 1976, p. 76.

32. Sabom, op. cit., 1982, p. 54.

33. William and Judith Guggenheim, *Hello from Heaven* (New York: Bantam Books, 1997).

34. Aziz, op. cit., 1990, p.111.

35. *Ibid.*, p. 112.

36. *Ibid.*, p. 113, 114.

37. *Ibid.*, p. 114.

38. C.G. Jung, *Memories, Dreams, Reflections*, ed. Aniela Jaffe (New York: Vintage Books, 1965), p. 156.

39. C.G. Jung, *Collected Works,* "Synchronicity: An Acausal Connecting Principle," vol. 8, par. 995, Trans. R.F.C. Hull (New Jersey: Princeton University Press, 1978), pp. 509-10.

40. Jung, op, cit., 1965, p. 291.

41. Michael Talbot, *The Holographic Universe* (New York: HarperPerennial, 1991), p. 146.

Chapter 13

1. Craig Chalquist, *Glossary of Jungian Terms* (http://www.tearsofllorona.com/jungdefs.html).

2. Violet Staub De. Laszlo, Ed., *The Basic Writings of C. G. Jung* (New York: The Modern Library, 1993), p. 585.

3. *Ibid.*, p. 96.

4. Charles M. Wynn and Arthur W. Wiggins, with cartoons by Sidney Harris, *Quantum Leaps in the Wrong Direction* (Washington, DC: Joseph Henry Press, 2001).

5. *The Journal of Parapsychology*, Volume 66, No. 3, September 2002 Pages 321-324.

Appendix B

1. Jane Piirto, *Synchronicity: An article for The Encyclopedia of Creativity* (Academic Press), 1999. http://www.ashland.edu/~jpiirto/synchronicity.htm.

2. C.G. Jung, *Synchronicity: An Acausal Connecting Principle*, Tr. R.F.C. Hull. Princeton (NJ: Princeton University Press, 1973), pp. 25-28.

3. A. Koestler, *The Roots of Coincidence* (New York: Random House, 1972), p. 664.

4. R. Sheldrake, *The Rebirth of Nature: The Greening of Science and God* (Rochester, VT: Park Street Press, 1994), p. 117.

5. *Ibid.* 141.

6. A. Combs & M. Holland, *Synchronicity: Science, Myth, and the Trickster* (New York: Marlowe & Company, 1996), p. xxxiii.

List of Photographs

Photo 1.	Typical Abduction Scoop Mark on author's tibia.	182
Photo 2.	Photograph of X-ray showing suspected nasal implant in author's nose.	204
Photo 3.	Close-up of suspected nasal implant in author's nose.	205

About the Author

Raymond E. Fowler was born in Salem, Massachusetts and received a B.A. degree (magna cum laude) from Gordon College of Liberal Arts. His career included a tour with the USAF Security Service and twenty-five years with GTE Government Systems as a Senior Planner for the Minuteman Intercontinental Missile Program. Ray has directed his own planetarium and observatory and teaches courses on Astronomy, Cosmology and UFOs.

Ray Fowler's contributions to UFOlogy are respected by UFO researchers throughout the world. Reports of his UFO investigations have been published in: Congressional Hearings on UFOs, military publications, newspapers, magazines and professional journals in the USA and abroad. Astronomer Dr. J. Allen Hynek, Chief Scientific Consultant for the USAF UFO Projects, called Raymond Fowler, "An outstanding UFO investigator...I know of no one who is more dedicated, trustworthy or persevering." Ray has served as an early warning coordinator for the USAF-contracted Colorado University UFO Study and as the Director of Investigations for the international Mutual UFO Network [MUFON].

Ray has been a guest on hundreds of radio and TV shows in the U.S.A. since 1963 including: *Dave Garroway, Dick Cavett, Mike Douglas, Good Morning America, Unsolved Mysteries, Sightings*, and has been a consultant to TV UFO Documentaries and *Time-Life* Books.

Ray has had 10 books on UFOs published in the USA between 1974 and 2002. Many of them have been reprinted in foreign languages. These are: *UFOs: Interplanetary Visitors, The Andreasson Affair, The Andreasson Affair—Phase Two, Casebook of a UFO Investigator, The Melchizedek Connection, The Watchers, The Allagash Abductions, Watchers II, The Andreasson Legacy* and *UFO Testament—Anatomy of an Abductee.*

0-595-31589-5

Printed in the United States
19941LVS00006B/208-234